Makers of the Western Tradition

PORTRAITS FROM HISTORY

VOLUME 1

Second Edition

J. KELLEY SOWARDS, editor

Makers of the Western Tradition

PORTRAITS FROM HISTORY

VOLUME 1

Second Edition

St. Martin's Press   New York

ACKNOWLEDGMENTS

AKHENATON: "Hymn to Aton" from "Egyptian Hymns and Prayers," translated by
John A. Wilson, in *Ancient Near Eastern Texts Relating to the Old Testament*, 3rd
edition, with Supplement, edited by James B. Pritchard. Omission of footnotes.
Copyright © 1969 by Princeton University Press. Reprinted by permission of
Princeton University Press. From *The Dawn of Conscience* by James Henry
Breasted. Copyright 1933 by James Henry Breasted. Reprinted by permission of
Charles Scribner's Sons. From *Ikhnaton: Legend and History* by F. J. Giles. Re-
printed by permission of the Hutchinson Publishing Group Ltd.
KING DAVID: Excerpts from the *Revised Standard Version Bible*. Reprinted by permis-
sion of the National Council of the Churches of Christ. From *Kingship and the
Gods: A Study of Ancient Near Eastern Religion as the Integration of Society and
Nature* by Henri Frankfort. Copyright 1948 by The University of Chicago Press.
Reprinted by permission of The University of Chicago Press. From *Archaeology
in the Holy Land*, 3rd edition, by Kathleen M. Kenyon. Copyright © Kathleen M.
Kenyon 1960, 1965, 1970 in London, England. Reprinted by permission of Praeger
Publishers, Inc. and Ernest Benn Limited.
SOCRATES: From *The Clouds* by Aristophanes, translated by William Arrowsmith.
Copyright © 1962 by William Arrowsmith. Reprinted by arrangement with The
New American Library, Inc., New York, New York. From "The Apology" from
The Dialogues of Plato, translated by Benjamin Jowett, 3rd edition, 1892. Also
published by Random House in 1937. Reprinted by permission of Oxford University
Press. From "The Image of Socrates" from *Heroes and Gods* by Moses Hadas and
Morton Smith, Volume Thirteen, Religious Perspectives, edited by Ruth Nanda
Anshen. Copyright © 1965 by Moses Hadas and Morton Smith.
ALEXANDER THE GREAT: "The Ancient Sources" from *The Campaigns of Alexander
by Arrian*, translated by Aubrey de Sélincourt (Penguin Classics, Revised Edition,
1971). © the Estate of Aubrey de Sélincourt 1958. From *The Geography of Strabo*,
translated by Horace Leonard Jones. "The Loeb Classical Library" published by
Harvard University Press and William Heinemann, Ltd., 1917. From *Plutarch's
Moralia*, translated by Frank Cole Babbitt. "The Loeb Classical Library" published
by Harvard University Press and William Heinemann, Ltd., 1936. From *Plutarch's
Lives*, translated by Bernadotte Perrin. "The Loeb Classical Library" published by
Harvard University Press and William Heinemann, Ltd. 1919. From "Alexander
the Great and the Unity of Mankind" by W. W. Tarn, published in *The British
Academy Proceedings*, 19 (1933). Reprinted by permission of The British Academy.
Excerpts from "W. W. Tarn and the Alexander Ideal" by Richard A. Todd, published in *The Historian*, 27 (1964), 48–55. Reprinted by permission of the author
and *The Historian*.
JULIUS CAESAR: From *The Lives of the Twelve Caesars by Seutonius*, edited by Joseph
Gavorse. Copyright 1931 and renewed 1959 by Modern Library, Inc. Reprinted by
permission of Random House, Inc. From Ronald Syme, *The Roman Revolution*
published in 1939; reprinted by permission of Oxford University Press.
AUGUSTINE: From *The Confessions of St. Augustine*, translated by Rex Warner. Copyright © 1963 by Rex Warner. Reprinted by permission of The New American
Library, Inc., New York, New York. From *Augustine of Hippo: A Biography* by
Peter Brown. Originally published by the University of California Press, 1967; reprinted by permission of The Regents of the University of California and Faber
and Faber Ltd. From *Thought and Letters in Western Europe, A.D. 500 to 900* by
M.L.W. Laistner. Copyright 1931 by M.L.W. Laistner; revised edition, Methuen &
Co. Ltd. and Cornell University Press, 1957. Used by permission of Cornell Uni-
versity Press.

CHARLEMAGNE: From *The Life of Charlemagne by Einhard*, translated from the *Monumenta Germaniae* by Samuel Epes Turner, 1960. Reprinted by permission of The University of Michigan Press. From *The Carolingian Empire: The Age of Charlemagne* by Heinrich Fichtenau, translated by Peter Munz. Harper Torchbooks, 1964. Translated from *Das Karolingische Imperium,* published by Fertz and Wasmuth Verlag A. G., Zurich. First English translation published by Basil Blackwell, Oxford, England, 1957. Reprinted by permission of Harper & Row, Publishers, Inc. and Basil Blackwell Publisher. From François Ganshof, "Charlemagne," *Speculum* 24 (1949), 523–527. Reprinted by permission of *Speculum,* published by the Mediaeval Academy of America.

ABELARD: From *The Story of My Misfortunes: The Autobiography of Peter Abelard,* translated by Henry Adams Bellow with an introduction by Ralph Adams Gram. Copyright 1922 by Thomas Alexander Boyd. Published by The Free Press, 1958. Reprinted by permission of Macmillan Publishing Co., Inc. From *The Renaissance of the Twelfth Century* by Charles Homer Haskins. Copyright 1927 by Charles Homer Haskins; renewed 1955 by Clare Allen Haskins. Reprinted by permission of Harvard University Press. From *The Evolution of Medieval Thought* by David Knowles, copyright © 1962. Reprinted by permission of Helicon Press, Inc.

ELEANOR OF AQUITAINE: From *William Archbishop of Tyre: A History of Deeds Done Beyond the Sea,* Vol. II, E. A. Babcock and A. C. Krey (translators), New York: Columbia University Press, 1943, reprinted by permission of Columbia University Press. From *The Historia Pontificalis of John of Salisbury* edited and translated by Marjorie Chinball, 1956. Reprinted by permission of Thomas Nelson & Sons Limited. From *Eleanor of Aquitaine and the Four Kings* by Amy Kelly. Copyright © 1950 by the President and Fellows of Harvard College; renewed 1978 by J. Margaret Malcolm. Reprinted by permission of Harvard University Press. From *Eleanor of Aquitaine* by Marion Meade. Copyright © 1977 by Marion Meade. All rights reserved. Reprinted by permission of Hawthorne Books, Inc. and James Seligmann.

DANTE: From *The Earliest Lives of Dante by Giovanni Boccaccio,* translated by James Robinson Smith, published by Frederick Ungar Publishing Company. From *The Medieval Mind: A History of the Development of Thought and Emotion in the Middle Ages,* Volume II, by Henry Osborn Taylor. Copyright Harvard University Press, 1925 (4th edition). Reprinted by permission of Harvard University Press. From "Dante's Relevance Today" by Philip McNair, *The Listener,* Vol. LXXIV, No. 1892 (July 1, 1965). Reprinted by permission of Professor Philip M. J. McNair, Serena Professor of Italian, University of Birmingham, England.

LEONARDO DA VINCI: From *Lives of the Most Eminent Painters, Sculptors and Architects.* Vol. IV, by Giorgio Vasari, translated by Gaston C. DeVere. Reprinted by permission of the Medici Society Ltd. Excerpts from "The Place of Leonardo da Vinci in the Emergence of Modern Science" by John H. Randall, Jr., published in *Journal of the History of Ideas,* 14 (1935). Reprinted by permission of *Journal of the History of Ideas.* From *Leonardo's Legacy: An International Symposium,* edited by C. D. O'Malley, "Leonardo da Vinci the Technologist: The Problem of Prime Movers" by Ladislao Reti. Copyright 1969 by the University of California Press. Reprinted by permission of the Regents of the University of California.

MARTIN LUTHER: Excerpts from *Luther's Works,* Vol. 54, edited and translated by Theodore G. Tappert, reprinted by permission of The Fortress Press. From *These Theses Were Not Posted: Luther Between Reform and Reformation* by Erwin Iserloh. Copyright © 1966 by Aschendorff, Munster. English translation and notes © by Jared Wicks, S. J. Reprinted by permission of Beacon Press.

To my parents, in love and gratitude

Preface

Are men and women able to force change upon history by their own skill and wits, their nerve and daring? Are they capable of altering its course by their own actions? Or are they hopelessly caught up in the grinding process of great, impersonal forces over which they have no real control?

Historians, like theologians, philosophers, and scientists, have long been fascinated by this question. People in every age have recognized great forces at work in their affairs, whether they perceived those forces as supernatural and divine, climatological, ecological, sociological, or economic. Yet obviously at least a few individuals—Alexander, Charlemagne, Napoleon, Hitler—were able to seize the opportunity of their time and compel the great forces of history to change course. Still other individuals—Moses, Jesus, Copernicus, Darwin, Einstein—were able, solely by the power of their thought or their vision, to shape the history of their period and of all later time more profoundly than the conquerors or military heroes could do.

The purpose of this book is to examine the careers and the impact of several figures who significantly influenced the history of Western civilization, or who embodied much that is significant about the periods in which they lived, and at the same time to introduce the student to the chief varieties of historical interpretation. Few personalities or events stand without comment in the historical record; contemporary accounts and documents, the so-called original sources, no less than later studies, are written by people with a distinct point of view and interpretation of what they see. Problems of interpretation are inseparable from the effort to achieve historical understanding.

The readings in this book have been chosen for their inherent interest and their particular way of treating their subject. Typically, three or four selections are devoted to each figure. The first selection is usually an autobiographical or contemporary biographical account; in a few instances, differing assessments by contemporaries are included. Next, a more or less orthodox interpretation is presented; it is often a selection from the "standard work" on the figure in question. The final selection offers a more recent view, which may reinforce the standard interpretation, revise it in the light of new evidence, or dissent from it completely. In some cases, two very different recent views are set side by side.

A book of this size cannot hope to include full-length biographies of all the individuals studied. Instead, each chapter focuses on an important interpretative issue. In some chapters, the figure's relative historical importance is at issue; in others, the significance of a major point mooted in the sources; in still others, the general meaning of the figure's career, as debated in a spread of interpretative positions. In every chapter, it is hoped, the problem examined is interesting and basic to an understanding of the figure's place in history.

Note to the Second Edition

The second edition was undertaken after some three years' experience with the book, both in my own classes and in those of colleagues across the country. Many of these colleagues generously responded to a questionnaire about the book and its usefulness to them, and on the basis of their suggestions as well as my own reactions after using it, revisions were made. In some instances only a single selection in a chapter was changed; in others whole chapters were deleted and totally different historical personalities were substituted. And in still other chapters the consensus was that no changes should be made. It is my sincere hope that the book is improved in its usefulness for teachers and students alike.

J.K.S.

Contents

**Martin Luther: Protestant Saint or
"Devil in the Habit of a Monk"?** **239**

Makers of the Western Tradition

PORTRAITS FROM HISTORY

VOLUME 1

Second Edition

Akhenaton:
The Heretic King

With the enormous distance in time that separates us from ancient Egypt and the Near East, the scale of individual human size is reduced nearly to the point of oblivion. Even the greatest kings and conquerors, high priests, viziers, queens and "chief wives" tend to be reduced to lists of properties and exploits, names without substance or dimension.

For Egypt in particular the problem is compounded by the fact that the Egyptian culture tended to stress timelessness and eternity rather than history or individuals. The Egyptians had no continuous chronology. The names of successive pharaohs and their identifying epithets were often run together, overlapped, and sometimes blandly falsified in records and inscriptions. The great modern British Egyptologist Sir Alan Gardiner, speaking of this maddening anonymity of Egyptian history, notes however that "in one case only, that of Akhenaten towards the end of Dyn. XVIII, do the inscriptions and reliefs bring us face to face with a personality markedly different from that of all his predecessors." [1]

This is the famous "heretic king," the most intriguing figure in Egyptian history.

[1] Sir Alan Gardiner, *Egypt of the Pharaohs* (Oxford: Oxford University Press; 1st ed., 1961; 1972), p. 55. The reader will note the first of several variations in the spelling of Akhenaton in this passage. Hieroglyphics did not write the vowels and there were consonant sounds we do not have. Hence considerable latitude in rendering names is to be expected.

A Hymn to Aton

There is no contemporary biographical account of this remarkable ruler, nor should we expect to find one. But what is more intriguing, conscious efforts apparently were made to obliterate every trace of him and of his reign. His name was systematically hacked out of official inscriptions and omitted from king lists. Even the genealogical lines, so important to Egyptian royal continuity, were altered. But a handful of inscriptions did remain, the most substantial being the Long Hymn to Aton, *from the tomb of one of Akhenaton's successors, Eye. Part of this inscription follows below. The hymn may not have been actually composed by Akhenaton, although he certainly may have written it. Nor is it about him. Rather, it is a hymn to the god Aton, the disk of the sun, to whom Akhenaton subordinated all the other myriad of Egyptian gods, "sole god, like whom there is no other!" This was the apostasy of "the heretic king." This was the offense that seems to have created the animus toward Akhenaton, unique in Egyptian history.*

THOU APPEAREST beautifully on the horizon of heaven
Thou living Aton, the beginning of life!
When thou art risen on the eastern horizon,
Thou has filled every land with thy beauty.
Thou art gracious, great, glistening, and high over every land;
Thy rays encompass the lands to the limit of all that thou hast made:
As thou art Re, thou reachest to the end of them;
(Thou) subduest them (for) thy beloved son.
. . . .
When thou settest in the western horizon,
The land is in darkness, in the manner of death.
Every lion is come forth from his den;
All creeping things, they sting.
Darkness *is a shroud,* and the earth is in stillness,
For he who made them rests in his horizon.

At daybreak, when thou arisest on the horizon,
When thou shinest as the Aton by day,
Thou drivest away the darkness and givest thy rays.
. . . .
All the world, they do their work.

All beasts are content with their pasturage;
Trees and plants are flourishing.
The birds which fly from their nests,
Their wings are (stretched out) in praise to thy *ka*.
All beasts spring upon (their) feet.
Whatever flies and alights,
They live when thou hast risen (for) them.
The ships are sailing north and south as well,
For every way is open at thy appearance.
The fish in the river dart before thy face;
Thy rays are in the midst of the great green sea.

. . . .

How manifold it is, what thou hast made!
They are hidden from the face (of man).
O sole god, like whom there is no other!
Thou didst create the world according to thy desire,
Whilst thou wert alone:
All men, cattle, and wild beasts,
Whatever is on earth, going upon (its) feet,
And what is on high, flying with its wings.

The countries of Syria and Nubia, the *land* of Egypt,
Thou settest every man in his place,
Thou suppliest their necessities:
Everyone has his food, and his time of life is reckoned.
Their tongues are separate in speech,
And their natures as well;
Their skins are distinguished,
As thou distinguishest the foreign peoples.
Thou makest a Nile in the underworld,
Thou bringest it forth as thou desirest
To maintain the people (of Egypt)
According as thou madest them for thyself,
The lord of all of them, wearying (himself) with them,
The lord of every land, rising for them,
The Aton of the day, great of majesty.

. . . .

Thou art in my heart,
And there is no other that knows thee
Save thy son Nefer-kheperu-Re Wa-en-Re,
For thou hast made him well-versed in thy plans and in thy strength.

The world came into being by thy hand,
According as thou hast made them.
When thou hast risen they live,

When thou settest they die.
Thou art lifetime thy own self,
For one lives (only) through thee.
Eyes are (fixed) on beauty until thou settest.
All work is laid aside when thou settest in the west.
(But) when (thou) risest (again),
[*Everything is*] made to flourish for the king, . . .
Since thou didst found the earth
And raise them up for thy son,
Who came forth from thy body:
the King of Upper and Lower Egypt, . . . Akh-en-Aton, . . . and
the Chief Wife of the King . . . Nefert-iti, living and youthful for-
ever and ever.

The Dawn of Conscience
JAMES H. BREASTED

*It was largely this hymn to Aton, so obviously similar in sentiment, even
in phrasing, to Psalm 104 of the Hebrew Old Testament, that intrigued
James H. Breasted and started him on his search to piece together the
story of Akhenaton, "the world's first monotheist."*

*Breasted was the pioneer figure in American Egyptology. He almost
singlehandedly created the Oriental Institute of the University of Chicago
in 1919, held the first chair of Egyptology in the United States,
and by his popular books, articles, and lectures was largely responsible
for the great vogue of things Egyptian in America in the 1920s and
1930s. But despite his other interests, Breasted kept returning in
fascination to Akhenaton. Here in brief is the story he recreated.*

*The pharaohs of the Eighteenth Dynasty had been a strong line of kings
who aggressively pushed Egyptian influence into western Asia to form
the Egyptian "empire" and who asserted their rights and powers
in Egypt with equal force. One of the strongest of these kings was
Amenhotep III. About 1380 B.C. the throne passed to his young and
immature son, who took the name Amenhotep IV and who, despite
his frail health, might have successfully continued his father's vigorous*

*policies. Instead, he became a religious revolutionary, promoting the
worship of his own private deity, Aton, at the expense of the other gods.
The young pharaoh in effect changed the state religion of Egypt
and in the process mortally offended the entrenched interests of the
powerful priesthoods, in particular the priests of Amon, who had come to
be regarded as the chief of the gods and the special tutelary god of
the pharaoh. His devotion to Aton led Amenhotep to change his own
regnal name—further offending Amon, whose name was part of his
own—to Akhenaton, meaning "Spirit of the Aton." He even abandoned
the site of the court at Thebes, where the worship of Amon particularly
flourished, and built a new capital city at Tell el-Amarna, which
he called Akhetaton, "Horizon of Aton." Akhenaton's attention was
riveted upon the service of his god. He was interested in nothing else,
neither the administration of his state nor the maintenance of his empire.*

In James H. Breasted's *most famous book, suggestively titled* The
Dawn of Conscience, *the story of Akhenaton is continued.*

ON A MOMENT'S reflection, such fundamental changes as these suggest
what an overwhelming tide of inherited thought, custom, and tradition had
been diverted from its channel by the young king who was guiding this
revolution. It is only as this aspect of his movement is clearly discerned
that we begin to appreciate the power of his remarkable personality. Before his time religious documents were commonly attributed to ancient
kings and wise men, and the power of a belief lay chiefly in its claim to
remote antiquity and the sanctity of immemorial custom. Until Ikhnaton
the history of the world had largely been merely the irresistible drift of
tradition. The outstanding exception was the great physician-architect, Imhotep, who introduced stone architecture and built the first stone masonry
pyramidal tomb of the Thirtieth Century B.C. Otherwise men had been but
drops of water in the great current. With the possible exception of Imhotep,
Ikhnaton was the first individual in history. Consciously and deliberately,
by intellectual process he gained his position, and then placed himself
squarely in the face of tradition and swept it aside. He appeals to no myths,
to no ancient and widely accepted versions of the dominion of the gods, to
no customs sanctified by centuries—he appeals only to the present and
visible evidences of his god's dominion, evidences open to all, and as for
tradition wherever it had left material manifestations of other gods in
records which could be reached, he endeavoured to annihilate it. A policy
so destructive was doomed to encounter fatal opposition. . . .

Here had been a great people, the onward flow of whose life, in spite of
its almost irresistible momentum, had been suddenly arrested and then
diverted into a strange channel. Their holy places had been desecrated,
the shrines sacred with the memories of thousands of years had been

closed up, the priests driven away, the offerings and temple incomes confiscated, and the old order blotted out. Everywhere whole communities, moved by instincts flowing from untold centuries of habit and custom, returned to their holy places to find them no more, and stood dumfounded before the closed doors of the ancient sanctuaries. On feast days, sanctified by memories of earliest childhood, venerable halls that had resounded with the rejoicings of the multitudes, as we have recalled them at Siut, now stood silent and empty; and every day as the funeral processions wound across the desert margin and up the plateau to the cemetery, the great comforter and friend, Osiris, the champion of the dead in every danger, was banished, and no man dared so much as utter his name. Even in their oaths, absorbed from childhood with their mothers' milk, the involuntary names must not be suffered to escape the lips; and in the presence of the magistrate at court the ancient oath must now contain only the name of Aton. All this to them was as if the modern man were asked to worship X and swear by Y. Groups of muttering priests, nursing implacable hatred, must have mingled their curses with the execration of whole communities of discontented tradesmen—bakers who no longer drew a livelihood from the sale of ceremonial cakes at the temple feasts; craftsmen who no longer sold amulets of the old gods at the temple gateway; hack sculptors whose statues of Osiris lay under piles of dust in many a tumbled-down studio; cemetery stone-cutters who found their tawdry tombstones with scenes from the Book of the Dead banished from the necropolis; scribes whose rolls of the same book, filled with the names of the old gods, or even if they bore the word god in the plural, were anathema; actors and priestly mimes who were driven away from the sacred groves on the days when they should have presented to the people the "passion play," and murmuring groups of pilgrims at Abydos who would have taken part in this drama of the life and death and resurrection of Osiris; physicians deprived of their whole stock in trade of exorcising ceremonies, employed with success since the days of the earliest kings, two thousand years before; shepherds who no longer dared to place a loaf and a jar of water under yonder tree, hoping thus to escape the anger of the goddess who dwelt in it, and who might afflict the household with sickness in her wrath; peasants who feared to erect a rude image of Osiris in the field to drive away the typhonic demons of drought and famine; mothers soothing their babes at twilight and fearing to utter the old sacred names and prayers learned in childhood, to drive away from their little ones the lurking demons of the dark. In the midst of a whole land thus darkened by clouds of smouldering discontent, this marvellous young king, and the group of sympathisers who surrounded him, set up their tabernacle to the daily light, in serene unconsciousness of the fatal darkness that enveloped all around and grew daily darker and more threatening.

In placing the movement of Ikhnaton against a background of popular discontent like this, and adding to the picture also the far more immediately

dangerous secret opposition of the ancient priesthoods, the still uncon-
quered party of Amon, and the powerful military group, who were dis-
affected by the king's peace policy in Asia and his lack of interest in imperial administration and maintenance, we begin to discern something of
the powerful individuality of this first intellectual leader in history. His reign
was the earliest attempt at a rule of ideas, irrespective of the condition and
willingness of the people upon whom they were to be forced. . . .

And so the fair city of the Amarna plain arose, a fatuous Island of the
Blest in a sea of discontent, a vision of fond hopes, born in a mind fatally
forgetful that the past cannot be annihilated. The marvel is that such a man
should have first arisen in the East, and especially in Egypt, where no man
except Ikhnaton possessed the ability to forget. Nor was the great Mediterranean World which Egypt now dominated any better prepared for an
international religion than its Egyptian lords. The imperial imagination of
Ikhnaton reminds one of that of Alexander the Great, a thousand years
later, but it was many centuries in advance of his own age. . . .

The fall of the great revolutionary is shrouded in complete obscurity.
The immediate result of his fall was the restoration of Amon and the old
gods whom the Amonite priesthood forced upon Ikhnaton's youthful and
feeble son-in-law, Tutenkhamon. The old régime returned. . . . In the
great royal lists recording on the monuments the names of all the past
kings of Egypt, the name of Ikhnaton never appears; and when under later
Pharaohs, it was necessary in a state document to refer to him, he was
called "the criminal of Akhetaton."

Ikhnaton, Legend and History
F. J. GILES

*It was inevitable that such an unequivocal and dramatic view as
Breasted's would attract critics. And those critics have found bases for
their objections not only in the materials Breasted used and in his rein-
terpretation of them but in substantial materials that have come to light
in more recent years. Among these finds was the discovery at Amarna
of an almost intact cache of diplomatic correspondence, some three
hundred fifty pieces, written on clay tablets and in cuneiform, including*

letters from the Hittite kings and other peoples of Syria-Palestine and western Asia. The discovery of even more Hittite records at the site of Bogazkoy in Turkey produced further information on aspects of Akhenaton's reign.

The tomb of Akhenaton's successor, Tutankamen, was discovered in 1922, probably the most sensational of all archaeological finds, for it is the only Egyptian royal tomb yet discovered that has not been rifled by tomb robbers. Breasted was among those who celebrated this discovery. But the analysis of the tomb furnishings and inscriptions extended beyond Breasted's time and continues today to produce important information relative to the Aton cult.

But perhaps more important than any single find, the continuing patient work of Egyptologists, archaeologists, linguists, and other scholars in studying, restudying, reclassifying, and comparing the material of old and new discoveries has produced a rather more complicated story about the events at Amarna and some cautious reservations about Akhenaton and his religious revolution.

The striking affinities between the hymn to Aton and the Old Testament remain. But James B. Pritchard, in Ancient Near Eastern Texts Relating to the Old Testament *and in his more recent* The Ancient Near East, Supplementary Texts and Pictures Relating to the Old Testament [2]*—as well as other scholars—has shown that the uniqueness of those affinities is considerably lessened by the discovery, both in the Near East and Egypt, of hundreds of other parallel sources, even a hymn to Aton's great rival Amon, that reveal the same exalted spirituality and seeming monotheism of the Aton hymn. It has even been suggested that the apparent monetheism of the Aton worship was no more than a mode of addressing any number of major Egyptian gods both before and after Akhenaton's supposed religious revolution. John A. Wilson, for example, believes that* "this is an adequate explanation of the similarity between the Aton hymn and the 104th Psalm. Hymns of this kind were current after the fall of Akh-en-aton, so that when Hebrew religion had reached a point where it needed a certain mode of expression it could find in another literature phrases and thoughts which would meet the need." [3]
Wilson also argues against the lofty monotheism of Akhenaton: at best, it was a henotheism—the ranking of the other gods below the new chief god Aton and thus simply a displacement of Amon; at worst, a selfish bigotry in which Akhenaton reserved the worship of Aton to himself and his family and was in turn worshipped as a god and the "prophet" of Aton by all other lesser folk.

Many critics have called attention to the highly unusual, even grotesque, artistic depiction of Akhenaton (found only at Amarna) and have raised

[2] (Princeton: Princeton University Press, 1969).
[3] John A. Wilson, *The Culture of Ancient Egypt* (Chicago: University of Chicago Press; 1st. ed., 1951; 1956), p. 229.

questions about the physical and mental competence of the king. The British Egyptologist Cyril Aldred, in his Akhenaten Pharaoh of Egypt— a New Study,[4] *denies that there was anything at all revolutionary in the social and political character of Akhenaton's reign.*

Much of this cumulative scholarship is reflected in a book by F. J. Giles, Ikhnaton, Legend and History. *Giles is one of the most insistent critics of the Breasted tradition, which, he claims, has created "a wholly legendary Ikhnaton, a kind of pre-Christian Christian in whose life and teachings scholars have found the germ of ideal Western morality."* [5] *His book has been called "a debunking book."* [6] *And it is certainly that. But it is also the most piquant, if not the most persuasive, recasting of the Akhenaton story we now have.*

Here is the story as Giles tells it.

BEFORE APPROACHING the major historical problems of the era, it is useful to turn for a moment to Ikhnaton himself and his environment.

We know him to have been the son of Amenhotep III and Queen Tiy from inscriptions on the Theban tomb of the official Heruef and from the funerary shrine which he presented to his mother. Probably he was their oldest son, and though it could be that an elder brother had died in childhood, it is more likely that he was from his youth the crown prince and heir to the throne of Egypt. This is in itself somewhat unusual, since Tiy could not have been the royal heiress, that is, the daughter of the preceding king.

Ikhnaton was apparently raised in Thebes and was extremely influenced by and interested in religious questions, especially the worship of the Aton, a cult which was increasing in importance during his formative years.

As soon as he was old enough he married a woman of uncertain origin named Nofretiti, and by his ninth regnal year had six daughters by her. His wife stood in the same relationship to him as had Tiy to Amenhotep III. She is shown at his side on all kinds of state occasions, her name was very frequently inscribed alongside his, and intimate scenes of their life together—at meals, enjoying their leisure, on journeys, and in company with their children—are depicted on the tombs of the Akhetaton necropolis to such an extent that these form far more a record of the existence of the royal family than of their owners.

Of the royal princesses the eldest, Meritaton, married Smenkhkare, the heir to the throne; the second, Meketaton, died before the end of her

[4] (New York: McGraw-Hill, 1968).
[5] F. J. Giles, *Ikhnaton, Legend and History* (London: Hutchinson, 1970), p. 6.
[6] By E. P. Uphill in the *Journal of Egyptian Archaeology,* 57 (1971), 219. But Uphill also finds the book "well done" and one that "opens new vistas."

father's reign; and a third, Ankhsenpaaton, married Tutankhamen, possibly
the next in line of succession to Smenkhkare. Nothing definite is known
of the other three. . . . For us it is sufficient that, by Egyptian standards,
Ikhnaton was at his accession either mature, or almost so, a married man,
at least once and perhaps twice a father, and certainly not a boy. . . .

. . . At his accession the young king was known as Neferkheperure
(Uanre usually present) Amenhotep the Divine King of Thebes, but by
the fifth year of his reign he had changed his name to Neferkheperure
Uanre Ikhnaton, by which he is generally known to us and which he retained until the end of his reign.

Ikhnaton was intimately concerned with the Aton cult as it developed
during his lifetime, and a number of the strange features of the belief
may have been his own idea. . . . In the fourth year of his reign, as he
declared on the boundary stele set up to mark the city limits, Ikhnaton
began to build his new capital of Akhetaton. It was not ready for permanent occupation until four more years had passed, which perhaps explains
the relatively few uses of the early form of the full name of the Aton in
the city. Here the king lived out the major remaining portion of his reign.
Here he built his tomb, here he sought to be buried, and here he still
may lie in a tomb yet undiscovered.

Varied scenes of life in the city during its brief heyday are shown on
the wall reliefs in the tombs of the nobles of the court. We see the great
temple of Aton, open to the rays of the sun, the great court filled with
offering tables, and we stand, as if among his subjects, looking up at the
great window of appearances from which the king with his family would
reward his servants. . . .

The plan of the major buildings of Akhetaton may well have altered
from time to time as its royal creator's ideas evolved, and the atelier of
the royal sculptor would certainly have been kept busy producing enough
decorative statuary and relief to keep up with the royal building.

Much has been written about the so-called revolutionary art style of
Amarna. True, Egyptian art had always maintained a stiff and rigid canon
of conventions—in which the peculiar Egyptian notion of perspective is
important—when portraying the human figure, but we must at the same
time remember that by far the greater part of their surviving pictorial art
was originally designed for use in tomb or temple, and hence had a religious
significance. Even at a very early period the portrayal of animals had
always been more natural than that of the human figure, and it is just this
treatment of human beings which is to a certain extent changed in the
Amarna style. In the paintings, statuary and relief of Akhetaton, and to
a very limited extent outside the city proper, the royal family and once
in a while members of its entourage, are depicted naturalistically. In pose
they are relaxed, they lounge and lean and slouch; all of this is anomalous
in religious or semi-religious art. The person of the king is specially treated:
the usual portrayal is more or less distorted and at time verges on a ma-

lignant caricature, as in the case of the colossal statues from Karnak. His head is enlarged and he is shown with a long, hanging jaw. His belly is pendulous and bloated, and his thighs very fat and feminine, and the lower part of his legs spindle-shanked. If Egyptian art has any historical value whatever, as I am sure it has, then this strange portrayal of Ikhnaton must have some origin in his actual physical condition. The art work, however, tends to exaggerate. This is shown particularly because this series of deformities is, as it were, catching. Nofretiti and her daughters are shown in a similar fashion, as is Smenkhkare. Such a great concatenation of gross malformity is a genetic absurdity, and stems from a kind of honorific transposition, whereby it is regarded as desirable for a subject to resemble his monarch even in that which is loathsome. . . .

. . . After the notion that Ikhnaton succeeded to the throne as a child has been disposed of, it becomes less improbable that the so-called Atonist heresy was his work alone. Nevertheless, there are enough references to the Aton, coming from the years before Ikhnaton's reign, to make careful investigation of his primary responsibility for Aton worship necessary.

There follows a lengthy passage in which Giles sifts the evidence—the Amarna letters, inscriptional material, temples and tombs and papyri— and puts together a substantial case on two points. First he argues for a long period of joint rule by Amenhotep III and Akhenaton at the beginning of the latter's reign, followed by a regency exercised by his mother, Queen Tiy, and, at the end of his reign, another regency with the Pharaoh Smenkhkare. Secondly he argues that the Aton worship was routinely practiced both before and after the "Amarna revolution" and was honored by the regents as well as by Akhenaton.

. . . The reign of Ikhnaton now takes shape as being two-thirds spent in a co-regency with Amenhotep III, after whose death Queen Tiy was apparently regent for her son. Then followed a short period of sole rule by Ikhnaton, and the last part of the reign was passed in a co-regency with his son-in-law.

The co-regency with Amenhotep III, from the evidence of the late Aton names used on the doubly inscribed objects, lasted at least nine years. The Gurob Papyri suggest approximately twelve years as the shortest period that will fit the chronology. This second figure agrees with my interpretation of the durbar depicted in the tombs of Huya and Meryre II at Amarna, as either the celebration of the start of Ikhnaton's sole rule, or the funeral and deification of Amenhotep III. The docket on the Amarna letter which Gardiner would read 2, actually must be read 12, and the presence of Ikhnaton in Thebes might well be in connection with the obsequies of Amenhotep III. The period when Tiy apparently held power could only be that immediately succeeding the death of her husband. Its duration is uncertain, but anything more than an outside limit of six months would make the period of Ikhnaton's sole rule very short indeed. We do not know how much longer Smenkhkare reigned after the graffito in the tomb of Pere was written, nor at what period in the year 17 Ikhnaton's reign ended, but late in the year 14 seems the most likely time at which the co-regency with Smenkhkare began. Thus Ikhnaton ruled alone two years, if the above figures are approximately accurate, and two and a half years if the figures are both erroneous to the largest extent possible in the existing circumstances.

Certainly the persecution of the Amen cult and the erasing of the names of other gods as well, which extended in a few cases even to the erasure of the plural noun "gods," could not have taken place while Amenhotep III was alive, since until his death he was building Luxor, a large temple to Amen. Besides, the shrine Ikhnaton presented to Tiy, which was certainly produced after the year 9 on his order by his own workmen, originally contained the Amen name of Amenhotep III. Tiy, in her steles to the Osiris Amenhotep III, used her husband's Amen name so that this policy was not a feature of her regency. By his third year Smenkhkare had a temple in Thebes, in which a scribe of the divine offerings of Amen officiated. Thus, the only period left at which the fanatical Atonism of the reign could have broken out was the period of Ikhnaton's sole rule, the two years between the latter part of years 12 and 14.

The fact is, then, that out of a reign of seventeen years, Ikhnaton ruled only between two and two and a half years by himself. The most obvious conclusion is that Ikhnaton was incompetent to rule. This was recognised by Amenhotep III, and by Tiy and the court officials after the death of the old king, and it resulted in the earliest possible opportunity being taken to put another ruler on the throne with Ikhnaton. This theory is corroborated by the fact that it was during the sole rule of Ikhnaton that such an outbreak of fanatical religious frenzy occurred, wherein workmen were travelling around Egypt chiselling gods' names out of inscriptions. The pictures of Ikhnaton, if they correspond in any way to his actual condition, certainly point in the same direction, for such a badly deformed body might indicate the presence of some mental abnormality as well.

It is scarcely reasonable to assume that Amenhotep III elevated his son to the co-regency knowing that he was completely incompetent to rule, hence if Ikhnaton was actually mentally deranged, he probably became so after his appointment as co-regent, his condition deteriorating to a point at which he could no longer be allowed to rule. It is possible that his father was aware of this, and let Akhetaton be built as a place where Ikhnaton might be kept out of trouble, and left him there hoping that his state of health might improve. It may also be that the Egyptians suffered a mad king as long as they were able, but finally for the safety of their state they had to remove him.

With all of this information in mind, it is possible now to attempt an explanation for the co-regency. We have already seen the extraordinary influence of Queen Tiy, and that she must have possessed quite a command over her husband's affections in order to achieve the position she did. Her origins were well known, indeed Amenhotep III published them far and wide, and there is no possibility whatever that she was the royal heiress, so that, in Egyptian eyes, her children would have no right to the throne. However, because of the affection which he held for his wife, Amenhotep III quite naturally wished that the son of their marriage might succeed him. To this end he elevated Ikhnaton to a position of power long before there was any question of his own health failing. He recognised that, despite his own wishes, the claims of Tiy's children were invalid by custom, and that if he died before Ikhnaton had grasped the reigns of power very firmly, some other prince might be accepted instead of the son whom he wished to succeed him. . . .[7]

. . . Until recently most scholars were very reluctant to admit that the Aton cult had any real historical background before the reign of Ikhnaton. An article of Marianne and Jean Doresse in 1941–2 was the first discussion in detail of the history of the cult, and even today there is no study of the surviving traces of the Aton cult after the Amarna period, or of the extent of its distribution throughout Egypt during that period.

At one time it was thought to have links with western Asia and particularly with the Mitannian sun cult, but there was no definite supporting evidence from either inside or outside Egypt, except rather improbable theories about the Asiatic ancestry of Queen Tiy or Nofretiti. Queen Tiy's father is alleged to have been a western Asiatic on no evidence whatever, and Nofretiti has been thought to be the Mitannian princess sent by Tushratta to Amenhotep III shortly before the latter's death. Mitannian, Babylonian and other princesses were taken in marriage by the king of Egypt, but such alliances would probably be political, the ladies having little influence with their husband.

Moreover, neither the nature nor the literature of the cult shows signs of foreign elements. It is true that the word "Adon" in Hebrew meant "lord" but such a comparison is of very little value since Hebrew appears as a literary language long after this period, and even parallels between the Aton hymns and Hebrew religious literature may well be the result of Egyptian influence on the Hebrews whose familiarity with the older culture is known.

It is enough to say here that the word Aton has an eminently respectable Egyptian history going back at least to the Middle Kingdom, and to mention that the title of the Amarna high priest "greatest of seers" is borne also by the high priests of Re at Heliopolis and at Southern On, whether

---

[7] Although there were relatively few reigning queens in Egyptian history, the claim to the throne passed through the female rather than the male line and thus a Pharaoh whose mother had been a "commoner" had a defective title.—ED.

the latter be identified with Hermonthis or Thebes. It is interesting, also, that the name of the Aton in its early form in Ikhnaton's reign is compounded with that of Re Harakhte. The Aton temple as preserved at Amarna and in pictorial form in the necropolis there is similar in appearance and structure to the sun temples of older times, and the sun hymns of the Aton are very similar to older sun hymns. The house of the benben (shrine) of the Aton temples in Amarna and Thebes is parallel to similar structures in sun temples. The Mnevis bull was held sacred at Amarna as it was in Heliopolis. It is also worth mention that the fanaticism of the Aton cult was not directed against the solar gods. Worship of the Aton was closely connected with, if not an offshoot from, that of Re.

From the earliest to the latest times there was a particular link between the monarch and the Re cult, the kings almost invariably compounding their praenomen with Re, and the cult figuring to a large extent in the royal burial rites. In the Fifth Dynasty it became pre-eminent throughout Egypt, a pre-eminence to some extent lost by the start of the Middle Kingdom, but still leaving the cult a very powerful church. The Amen cult, perhaps wishing to take advantage of this established reputation, made a syncretic identification between Amen and Re, and Amen is very frequently called Amen-Re. Which cult derived the most benefit from this association is not clear. The Amen priesthood may have regarded the connection as necessary, because of the particular attachment of the king to the Re cult, which manifested itself especially in the Atonist fanaticism under Ikhnaton, but it may well have been a factor in royal policy since the beginning of the dynasty, either because of the close connection of the Re cult with the burial ritual, or as a means of fostering the interests of the king in Lower Egypt where it was the most important church.

It is possible to trace the god Aton back to the Middle Kingdom. References exist from the early Eighteenth Dynasty, but as yet no monuments have been discovered which are connected directly or indirectly with the Aton church apparatus before the reign of Amenhotep III. It is arguable that if the Aton cult were the private religion of the monarch, as it appears to have been at the time of Ikhnaton, references to it would not need to be very numerous. In addition, both Amenhotep II and Thutmose IV had close connections with Lower Egypt, Amenhotep II having been born there and Thutmose IV recording on the "Dream Stele" a prophecy received while he was living in Lower Egypt that he would be king.

It is certainly conceivable, if not probable, that the kings might have played one cult against another, but this idea can be overworked since all the kings concerned constructed portions of Karnak, and Amenhotep III probably constructed more buildings in honour of Amen than any previous king.

On balance, it would seem that the fanaticism of Ikhnaton resulted more from a disordered brain than policy. The Egyptian king was always considered a god and an incarnation of god, but it is worth considering whether Ikhnaton might not have taken this idea literally where other more stable monarchs took it figuratively. In other words, he identified himself with the Aton whose high priest he became at the beginning of his reign, considering himself Egypt's paramount god, and attempted to destroy the worship of all the gods except those connected with Aton (that is himself). If all the data were available it might prove that too much emphasis has been given to his destruction of the name of Amen. He made an effort to destroy the names of other gods than the Theban Triad: Amen, Mut and Khonsu, and these may only have received the most attention because Thebes was a most important centre, because a relatively large number of Amen buildings have survived from this period, and because the Amen cult was probably, except for that of Re, the most powerful in Egypt. We have also seen that Ikhnaton did not destroy the names of the gods over a long period of time, such a policy only being put into practice over a two-year period, from the death of Amenhotep III until the elevation of Smenkhkare as co-regent.

To see the end of the Amarna period as the triumph of the Amen cult is a mistake, for the Amarna period was a complete disaster not only for the Amen cult but for Thebes. Never again did the city enjoy the position which it had held until the reign of Ikhnaton. Where Tutankhamen (for the latter part of his reign) and Eye made their headquarters is not definitely known. Haremhab, the so-called violent proponent of Amen, probably spent much of his time in Lower Egypt, and the Nineteenth Dynasty which succeeded him seemed to regard Thebes as no more than a religious centre. From this I venture to argue that the role of the Amen cult in this situation may have been overemphasised. The Amarna revolt was neither against the power of the Amen priesthood nor against Thebes, and its end was no triumph for either. . . .

. . . Material dealing with the Aton cult after the end of the reign of Ikhnaton is very scanty, but it does exist. Bouriant noted, though without adducing evidence, that both Eye and Tutankhamen added to the Aton temple in Thebes, but a full report of this Theban material is as yet not published.

Nevertheless, the fact that Tutankhamen did not change his name from Tukankhaton until quite some time after his accession, indicates that he, or more likely his advisers, were still interested in the new cult. The royal residence was not removed from Akhetaton to Thebes until the reign had well started, and in the tomb of Tutankhamen a number of objects inscribed in the Atonist fashion were found. However, except for Bouriant's statement, no evidence of Aton buildings of this reign exists, unless the remark that the Kawa temple of Tutankhamen was first planned as an Aton structure, and only later changed to an Amen temple, be literally correct. In the inscriptions of this temple the phrase "rule what the Aton encircles" occurs, and a noble who calls himself "a child of the court, the overseer of the southern countries, fan bearer on the king's right,"

Khay, uses the epithet "the chosen one of the Aton" on a stele. . . .

Other miscellaneous items include the dual reading cartouche ring of Tutankhamen found by Petrie; a peculiar stele of Pareemheb, a Heliopolitan priest, which was originally a normal Amarna product showing Ikhnaton and a daughter but was usurped for the reigning king, Haremhab, though the sun disc with hands—symbol of the Aton—is left untouched; and the frequent writing, in the Ramesside manuscripts of the Book of the Dead of the word of Aton with the divine determinative and, on occasion, a cartouche. It is also worth noting that Kawa in Nubia was known as late as the reign of the Nubian king Aspelta in the sixth century B.C. as Pergematon.

Yet it is noticeable that after Ikhnaton the Atonists were no longer fanatical. In almost all of the quoted examples the name of Amen appears as well as that of Aton, and it is obvious that at least by the reign of Haremhab the cult apparatus of the Aton has disappeared. There seems, however, to have been no attempt to destroy the emblem of the god, although there was undoubted enmity on the part of some against Ikhnaton. By the reign of Haremhab the buildings which were erected to the Aton had become handy sources of stone for filling between wall spaces or other such purposes. Whatever officially fostered pro-Aton party had existed between the reigns of Amenhotep II and Tutankhamen had largely died out by the time of Haremhab's death.

It should be stressed, however, that the decline of the Aton cult did not result in the triumph of Amen, since even though Atonism disappeared as a popular religion—though probably not as an article of worship—Amenism never recovered the pre-eminent position it had enjoyed during the first three-quarters of the Eighteenth Dynasty. The kings from Haremhab onward had their main royal residence in Lower Egypt, Thebes ceasing to be the major administrative headquarters of the government, and becoming only a religious centre.

What the disappearance of Atonism from the records signifies is as much of a mystery as its original appearance. If my idea that it was an attempt to construct an empire-wide religion from above has any merit, then its disappearance was a consequence of the failure of a policy of religious nationalism. Since it seems, from what traces remain, that the cult was constructed for personal or political purposes by the rulers rather than evoked as a response to some particular religious need, its disappearance for all practical purposes was not surprising. . . .

. . . The idea that Iknaton, through innate pacifism and devotion to his religion, allowed his empire in Asia to collapse derives directly from an interpretation of the Tell el Amarna letters. It is easy enough when reading them to find the material on which this view is based, but even a cursory examination shows that grounds exist, perhaps far better grounds, for an entirely different interpretation. . . . [For example] in his final letter written towards the end of Ikhnaton's reign, [the Babylonian king]

Burnaburiash objects to the Egyptian king sending an escort of five chariots to fetch the Babylonian princess who is being given to him in marriage. This is not the protest of a father anxious for his daughter's safety on a long and dangerous route through hostile territory; the ground of his objection is simply that five chariots constitutes insufficient pomp and circumstance for the transport of a future queen of Egypt. It is evident that he considers the country safe enough for a small expedition to cross from Egypt to Babylon, and also for the letters themselves to be sent from one court to the other. Nowhere, either in the letters of Burnaburiash or those of other kings, is there any mention of marauding tribes, such as those Khabiru or SA-GAZ peoples to whom various princes subject to Egypt, notably Abdi Hilba, the ruler of Jerusalem, refer. . . .

Only two letters are preserved from the king of the Hittites: one is directed to Ikhnaton, but the other is too badly broken for either salutation or context to provide a clue to the addressee. However, both indicate that relations between the two states have been uniformly good for some time, and the second refers in unambiguous terms to an alliance.

The letters from Alashia and to (as well as perhaps from) Arzawa contain little positive information for the general conditions of the period, but it is interesting to see that Amenhotep's habit of diplomacy by matrimony extended as far as Arzawa. One letter from Alashia gives advice that no treaties should be made by Egypt with the Hittites or the land of Sankhar, but this is an isolated comment with no further references. With both these powers—Alashia and Arzawa—communication would have to be by sea, and transit seems to have been unhindered by hostilities here also.

In short, except for the remarks of Tushratta in what was obviously the earliest of his letters to Amenhotep III, there is no reference in the surviving royal letters indicating a state of war among any of the current great powers. All countries in correspondence with Egypt seem simply to have been in competition for gifts of gold, and the period seems to have been one of unparalleled prosperity with no hint of a collapsing Egyptian Empire. . . .

We also learn from this material that the frontier of the Egyptian hegemony in Western Asia at the end of the reign of Tutankhamen remained the same as when the scene opened on the Tell el Amarna letters. This, of course, lays the ghost of the second part of the Amarna legend: the king can no longer be seen as a pacifist, who spent his time in Amarna composing hymns while his empire fell to pieces. . . .

Suggestions for Further Reading

FOR ALL THE antiquity of its subject, the Akhenaton controversy is essentially a modern one, a continuing dispute among Egyptologists about nearly everything connected with the so-called Amarna period of Eighteenth Dynasty Egyptian history and its central figure. F. J. Giles, whose *Ikhnaton, Legend and History* (London: Hutchinson, 1970) is excerpted in this chapter, represents one view. The British archaeologist Cyril Aldred, in the *Akhenaten—A New Study* (New York: McGraw-Hill, 1968), represents a radically different one. Although Aldred's book is in a series on popular archaeology, it is nevertheless somewhat technical. Students may prefer a further popularization of his views in the work of Joy Collier, *King Sun, In Search of Akhenaten* (London: Ward Lock, 1970), also published under the title *The Heretic Pharaoh* (New York: John Day, 1970). Also dissenting from the Giles view is Donald B. Redford, *History and Chronology of the Eighteenth Dynasty of Egypt, Seven Studies* (Toronto: University of Toronto Press, 1967). The last three of the seven deal with Akhenaton and, while somewhat difficult and detailed, illuminate the way Egyptologists come to their conclusions and the grounds for their often considerable disagreements—excellent reading in parallel with Giles. Much easier to read is Eléanore Bille-De Mot, *The Age of Akhenaten*, tr. Jack Lindsay (New York and Toronto: McGraw-Hill, 1966), which deals interestingly as well with Akhenaton's queen, Nefrititi. The Pulitzer Prize-winning novelist Allen Drury has written a novel dealing with Akhenaton, *A God Against the Gods* (New York: Doubleday, 1976) and one about his successor, Tutankamen, *Return to Thebes* (New York: Doubleday, 1977). They are both first-rate historical novels, dealing with the perennial problems of political power and based upon respectable research.

For the larger setting of the Akhenaton problem, three works by outstanding American, British, and French Egyptologists can be recommended. John A. Wilson, *The Burden of Egypt, An Interpretation of Ancient Egyptian Culture* (Chicago: University of Chicago Press, 1951), republished under the title *The Culture of Ancient Egypt* (Chicago: Phoenix, 1971), while somewhat dated in its research, is still valuable for its insights and an eminently readable book. More up-to-date and equally readable is Sir Alan Gardiner, *Egypt of the Pharaohs, An Introduction* (London and New York: Oxford University Press, 1972 [1961]) which also treats the Amarna period more centrally. Pierre Montet, *Lives of the Pharaohs* (Cleveland and New York: World Publishing Co., 1968) is, with its biographical organization, the most popularly conceived of the

three. Finally, to understand more fully the profound nature of Akhenaton's religious revolt, students should read Henri Frankfort, *Ancient
Egyptian Religion, An Interpretation* (New York: Columbia University
Press, 1948; republished by Harper Torchbooks, 1961), a popular but
authoritative essay, and very readable.

King David: "The Lord's Anointed"

In dealing with Akhenaton we noted the fact—on which there is some degree of consensus—that he is the earliest "individual" we can find in human history. If we take "history" in a slightly broader sense and view the Bible as a species of history, this is not quite true. The Hebrew religion was, from an early time, a religion moving through history and seeing history as the record of God's relationship with his special people, "the sons of Abraham, Isaac, and Jacob."

The history that the Hebrews recorded is admittedly a parochial one, dealing almost exclusively with its own subject and touching only in the most superficial fashion the histories of the "great peoples" of the ancient Near East with whom the Hebrews came in contact. But it does reveal a series of strongly marked protohistorical, even mythohistorical, figures; we find not only Abraham, Isaac, and Jacob but also—at the point where myth and protohistory edge into history—the most interesting and fully rounded personality in the Old Testament, King David.

The Biblical David

*The story of David is found in the Old Testament books of I and II Samuel
and the opening verses of I Kings. The story is very old, preserved in
the religiohistorical tradition from the time of the events themselves,
shortly after the year 1000 B.C., and probably first written down when
the monarchy had finally fallen and the kingdom itself had been swept
away, Israel caught up in the advance of the brutal Assyrians in 722 B.C.
and Judah "carried away captive" to Babylon in 586 B.C. It was a time
of despair, a time when the Hebrew priests and scribes looked back
with longing to the age of their hero-king David, when God had been
gracious to them. David thus took on a special significance in Hebrew
history, which he was never to lose. And it is in terms of this special
significance and unique character of David, as well as against the backdrop
of historic events, that we must examine the story of the founder of
Israel's holy monarchy.*

*The story of David is rich in anecdote and detail. One need only recall
his single combat with the Philistine champion Goliath, or his coming
by night to Saul's camp, standing by the head of the sleeping king,
and sparing his life. The character of David is developed with equal
richness. David's response when he heard that Saul and Jonathan had died
in battle against the Philistines on Mount Gilboa is described in
II Samuel 1:17–27, from the* Revised Standard Version Bible.

DAVID LAMENTED with this lamentation over Saul and Jonathan his son,
and he said it should be taught to the people of Judah; behold, it is written
in the Book of Jashar. He said:

"Thy glory, O Israel, is slain upon thy high places!
How are the mighty fallen!
Tell it not in Gath,
publish it not in the streets of Ash'kelon;
lest the daughters of the Philistines rejoice,
lest the daughters of the uncircumcised exult.

"Ye mountains of Gilbo'a,
let there be no dew or rain upon you,
nor upsurging of the deep!
For there the shield of the mighty was defiled,
the shield of Saul, not anointed with oil.

"From the blood of the slain,
   from the fat of the mighty,
the bow of Jonathan turned not back,
   and the sword of Saul returned not empty.

"Saul and Jonathan, beloved and lovely!
   In life and in death they were not divided;
they were swifter than eagles,
   they were stronger than lions.

"Ye daughters of Israel, weep over Saul,
   who clothed you daintily in scarlet,
   who put ornaments of gold upon your apparel.

"How are the mighty fallen
   in the midst of the battle!

"Jonathan lies slain upon thy high places.
I am distressed for you, my brother Jonathan;
very pleasant have you been to me;
   your love to me was wonderful,
   passing the love of women.

"How are the mighty fallen,
   and the weapons of war perished!"

The preceding passage, one of the finest lyric passages of the Old Testament, reveals David the singer, the lyre-player, the psalmist. But the passage contrasts sharply with the account of how David ordered the execution of the messenger who had come to report that he had helped Saul end his life on the battlefield, even though the man pleaded that he acted only out of mercy for the old, wounded king. But that did not matter to David, "for your mouth has testified against you, saying 'I have slain the Lord's anointed.' " (II Sam. 1:16). Nor is this the only such contradiction of character in the story of David. The incident of Uriah the Hittite and David's desire for his handsome wife Bathsheba is an account of the king's human weakness. In another instance, we hear the plaint for David's dead rebel son Absalom that his battle commander, the rough and outspoken Joab, finds so hard to understand.

   Despite the rich and varied detail that makes David live so vividly for us, the emphasis in the account of II Samuel is less upon the man than upon his special relationship—and the special relationship of the monarchy—with God. David stood very close to the beginning of the monarchy itself. It was, after all, less than a generation since the scattered tribes of Hebrews, presided over by their "judges" and halted in their uneven conquest of their promised land, had turned to the aged prophet Samuel and asked him to "appoint for us a king to govern us like all the nations," "to go out before us and fight our battles." (I Sam. 8:4–6). Samuel had appointed Saul, to be succeeded by David. But the choice both of Saul and of David had not been Samuel's; he was simply the vehicle of God's will. As a learned, modern German critic has put it, ". . . the king set over the people of God must be a man of God's grace, called by him and a real instrument in his hand. . . . Only the man 'on whom the spirit of the Lord shall rest' (Isa. 11:2) can really be the king in Israel. . . . Only he who allows God to be wholly king, and who is therefore himself completely obedient, can be king over the people of God." [1]

The special character of David as the instrument of God's will is stressed from the beginning of the biblical narrative. When, following God's direction, Samuel hesitated to choose the young shepherd boy David, God told him, "The Lord sees not as man sees. Anoint him; for this is he." (I Sam. 16:12).

David brought his people together in victory over the Philistines; he captured Jerusalem and established his capital there, calling it "the city of David."

. . . David became greater and greater, for the LORD, the God of hosts, was with him.

And Hiram king of Tyre sent messengers to David, and cedar trees, also carpenters and masons who built David a house. And David perceived that the LORD had established him king over Israel, and that he had exalted his kingdom for the sake of his people Israel. . . .

Now when the king dwelt in his house, and the LORD had given him rest from all his enemies round about, the king said to Nathan the prophet, "See now, I dwell in a house of cedar, but the ark of God dwells in a tent." And Nathan said to the king, "Go, do all that is in your heart; for the LORD is with you."

But that same night the word of the LORD came to Nathan, "Go and tell my servant David, 'Thus says the LORD: Would you build me a house to dwell in? I have not dwelt in a house since the day I brought up the people of Israel from Egypt to this day, but I have been moving about in a tent for my dwelling. In all places where I have moved with all the people of Israel, did I speak a word with any of the judges of Israel, whom I commanded to shepherd my people Israel, saying, "Why have you not built me a house of cedar?" ' Now therefore thus you shall say to my servant David, 'Thus says the LORD of hosts, I took you from the pasture, from following the sheep, that you should be prince over my people Israel; and I have been

[1] Hans Wilhelm Herzberg, *I & II Samuel, A Commentary*, J. S. Bowden, trans. (Philadelphia: Westminster Press, 1964), pp. 133–134.

with you wherever you went, and have cut off all your enemies from before you; and I will make for you a great name, like the name of the great ones of the earth. And I will appoint a place for my people Israel, and will plant them, that they may dwell in their own place, and be disturbed no more; and violent men shall afflict them no more, as formerly, from the time that I appointed judges over my people Israel; and I will give you rest from all your enemies. Moreover the LORD declares to you that the LORD will make you a house. When your days are fulfilled and you lie down with your fathers, I will raise up your offspring after you, who shall come forth from your body, and I will establish his kingdom. He shall build a house for my name, and I will establish the throne of his kingdom for ever. I will be his father, and he shall be my son. When he commits iniquity, I will chasten him with the rod of men, with the stripes of the sons of men; but I will not take my steadfast love from him, as I took it from Saul, whom I put away from before you. And your house and your kingdom shall be made sure for ever before me; your throne shall be established for ever.'" In accordance with all this vision, Nathan spoke to David.

Then King David went in and sat before the LORD, and said, "Who am I, O Lord GOD, and what is my house, that thou hast brought me thus far? And yet this was a small thing in thy eyes, O Lord GOD; thou hast spoken also of thy servant's house for a great while to come, and hast shown me future generations, O Lord GOD! And what more can David say to thee? For thou knowest thy servant, O Lord GOD! Because of thy promise, and according to thy own heart, thou has wrought all this greatness, to make thy servant know it. Therefore thou art great, O LORD God; for there is none like thee, and there is no God besides thee, according to all that we have heard with our ears. What other nation on earth is like thy people Israel, whom God went to redeem to be his people, making himself a name, and doing for them great and terrible things, by driving out before his people a nation and its Gods? And thou didst establish for thyself thy people Israel to be thy people for ever; and thou, O LORD, didst become their God. And now, O LORD God, confirm for ever the word which thou has spoken concerning thy servant and concerning his house, and do as thou hast spoken; and thy name will be magnified for ever, saying, 'The LORD of hosts is God over Israel,' and the house of thy servant David will be established before thee. For thou, O LORD of hosts, the God of Israel, hast made this revelation to thy servant, saying, 'I will build you a house'; therefore thy servant has found courage to pray this prayer to thee. And now, O Lord GOD, thou art God, and thy words are true, and thou hast promised this good thing to thy servant; now therefore may it please thee to bless the house of thy servant, that it may continue for ever before thee; for thou, O Lord GOD, hast spoken, and with thy blessing shall the house of thy servant be blessed for ever."

As David grew "old and advanced in years," his servants sought of him, "who should sit on the throne of my lord the king after him?"

Then King David answered, "Call Bathshe'ba to me." So she came into the king's presence, and stood before the king. And the king swore, saying, "As the LORD lives, who has redeemed my soul out of every adversity, as I swore to you by the LORD, the God of Israel, saying, 'Solomon your son shall reign after me, and he shall sit upon my throne in my stead'; even so will I do this day." Then Bathshe'ba bowed with her face to the ground, and did obeisance to the king, and said, "May my lord King David live for ever!"

King David said, "Call to me Zadok the priest, Nathan the prophet, and Benai'ah the son of Jehoi'ada." So they came before the king. And the king said to them, "Take with you the servants of your lord, and cause Solomon my son to ride on my own mule, and bring him down to Gihon; and let Zadok the priest and Nathan the prophet there anoint him king over Israel; then blow the trumpet, and say, 'Long live King Solomon!'

You shall then come up after him, and he shall come and sit upon my throne; for he shall be king in my stead; and I have appointed him to be ruler over Israel and over Judah." And Benai'ah the son of Jehoi'ada answered the king, "Amen! May the LORD, the God of my lord the king, say so. As the LORD has been with my lord the king, even so may he be with Solomon, and make his throne greater than the throne of my lord King David."

Kingship and the Gods
HENRI FRANKFORT

We turn now from the ancient scriptural account of King David to modern scholarship and the work of one of the most eminent of Near Eastern scholars, Henri Frankfort (d. 1954). Although Frankfort was European-born and trained, he spent most of his career at the University of Chicago as Field Director and Research Professor of Oriental Archaeology. But Henri Frankfort's real talent was his ability to move beyond the stones and shards of ancient material culture to speculate—as his great Chicago predecessor James H. Breasted had done—on the nature of ancient Near Eastern thought, ancient philosophical and religious beliefs, and the substance they gave to the forms of ancient institutions such as kingship.

One of Frankfort's most provocative books in this respect is **Kingship** and the Gods. *In this book he argues that the ancient Near Eastern peoples considered kingship to be the very basis of civilization. "Only savages could live without a king" to bring security, peace, and justice. And yet the ancient Egyptians and Mesopotamians regarded kingship as a religious, rather than a political, institution. These peoples "experienced human life as part of a widely spreading network of connections that reached beyond the local and the national communities into the hidden depths of nature, the powers that rule nature."* [2] *The king was the necessary link between the dangerous and potentially destructive power of nature—that is, the gods—and human survival. As either chief priest (as he was in Mesopotamia) or fellow god of the gods themselves (as he was in Egypt), it was the king who maintained the rituals necessary to secure the continued benefactions of the gods. The maintenance of life itself was in the hands of the king.*

At first glance this view would seem to concur, to a large extent, with what we have already seen of David and the ancient Hebrew monarchy. But Henri Frankfort does not agree.

THE ANCIENT Near East knew a third kind of king. In addition to the god incarnate who was Pharaoh and the chosen servant of the gods who ruled Mesopotamia, we find a hereditary leader whose authority derived from descent and was originally coextensive with kinship. This is a more primitive kind of monarchy, a product rather of nature than of man, based on the facts of consanguinity, not on any conception of man's place in the universe. Yet it was the equal of the Egyptian and Mesopotamian institutions in that it formed an integral part of the civilizations in which it occurred. For the type of rulership we are now to discuss is found among people who acknowledged kinship above every other bond of loyalty and whose coherence derived from a shared nomadic past rather than from what they had achieved as a settled community. It is found, significantly, in the peripheral regions of the ancient Near East where autochthonous civilization was feeble. Palestine and Syria, Anatolia and Persia, were overrun by foreign peoples on many occasions, and, furthermore, the newcomers succeeded in taking charge. In this respect the contrast between the peripheral regions and the centers of the ancient Near East is striking. Foreigners could rise to power in Egypt, but on condition that they were completely assimilated. When large groups of immigrants—Amorites, Kassites, Aramaeans—were absorbed by Mesopotamia, they insinuated themselves in the traditional fabric of Mesopotamian culture which henceforth determined their behavior. But the peripheral regions lacked cultural individuality, and once immigrants had asserted their power their mastery

[2] Henri Frankfort, *Kingship and the Gods, A Study of Ancient Near Eastern Religion as the Integration of Society and Nature* (Chicago: University of Chicago Press, 1948), p. 3.

was complete. The Philistines and Hebrews put their stamp on Palestine; Hittites, Mitanni, Medes, and Persians on other peripheral regions.

The position of these new arrivals was anomalous. They brought with them hereditary tribal institutions, such as rulership based on descent. But settling in civilized lands, they faced problems for which their nomadic existence had not prepared them. . . .

Our knowledge of Hittite, Syrian, and Persian kingship is so incomplete that we cannot pass beyond generalities. But we know more about the Hebrew monarchy. This was also based upon descent but possessed a peculiar character of its own which makes it an effective foil for the material we have discussed in this book; for the Hebrews, though in the Near East, were only partly of it. Much is made nowadays of Canaanite and other Near Eastern elements in Hebrew culture. . . . But it should be plain that the borrowed features in Hebrew culture, and those which have foreign analogies, are least significant. In the case of kingship they are externalities, the less important since they did not affect the basic oddness of the Hebrew institution. If kingship counted in Egypt as a function of the gods, and in Mesopotamia as a divinely ordained political order, the Hebrews knew that they had introduced it on their own initiative, in imitation of others and under the strain of an emergency. When Ammonite oppression was added to the Philistine menace, the people said: "Nay; but we will have a king over us; that we also may be like all the nations; and that our king may judge us, and go out before us, and fight our battles" (I Sam. 8:19–20).

If the Hebrews, like the Mesopotamians, remembered a kingless period, they never thought that "kingship descended from heaven." Hence the Hebrew king did not become a necessary bond between the people and the divine powers. On the contrary, it was in the kingless period that the people had been singled out by Yahweh and that they had been bound, as a whole, by the Covenant of Sinai. It was said in the Law: "Ye are the children of the Lord your God: . . . and the Lord hath chosen thee to be a peculiar people unto himself, above all the nations that are upon earth" (Deut. 14:1–2). Moses said to Pharaoh: "Thus saith the Lord, Israel is my son, even my firstborn: and I say unto thee, Let my son go, that he may serve me" (Exod. 4:22–23). For the service of God was part of the Covenant, which the people must keep even though it imposes a moral obligation which man's inadequacy makes forever incapable of fulfilment: "Now therefore, if you will obey my voice indeed, and keep my covenant, then ye shall be a peculiar treasure unto me above all people: for all earth is mine: And ye shall be unto me a kingdom of priests and an holy nation" (Exod. 19:5–6).

The conviction of the Hebrews that they were a chosen people is the one permanent, as it is the most significant, feature in their history. The tenacity of the Hebrew struggle for existence in the sordid turmoil of the Levant was rooted in the consciousness of their election. This animated the leaders of the people, whether they were kings like David and Hezekiah, or prophets opposing kings in whom belief in the unique destiny of Israel had been compromised. But this intimate relationship between the Hebrew people and their god ignored the existence of an earthly ruler altogether. Hebrew tradition, vigorously defended by the great prophets and the post-Exilic leaders, recognized as the formative phase of Hebrew culture the sojourn in the desert when Moses, the man of God, led the people and gave them the law. Kingship never achieved a standing equal to that of institutions which were claimed—rightly or wrongly—to have originated during the Exodus and the desert wandering.

The antecedents of Saul's kingship were known. The settlement in Canaan left the tribal divisions intact, and the Book of Judges shows the varying ranges of power to which individual chieftains might aspire. . . .

The tribesmen recognized the bond of blood alone, and it was exceedingly difficult to envisage a loyalty surpassing the scope of kinship. Nevertheless, when the separate tribes were threatened with extinction or enslavement, Saul was made king over all. Samuel anointed Saul, thereby expressing Yahweh's approval of the initiative of the people who had in any case sought advice from the seer. But royalty received little sanctity from this involvement. It is true that David shrank from buying personal immunity at the price of laying hands "upon the Lord's anointed" (I Sam. 24:10); but such scruples are perhaps more revealing for David's character than for the esteem in which kingship was held among the Hebrews. And the tragic sequel of Saul's history proves how little Yahweh's initial approval protected office and officeholder. In fact, once kingship had been established, it conformed to the tribal laws which treat relatives as one, for better or for worse. Saul's "house" was exterminated by David (II Sam., chap. 21) on Yahweh's orders. David's "house" was promised lasting dominion by Yahweh through the mouth of the prophet Nathan (see below). It is very significant that in actual fact the Davidian dynasty was never dethroned in Judah. But David belonged to Judah; and when Solomon died and his son Rehoboam was ill advised and refused to alleviate the burdens imposed by Solomon's splendor, ten of the tribes refused to acknowledge him: "So when all Israel saw that the king hearkened not unto them, the people answered the king, saying, What portion have we in David? neither have we an heritance in the son of Jesse: to your tents O Israel: now see to thine own house, David" (I Kings 12:16). No voice was raised to decry the rejection of David's grandson as an impious act. On the contrary, even David, Yahweh's favorite, had been confirmed in his rulership by the elders of all the tribes who, in accepting him, began by acknowledging their consanguinity:

> Then came all the tribes of Israel to David unto Hebron, and spake, saying, Behold we are thy bone and thy flesh. . . . So all the elders of Israel came to the king to Hebron, and King David made a league with them in Hebron before the Lord: and they anointed David king of Israel [II Sam. 5:1, 3]).

In the light of Egyptian, and even Mesopotamian, kingship, that of the
Hebrews lacks sanctity. The relation between the Hebrew monarch and
his people was as nearly secular as is possible in a society wherein religion
is a living force. The unparalleled feature in this situation is the independence, the almost complete separation, of the bonds which existed
between Yahweh and the Hebrew people, on the one hand, and between
Yahweh and the House of David, on the other. Yahweh's covenant with
the people antedated kingship. His covenant with David concerned the
king and his descendants, but not the people. Through Nathan, Yahweh
promised David:

> I will set up thy seed after thee. . . . I will be his father, and he shall
> be my son. If he commits iniquity, I shall chasten him with the rod of
> men, and with the stripes of the children of men: But my mercy shall
> not depart from him, as I took it from Saul, whom I put away before
> thee. And thine house and thy kingdom shall be established for ever
> before thee: thy throne shall be established for ever [II Sam. 7:12–16].

Only in later times, when this promise was made the foundation of
Messianic expectations, did the people claim a share in it. As it was made,
it was as simple and direct a pledge to David as the earlier divine promises
had been to the Patriarchs (e.g., Gen. 15:18–21). It committed Yahweh
solely to maintain the greatness of the House of David. It can be argued
that this implied the greatness of the Hebrew people, or at least of Judah;
but the conclusion is not inevitable. Nowhere else in the Near East do we
find this dissociation of a people from its leader in relation to the divine;
with the Hebrews we find parallelism while everywhere else we find coin-
cidence. In the meager information about Hebrew ritual it has been attempted to find indications that the king fulfilled a function not unlike
that of contemporary rulers. But even if we take an exceptional and apparently simple phrase, "[Solomon] sat on the throne of the Lord as king,
instead of David, his father" (I Chron. 29:23), we need only compare
this with the corresponding phrases "throne of Horus" or "throne of
Atum" to realize that the Hebrew expression can only mean "throne
favored by the Lord," or something similar. The phrase confirms what the
account of Saul's elevation and David's scruples showed in the first place
—namely, that there is interplay between the king's person and sancity, as
there was a connection between the king's fate and the national destiny.
But these relations were not the nerve center of the monarchy, as they were
in Egypt and Mesopotamia, but rather cross-currents due to the religious
orientation of Hebrew society; and their secondary nature stands out most
clearly when we consider the functions of the Hebrew king.

The Hebrew king normally functioned in the profane sphere, not in the
sacred sphere. He was the arbiter in disputes and the leader in war. He
was emphatically not the leader in the cult. The king created the conditions
which made a given form of worship possible: David's power allowed
him to bring the Ark to Jerusalem; Solomon's riches enabled him to build

the temple; Jeroboam, Ahab, Manasseh, and others had idols made and arranged for "groves" and "high places" for the cult of the gods of fertility. But the king played little part in the cult. He did not, as a rule, sacrifice; that was the task of the priests. He did not interpret the divine will; that, again, was the task of the priests, who cast lots for an oracle. Moreover, the divine intentions were sometimes made known in a more dramatic way when prophets—men possessed—cried, "Thus saith the Lord." These prophets were often in open conflict with the king precisely because the secular character of the king entitled them to censor him.

The predominant accusation of the prophets against the kings was faithlessness to Yahweh, a "seduction" of his chosen people (e.g., II Kings 21:9–11) so that they followed the ways of the gentiles. Said the prophet Jehu in the name of Yahweh to Baasha, king of Israel: "Forasmuch as I exalted thee out of the dust, and made thee prince over my people Israel; and thou hast walked in the way of Jeroboam, and hast made my people Israel to sin, to provoke me to anger with their sins" (I Kings 16:2). Such accusations recur with monotonous regularity throughout the Books of Kings. Most rulers "did evil in the sight of the Lord"; and we cannot discuss Hebrew kingship without considering this evil which seems to have attached to it. If the kings seduced the people, we must admit, in the light of the Egyptian and Mesopotamian evidence, that they offered the people something eminently desirable. The keeping of Yahweh's covenant meant relinquishing a great deal. It meant, in a word, sacrificing the greatest good ancient Near Eastern religion could bestow—the harmonious integration of man's life with the life of nature. The biblical accounts stress the orgiastic joys of the Canaanite cult of natural powers; we must remember that this cult also offered the serene awareness of being at one with the universe. In this experience ancient oriental religion rewarded its devotees with the peace of fulfilment. But the boon was available only for those who believed that the divine was immanent in nature, and Hebrew religion rejected precisely this doctrine. The absolute transcendence of God is the foundation of Hebrew religious thought. God is absolute, unqualified, ineffable, transcending every phenomenon, the one and only cause of all existence. God, moreover, is holy, which means that all values are ultimately his. Consequently, every concrete phenomenon is devaluated. We have discussed elsewhere this austere transcendentalism of Hebrew thought, which denied the greatest values and the most cherished potentialities of contemporary creeds, and have offered an explanation of its origin. Here we must point out that it bereft kingship of a function which it exercised all through the Near East, where its principal task lay in the maintenance of the harmony with the gods in nature. And so we observe—now for the third time—the inner logic and consistency of ancient Near Eastern thought. We have described the peculiar nature of Hebrew kingship, starting from its relation to the people and their past; it would have appeared with the same characteristics if we had taken our stand on Hebrew theology. The transcendentalism of Hebrew religion prevented kingship from assuming the profound significance which it possessed in Egypt and Meso-potamia. It excluded, in particular, the king's being instrumental in the integration of society and nature. It denied the possibility of such an integration. It protested vehemently—in the persons of the great prophets —that attempts by king and people to experience that integration were incompatible with their avowed faithfulness to Yahweh. To Hebrew thought nature appeared void of divinity, and it was worse than futile to seek a harmony with created life when only obedience to the will of the Creator could bring peace and salvation. God was not in sun and stars, rain and wind; they were his creatures and served him (Deut. 4:19; Psalm 19). Every alleviation of the stern belief in God's transcendence was corruption. In Hebrew religion—and in Hebrew religion alone—the ancient bond between man and nature was destroyed. Those who served Yahweh must forego the richness, the fulfilment, and the consolation of a life which moves in tune with the great rhythms of earth and sky. There were no festivals to celebrate it. No act of the king could promote it. Man remained outside nature, exploiting it for a livelihood, offering its first-fruits as a sacrifice to Yahweh, using its imagery for the expression of his moods; but never sharing its mysterious life, never an actor in the perennial cosmic pageant in which the sun is made "to rise on the evil and on the good" and the rain is sent "on the just and the unjust."

Kingship, too, was not, for the Hebrews, anchored in the cosmos. Except by way of contrast, it has no place in a "study of ancient Near Eastern religion as an integration of society and nature." The Hebrew king, as every other Hebrew, stood under the judgment of God in an alien world, which—as the dying David knew (II Sam. 23:3–4)—seems friendly only on those rare occasions when man proves not inadequate: "He that ruleth over men must be just, ruling in the fear of God. And he shall be as the light of the morning, when the sun riseth, even a morning without clouds; as the tender grass, springing out of the earth by clear shining after rain."

The Evidence of Archaeology
KATHLEEN M. KENYON

The most significant omission in the biblical account of the Davidic monarchy, and even in Frankfort's brilliant conceptualization, is the

setting in which the events of David's reign occurred. The scriptural
record mentions some peoples, like the Ammonites, the Amalekites, and
the Moabites, about whom we have virtually no other records, and
others, like the Philistines and the Hittites, for whom we are only now
beginning to gain substantial information. It cites battles and events and
persons with an easy familiarity that seems to reflect an accurate
history. But in the parallel records, admittedly fragmentary, of the other
contemporary peoples, there is not a shred of evidence to verify any
of the events that loom so large in the narrative of Samuel, nor is there
mention of any name that could be equated to Saul or David or
even Solomon. To fill the gap we must turn to another kind of reconstruc-
tion, that of modern archaeology, to see what we can tell about the
setting of the Hebrew monarchy, the contemporary physical and
political world, the other peoples of Palestine, and the way men lived.

For that purpose we sample the work of one of the foremost
contemporary Near Eastern archaeologists, Dr. Kathleen M. Kenyon,
who won such well-deserved acclaim for the excavations at Jericho. The
following excerpts are from her Archaeology in the Holy Land.

. . . ARCHAEOLOGY HAS NOT yet given us a clear picture of the Philistines, for none of their important cities has as yet been sufficiently excavated for any generalisations as to Philistine or non-Philistine traits to be
made. . . .

Such exact evidence as there is suggests that an initial settlement on
the coast was followed by a more gradual conquest of towns farther inland,
up to the edge of the central ridge, which they never settled, though in
the 11th century B.C. they exercised some degree of suzerainty over the
Israelites there. The evidence comes from the relation of the appearance
of the Philistine pottery to the termination of the 13th century Cypriot
and Mycenaean imports, which has been described above and which
must be ascribed to the disruption of trade caused by the movements of
the Peoples of the Sea. . . .

Thus the area of Philistine occupation was a limited one, though ultimately their political control extended considerably beyond this. For a
hundred years or so they lived side by side with their Canaanite and Israelite predecessors. As has already been said, there is no archaeological
evidence to decide which sites belong to which of these two groups. It
is only on historical grounds, for instance the mention of the people Israel
by Merneptah, that we know in fact that the Israelites were by now firmly
established in the land, in two groups, divided by the Canaanite wedge
round Jerusalem.

Our fullest evidence concerning non-Philistine areas at this period
does, however, come from sites which were certainly not Israelite, notably

Megiddo. There is actually no mention in the Bible of when this important city came to be part of Israel. It is included in the list of those that remained under the Canaanites in the initial conquest, while it was Israelite by the time of Solomon. It may well be that it came under Israelite control during the 11th century, during much of which period the site was unoccupied, and therefore no particular importance was attached to the fact. . . .

All the sites so far described lie outside the area at this period occupied by the Israelites. It must in fact be admitted that we know tantalisingly little about the early Israelite settlements. The reason for this is partly owing to the limitations of archaeological evidence, partly owing to the limitations of the culture of the Israelites themselves.

The archaeological limitations arise from the fact that the area in which these settlements lie is the hill country. Sites in such districts do not present the same thick deposits of successive strata as do the sites in the plains. The buildings are naturally constructed of stone, which is readily available all over the area. As a result, when buildings of one period decay, their walls are apt to be dismantled and the stones re-used in their successors. Thus instead of the ruins being buried intact beneath a mass of collapsed mud-brick, the usual material for the superstructure in the plains, they are disturbed and destroyed to the very base of the walls. The story of the successive phases is thus very much more difficult to deduce. The excavation of the great site of Gezer, for instance, carried out before modern refinements of archaeological technique had been introduced, did little to give us a detailed picture of its history, since the buildings could not be ascribed to definite periods. The same drawback applies to the results of the excavation of many other sites in the hill country.

The character of the settlements is the second factor which limits our information. The period is undoubtedly that in which the national consciousness of the Israelites is developing greatly. The biblical narrative shows how the groups were gradually combining together, with tentative efforts at temporal unification under the Judges and the stronger spiritual link of a national religion, with the high priest at times exercising temporal power. It is during these centuries that the groups allied by race, but differing in the manner and time of their settlement in Palestine, . . . must have come to combine their ancestral traditions together under the influence of the Yahwehistic religion, and to believe that all their ancestors took part in the Exodus. The nation was thus emerging, but its culture was as yet primitive. Its settlements were villages, its art crude, and the objects of everyday use homely and utilitarian. . . .

For something like a hundred years the Philistines and the Israelites lived side by side, the Philistines in the rich coastal plain, the Israelites in the more barren hill country. About 1080 B.C. the Philistines began trying to extend their control over the hill country, and this is the period of oppression by the Philistines of which the Bible gives such a vivid account. The period was one of oppression, but it was also one that gave a stimulus towards nationhood. Saul, leading a revolt which started about 1030 B.C., became the acknowledged leader of the whole country in the struggle, and though his success was varying, and marred by quarrels with the religious leaders and with David, and terminated by defeat on Mount Gilboa, it was on the foundations of the unity that he achieved that David was able to establish the free and united kingdom of Israel. . . .

The united kingdom of Israel had a life span of only three-quarters of a century. It was the only time in which the Jews were an important political power in western Asia. Its glories are triumphantly recorded in the Bible, and the recollection of them profoundly affected Jewish thought and aspirations. Yet the archaeological evidence for the period is meagre in the extreme.

After the disaster on Mount Gilboa, when the bodies of Saul and Jonathan were exhibited as trophies at Beth-shan, the Philistines set up two vassal kingdoms, with David as ruler at Hebron and Ishbaal in the north. In between the two lay Jerusalem, still occupied by the Canaanite tribe of Jebusites. But David, though he had taken refuge with the Philistines when Saul had turned against him, was not prepared to continue as a vassal now that his old leader was dead. He succeeded in defeating Ishbaal, apparently without intervention by the Philistines, thus reuniting the kingdom of Saul, and he threw off the Philistine overlordship. He then achieved the crucial success of capturing Jerusalem.

The control of Jerusalem was essential to the control of a united Palestine, as it lies on the central ridge which is the only convenient route north and south through the hill country. . . .

The previous lack of cohesion among the Israelites is well illustrated by the fact that this Canaanite enclave had been allowed to persist in their midst for centuries. Without its possession, political unity was impossible. Once it was secured, the great period of Israelite history begins. But the effect of the long division of the Israelites into two groups, added to that of probable difference of origin between the northern and southern tribes, was permanent and contributed to the renewed division into Israel and Judah at the end of the 10th century B.C. . . .

The capture of Jerusalem is to be dated c.995 B.C. By it, David's position was assured. His growing power inevitably aroused the hostility of the Philistines. Their defeats at Baal-Perazim and Rephaim caused their withdrawal once more to the coastal plain, and they ceased to be a permanent menace. But though David now started on a policy of expansion, he never annexed Philistia. It may be conjectured that Egypt, in spite of its weakness at this time, gave sufficient support to deter him. The coastal plain in fact never became part of the Israelite domain, and the Philistines reappear in the 8th and 7th centuries B.C. as an independent group.

David followed up his success against the Philistines by attacking other ancient enemies. The various "oppressors" were now oppressed in their turn. Moab, Ammon, Edom, were all subjugated, and the most surprising expansion is the defeat of the Aramaeans and the annexation of Damascus. The Israelites thus controlled a large part of the country from the Euphrates to the borders of Egypt, though the Phoenician towns on the Syrian coast remained independent.

This unification and expansion inevitably brought about a revolution in the culture of the country. The people of simple hill villages, united in reality only by religious ties, became part of an organised kingdom. The transfer of the religious centre to Jerusalem established a combined political and religious focus, and strengthened the monarch at the expense of the priesthood. The international contacts of the Israelites were opened up for the first time. Instead of being circumscribed within their limited area, they were brought into touch with the main currents of civilisation of the period. In particular, they were brought into touch with the Phoenicians. Recent archaeological research in Syria and the adjacent countries has shown that Phoenicia at this time had a highly developed civilisation, manifesting itself in fine buildings and a distinctive (though eclectic rather than original) art, and a remarkable development in literature, as well as in the trading and colonising ventures for which they have long been famous. Research in Palestine is beginning to show how strong Phoenician influence was in the process which began under David, which was in fact the civilising of Israel.

This process was indeed begun under David, but he only provided the groundwork for the great developments under Solomon. There is little in the record, either literary or archaeological, to show that much progress towards civilisation was made during David's reign. For Solomon's reign there is considerable literary evidence, but not much archaeological. Many attempts have been made to reconstruct on paper the Temple Solomon built at Jerusalem on the hill north of Ophel. Finds on other sites make it easier to understand the description and to visualise some of the details, but the area of the Temple and that of the extension of the city under the Israelites lie beneath modern Jerusalem, beyond the reach of the archaeologist's spade.

Suggestions for Further Reading

THE PRIMARY account of King David is, of course, I and II Samuel and the first part of I Kings in the Old Testament, and students are encouraged to read the entire story. There are many versions and editions of the Bible, but students will find particularly attractive *The Bible Designed To Be Read as Living Literature,* ed. Ernest S. Bates (New York: Simon and Schuster, 1937) and *The Modern Reader's Bible,* ed. Richard G. Moulton (New York: Macmillan, 1924) because of their organization and format. *The Dartmouth Bible,* ed. R. B. Chamberlain and Herman Feldman (Boston: Houghton Mifflin, 1950), *The Oxford Annotated Bible,* and the appropriate sections of vols. 2 and 3 of *The Interpreter's Bible* (New York and Nashville: Abingdon-Cokesbury Press, 1953–1954) have exhaustive and useful notes. Useful too is the brief section on the David monarchy in Harold H. Watts, *The Modern Reader's Guide to the Bible* (New York: Harper, 1949), with its emphasis upon literary rather than biblical criticism. There is also an attractive, solidly researched historical novel by Laurence Chambers Chinn, *The Unanointed* (New York: Crown, 1959), featuring as its central character David's friend Joab.

The greatest modern authority on the history and archaeology of Palestine is William Foxwell Albright. His most famous book is *From the Stone Age to Christianity, Monotheism and the Historical Process* (Baltimore: Johns Hopkins University Press, 1940), reprinted in a revised second edition by Anchor, 1957; chs. 4 and 5 are especially useful for the early monarchy. More recent and popular is his *The Biblical Period from Abraham to Ezra, an Historical Survey* (New York: Harper Torchbooks, 1963 [1949]), chs. 3–6. Somewhat more specialized but still very readable is his revised edition of *Archaeology and the Religion of Israel* (Baltimore: Johns Hopkins University Press, 1968), ch. 4. For one of the neighboring people of the ancient Hebrews, students should find useful John Gray, *The Canaanites* (New York: Praeger, 1964), a first-class popularization and updating of scholarship, an attractive book in an attractive and authoritative series. Students may also wish to read any of the several specialized essays in *The Biblical Archaeologist Reader,* vol. 3, ed. E. F. Campbell, Jr., and David N. Freedman (New York: Doubleday Anchor, 1970). H. and H. A. Frankfort, John A. Wilson, Thorkild Jacobsen, and William A. Irwin, *The Intellectual Adventure of Ancient Man, An Essay on Speculative Thought in the Ancient Near East* (Chicago: University of Chicago Press, 1946), is a famous book, a pioneering work in the intellectual history of the ancient Near East; students should see especially chs. 10–12.

Recommended finally is *The Cambridge History of the Bible,* vol. I, *From the Beginnings to Jerome,* ed. P. R. Ackroyd and C. F. Evans (Cambridge, England: Cambridge University Press, 1970), a fascinating book about the Bible as a book.

The Image of Socrates: Man or Myth?

By the lifetime of Socrates, in the late fifth century B.C., Greek civilization was almost at an end. This historic civilization was centered in Socrates' own city of Athens, which Pericles proudly called "the school of Hellas." But that magnificent city, which has so captivated our imagination, was widely regarded by her fellow city-states as a threat to their own independence—and with more than a little justification.

This threat led to the great Peloponnesian War, so vividly recounted in the pages of Socrates' contemporary, the historian Thucydides. Athens and her subject states were set against her arch-rival Sparta and Sparta's allies, the Peloponnesian League. It was a long, costly, and enervating war of almost thirty years' duration. And Athens finally lost it. She was humiliated, forced to accept her enemies' terms, and stripped of her subject states, her wealth, her navy. The buoyant optimism that had earlier characterized the city was one of the prime casualties of the war, along with confidence in her institutions and even in many of the presuppositions of her public life and private morality. It is in the backwash of these events that we must seek the life, and the death, of Socrates.

Socrates was surely the most famous Athenian of his age. Yet despite that fame, the facts of his life remain stubbornly vague. He was not a public official; hence we do not have archival records to rely on. And though he is a famous figure in literature, he actually wrote nothing

39

himself to which we can refer. There are scattered references to him
in Aristotle; a substantial (though prosaic) account in the works of
Xenophon, who knew him; and, of course, the principal source of our
information about him, the dialogues of the great philosopher Plato,
who was Socrates' adoring pupil and disciple and made him the main
character in most of his dialogues. And there are references and anecdotes
from a considerable number of near contemporary accounts of Socrates
that have been preserved, although the original sources are now lost.

What we know about Socrates is this. He was born an Athenian citizen
about 470 B.C. His family belonged to the class of small artisans;
his mother was a midwife and his father a stone mason. Socrates himself
followed his father's trade. Rather late in life he married Xanthippe,
and they had three sons, two of them still very young at the time of their
father's death. Like most able-bodied Athenians of his time, Socrates
was a veteran of the Peloponnesian War and even served with some
distinction. On two occasions he seems to have held office on the large
civic boards and commissions that carried on the business of the city.
But generally he avoided public life. From a number of surviving
descriptions and portrait busts we know what Socrates looked like—small
and bald and ugly, anything but the Greek ideal of physical beauty.
And we also know that he spent most of his time going about the city,
trailed by a delighted and curious crowd of bright young aristocrats,
asking often embarrassing questions of people who interested him, usually
public officials and men of substance and position. This practice was
to the detriment of his own family and his own trade. Socrates was
a poor man.

The Clouds
ARISTOPHANES

The preceding bare account of Socrates is supplemented—one must almost say contradicted—by a single additional source, The Clouds *of Aristophanes. This work is of considerable value in that it is the only really substantial account of Socrates by a mature contemporary. Even Plato, our principal source of information, was forty years younger than Socrates, knew him only as an old man, and wrote* The Dialogues *many years after Socrates' death.* The Clouds *is, of course, not a biography. It is a play, by the greatest of Greek comic dramatists, in which Socrates is not only one of its chief characters but also the object of its satire.*

Aristophanes was a conservative, and his plays are a catalog of his objections to the management of the war and public policy, the state of literature and philosophy, the subversion of the stern old virtues "of our forefathers," and the "new morality" that he saw about him. In The Clouds *he accused Socrates of being a professional teacher who received, nay extracted, money for his "lessons"—which was not true. He denounced him as a cynical, opportunistic atheist—which was also apparently not the case. He attributed to him an expert competence in natural philosophy—which was highly unlikely. And in what was perhaps the most unfounded of all his charges, he portrayed Socrates as being the chief of the Sophists.*

The Sophists were a school of professional teachers, then very popular in Athens, who taught young men of wealth and position (usually for substantial fees) the techniques of public life, mostly logic and oratorical persuasion. The Sophists also tended to a flexible morality in which success was to be preferred to virtue, victory to either morality or philosophic consistency. It is a more than Socratic irony that Socrates should have been depicted as one of them, for it was squarely against the Sophists and their moral relativism that he had taken his stand. The whole point of his life, the reason he engaged other people in his famous questioning and endured their animosity, the entire "Socratic method" was an attempt to make people understand that there are moral absolutes, unchanging abstract principles of conduct to which they must ultimately resort.

Why Aristophanes portrayed Socrates in this fashion we do not know. Perhaps he genuinely believed that Socrates was a Sophist. Or perhaps he knew the truth but simply did not care, and made use of Socrates'

*notoriety in Athens to score his own point about the scandalous decline
of education and what he regarded as philosophic quackery.*

*In any event, the play is cruel, mean, and malicious, but it is also
outrageously funny. And it gives us a view, however hostile, of the historic
Socrates.*

The Clouds *opens in the house of Strepsiades, a foolish old farmer,
whose son's extravagant passion for racehorses—his name is even
Pheidippides, "lover of horses"—has piled up so many debts that the old
man is faced with ruin. One night, unable to sleep, Strepsiades decides
to enroll the boy in the Sophist's school down the street. He calls it
the "Thinkery." But Pheidippides will have nothing to do with "those
filthy charlatans you mean—those frauds, those barefoot pedants with
the look of death. Chairephon and that humbug, Sokrates."*

*The old man then decides to go to the school himself. He kicks on the
door, and a student-doorman answers. As they stand at the door, the
student extols the wisdom of his master Socrates, citing a number of
examples, not the least of which is Socrates' resolution of the problem
of how the gnat hums. "According to him, the intestinal tract of the gnat
is of puny proportions, and through this diminutive duct the gastric gas
of the gnat is forced under pressure down to the rump. At that point
the compressed gases, as through a narrow valve, escape with a whoosh,
thereby causing the characteristic tootle or cry of the flatulent gnat."*

*Strepsiades is suitably impressed. "Why, Thales himself was an amateur
compared to this! Throw open the Thinkery! Unbolt the door and let
me see this wizard Sokrates in person. Open up! I'm MAD for education!"
And Strepsiades enters the school.*

STREPSIADES

Look: who's that dangling up there in the basket?

STUDENT

Himself.

STREPSIADES

Who's Himself?

STUDENT

Sokrates.

STREPSIADES

SOKRATES!
Then call him down. Go on. Give a great big shout.

STUDENT

Hastily and apprehensively taking his leave.

Er . . . *you* call him. I'm a busy man.

Exit Student.

STREPSIADES

O Sokrates!

No answer from the basket.

Yoohoo. Sokrates!

SOKRATES

From a vast philosophical height.

Well, creature of a day?

STREPSIADES

What in the world are you doing up there?

SOKRATES

Ah, sir,
I walk upon the air and look down upon the sun
from a superior standpoint.

STREPSIADES

Well, I suppose it's better
that you sneer at the gods from a basket up in the air
than do it down here on the ground.

SOKRATES

Precisely. You see,
only by being suspended aloft, by dangling
my mind in the heavens and mingling my rare thought
with the ethereal air, could I ever achieve strict
scientific accuracy in my survey of the vast empyrean.
Had I pursued my inquiries from down there on the ground,
my data would be worthless. The earth, you see, pulls down
the delicate essence of thought to its own gross level.

As an afterthought.

Much the same thing happens with watercress.

STREPSIADES

Ecstatically bewildered.

You don't say?
Thought draws down . . . delicate essence . . . into
watercress. O dear little Sokrates, please come down.
Lower away, and teach me what I need to know!

Sokrates is slowly lowered earthwards.

SOKRATES

What subject?

STREPSIADES

Your course on public speaking and debating techniques.
You see, my creditors have become absolutely ferocious.
You should see how they're hounding me. What's more,
Sokrates, they're about to seize my belongings.

SOKRATES

How in the
world could you fall so deeply in debt without realizing it?

STREPSIADES

How? A great, greedy horse-pox ate me up, that's how.
But that's why I want instruction in your second Logic,
you know the one—the get-away-without-paying argument.
I'll pay you *any* price you ask. I swear it.
By the gods.

SOKRATES

By the gods? The gods, my dear simple fellow,
are a mere expression coined by vulgar superstition.
We frown upon such coinage here.

STREPSIADES

What do *you* swear by?
Bars of iron, like the Byzantines?

SOKRATES

                    Tell me, old man,
would you honestly like to learn the truth, the *real* truth,
about the gods?

STREPSIADES

              By Zeus, I sure would. The *real* truth. . . .

[*At this point the chorus of clouds enters, singing.*]

STREPSIADES

Holy Zeus, Sokrates, who were those ladies that sang
that solemn hymn? Were they heroines of mythology?

SOKRATES

                              No, old man.
Those were the Clouds of heaven, goddesses of men of
leisure and philosophers. To them we owe our repertoire of
verbal talents: our eloquence, intellect, fustian, casuistry,
force, wit, prodigious vocabulary, circumlocutory skill—

.   .   .   .

[*The leader of the chorus greets them.*]

KORYPHAIOS

                    Hail, superannuated man!
Hail, old birddog of culture!

To Sokrates.

                    And hail to you, O Sokrates,
high priest of poppycock!
                    Inform us what your wishes are.
For of all the polymaths on earth, it's you we most prefer—
.   .   .   .
sir, for your swivel-eyes, your barefoot swagger down the
street, because you're poor on our account and terribly
affected.

STREPSIADES

Name of Earth, what a voice! Solemn and holy and awful!

SOKRATES

These are the only gods there are. The rest are but figments.

STREPSIADES

Holy name of Earth! Olympian Zeus is a figment?

SOKRATES

Zeus?
    What Zeus?
        Nonsense.
            There is no Zeus.

STREPSIADES

                No Zeus?
Then *who* makes it rain? Answer me that.

SOKRATES

              Why, the Clouds,
of course.
    What's more, the proof is incontrovertible.
              For instance,
have you ever yet seen rain when you didn't see a cloud?
But if your hypothesis were correct, Zeus could drizzle
  from an empty sky
while the clouds were on vacation.

STREPSIADES

           By Apollo, you're right. A pretty
  proof.
And to think I always used to believe the rain was just Zeus
pissing through a sieve.
          All right, *who* makes it thunder?
Brrr. I get goosebumps just saying it.

SOKRATES

            The Clouds again,
of course. A simple process of Convection.

STREPSIADES

            I admire you,
but I don't follow you.

SOKRATES

    Listen. The Clouds are a saturate water-solution.

Tumescence in motion, of necessity, produces precipitation.
When these distended masses collide—*boom!*
                                        Fulmination.

STREPSIADES

But who makes them move before they collide? Isn't that
Zeus?

SOKRATES

Not Zeus, idiot. The Convection-principle!

STREPSIADES

                                        Convection? That's
a new one.
Just think. So Zeus is out and Convection-principle's in.
Tch, tch.
            But wait: you haven't told me who makes it thunder.

SOKRATES

But I just *finished* telling you! The Clouds are water-packed;
they collide with each other and explode because of the
pressure.

STREPSIADES

            Yeah?
And what's your proof for *that?*

SOKRATES

                        Why, take yourself as example.
You know that meat-stew the vendors sell at the Pana-
thenaia? [1] How it gives you the cramps and your stomach
starts to rumble?

STREPSIADES

                                                Yes,
by Apollo! I remember. What an awful feeling! You feel
sick and your belly churns and the fart rips loose like
thunder. First just a gurgle, *pappapax;* then louder, *pappa-
PAPAXapaX,* and finally like thunder, *PAPAPAPAXA-
PAXAPPAPAXapap!*

SOKRATES

Precisely.
First think of the tiny fart that your intestines make.

[1] The quadrennial festival of Athena, the patron goddess of Athens.—ED.

Then consider the heavens: their infinite farting is thunder.
For thunder and farting are, in principle, one and the same.

[*Strepsiades is convinced and is initiated into Socrates' school. But, alas,
he is incapable of learning the subtleties Socrates sets out to teach him and
is contemptuously dismissed from the school. Then the leader of the chorus
suggests that he fetch his son to study in his place. A splendid idea! As
Strepsiades drags his son on to the scene, Pheidippides protests.*]

PHEIDIPPIDES

                              But Father,
what's the matter with you? Are you out of your head?
Almighty Zeus, you must be mad!

STREPSIADES

                              "Almighty Zeus!"
What musty rubbish! Imagine, a boy your age.
still believing in Zeus!

PHEIDIPPIDES

                    What's so damn funny?

STREPSIADES

It tickles me when the heads of toddlers like you
are still stuffed with such outdated notions. Now then,
listen to me and I'll tell you a secret or two
that might make an intelligent man of you yet.
But remember: you mustn't breathe a word of this.

PHEIDIPPIDES

A word of what?

STREPSIADES

                    Didn't you just swear by Zeus?

PHEIDIPPIDES

I did.

STREPSIADES

     Now learn what Education can do for *you:*
Pheidippides, there is no Zeus.

PHEIDIPPIDES

                    There is no Zeus?

STREPSIADES

No Zeus. Convection-principle's in power now.
Zeus has been banished.

PHEIDIPPIDES

Drivel!

STREPSIADES

Take my word for it,
it's absolutely true.

PHEIDIPPIDES

Who says so?

STREPSIADES

Sokrates.
And Chairephon too. . . .

PHEIDIPPIDES

Are you so far gone on the road to complete insanity
you'd believe the word of those charlatans?

STREPSIADES

Hush, boy.
For shame. I won't hear you speaking disrespectfully
of such eminent scientists and geniuses. And, what's more,
men of such fantastic frugality and Spartan thrift,
they regard baths, haircuts, and personal cleanliness
generally as an utter waste of time and money—whereas
you, dear boy, have taken me to the cleaner's so many times,
I'm damn near washed up. Come on, for your father's sake,
go and learn.

[*Some time later*]
*Enter Strepsiades from his house, counting on
his fingers.*

STREPSIADES

Five days, four days, three days, two days, and then
that one day of the days of the month
I dread the most that makes me fart with fear—
the last day of the month, Duedate for debts,
when every dun in town has solemnly sworn
to drag me into court and bankrupt me completely.

And when I plead with them to be more reasonable—
"But PLEASE, sir. Don't demand the whole sum now.
Take something on account. I'll pay you later."—
they snort they'll never see the day, curse me
for a filthy swindler and say they'll sue.
                                        Well,
let them. If Pheidippides has learned to talk,
I don't give a damn for them and their suits.
                                        Now then,
a little knock on the door and we'll have the answer.

He knocks on Sokrates' door and calls out.

Porter!
        Hey, porter!

Sokrates opens the door.

SOKRATES
                        Ah, Strepsiades. Salutations.

STREPSIADES

Same to you, Sokrates.

He hands Sokrates a bag of flour.

                        Here. A token of my esteem.
Call it an honorarium. Professors always get honorariums.

Snatching back the bag.

But wait: has Pheidippides learned his rhetoric yet—. . . .

SOKRATES

Taking the bag.

He has mastered it.

STREPSIADES
                        O great goddess Bamboozle!

SOKRATES

Now, sir, you can evade any legal action you wish to.

[*But instead of help with his creditors, Strepsiades gets a very different kind of treatment from his son.*]

With a bellow of pain and terror, Strepsiades
plunges out of his house, hotly pursued by Pheidip-
pides with a murderous stick.

STREPSIADES

OOOUUUCH!!!
                    HALP!
                        For god's sake, help me!

Appealing to the Audience.

                                                Friends!
Fellow-countrymen! Aunts! Uncles! Fathers! Brothers!
To the rescue!
            He's beating me!
                        Help me!
                            Ouuch!
O my poor head!

            Ooh, my jaw!

To Pheidippides.
                        —You great big bully,
Hit your own father, would you?

PHEIDIPPIDES

                        Gladly, Daddy.

STREPSIADES

You hear that? The big brute *admits* it.

PHEIDIPPIDES

                        Admit it? Hell,
I *proclaim* it. . . .
                    Would a logical demonstration
convince you?

STREPSIADES

        A logical demonstration? You mean to tell me
you can *prove* a shocking thing like that?

PHEIDIPPIDES

                                    Elementary, really.
What's more, you can choose the logic. Take your pick.
Either one.

STREPSIADES

                    Either *which?*

PHEIDIPPIDES

                              Either *which?* Why,
Socratic logic or pre-Socratic logic. Either logic.
Take your pick.

STREPSIADES

                    Take my pick, damn you? Look,
who do you think paid for your shyster education anyway?
And now you propose to convince *me* that there's nothing
wrong in whipping your own father?

PHEIDIPPIDES

                                    I not only propose it:
I propose to *prove* it. Irrefutably, in fact. Rebuttal
is utterly inconceivable. . . .

[*Phedippides then "proves" that since his father beat him as a child "for
your own damn good" "because I loved you," then it is only* "a fortiori"
*logic that the father be beaten by the son, since "old men logically deserve
to be beaten more, since at their age they have clearly less excuse for the
mischief that they do."*]

*There is a long tense silence as the full force of this
crushing argument takes its effect upon Strepsiades.*

STREPSIADES

                                        What?
                                    But how . . .?
                                        Hmm,
by god, you're right!

To the Audience.

                    —Speaking for the older generation,
gentlemen, I'm compelled to admit defeat. The kids have
proved their point: naughty fathers should be flogged. . . .

[*But this arrogance is too much, logic or no logic, for Strepsiades.*]

STREPSIADES

        O Horse's Ass, Blithering Imbecile,
Brainless Booby, Bonehead that I was to ditch the gods
for Sokrates!

*He picks up Pheidippides' stick and savagely
smashes the potbellied model of the Universe in front
of the Thinkery. He then rushes to his own house
and falls on his knees before the statue of Hermes.*

        —Great Hermes, I implore you!

[*Strepsiades and his slave set fire to the Thinkery and he beats the choking,
sputtering Socrates and his pallid students off the stage.*]

The Apology
PLATO

In 399 B.C., twenty-five years after The Clouds, *Socrates stood before
the great popular court of Athens. He was accused of much the same
charges that had been leveled at him by Aristophanes, specifically "that
Socrates is a doer of evil, who corrupts the youth; and who does not
believe in the gods of the state, but has other new divinities of his own."
The charges were brought by three fellow Athenians, Meletus, Lycon, and
Anytus. Although only one of the accusers, Anytus, was a man of any
importance, and he only a minor political figure, the charges carried
the death penalty if the court so decided. Indeed, this was the intent
of the accusers.
    The man, now seventy years old, who rose to speak in his own defense
was not the pettifogging buffoon of* The Clouds. *Perhaps that man never
really existed. By the same token, did the speaker at the trial ever
exist? The trial is Socrates', but the account of it is Plato's.* The Apology,
from The Dialogues of Plato, *is the "defense" of Socrates at his trial.*

HOW YOU, O Athenians, have been affected by my accusers, I cannot tell; but I know that they almost made me forget who I was—so persuasively did they speak; and yet they have hardly uttered a word of truth. But . . . first, I have to reply to the older charges and to my first accusers, and then I will go on to the later ones. For of old I have had many accusers, who have accused me falsely to you during many years; and I am more afraid of them than of Anytus and his associates, who are dangerous, too, in their own way. But far more dangerous are the others, who began when you were children, and took possession of your minds with their falsehoods, telling of one Socrates, a wise man, who speculated about the heaven above, and searched into the earth beneath, and made the worse appear the better cause. The disseminators of this tale are the accusers whom I dread; for their hearers are apt to fancy that such enquirers do not believe in the existence of the gods. And they are many, and their charges against me are of ancient date, and they were made by them in the days when you were more impressible than you are now—in childhood, or it may have been in youth—and the cause when heard went by default, for there was none to answer. And hardest of all, I do not know and cannot tell the names of my accusers; unless in the chance case of a Comic poet. . . .

I dare say, Athenians, that some one among you will reply, 'Yes, Socrates, but what is the origin of these accusations which are brought against you; there must have been something strange which you have been doing? All these rumours and this talk about you would never have arisen if you had been like other men: tell us, then, what is the cause of them, for we should be sorry to judge hastily of you.' Now I regard this as a fair challenge, and I will endeavour to explain to you the reason why I am called wise and have such an evil fame. . . .

. . . I will refer you to a witness who is worthy of credit; that witness shall be the God of Delphi—he will tell you about my wisdom, if I have any, and of what sort it is. You must have known Chaerephon; he was early a friend of mine. . . . Well, Chaerephon, as you know, was very impetuous in all his doings, and he went to Delphi and boldly asked the oracle to tell him whether—as I was saying, I must beg you not to interrupt —he asked the oracle to tell him whether any one was wiser than I was, and the Pythian prophetess answered, that there was no man wiser. Chaerephon is dead himself; but his brother, who is in court, will confirm the truth of what I am saying.

Why do I mention this? Because I am going to explain to you why I have such an evil name. When I heard the answer, I said to myself, What can the god mean? and what is the interpretation of his riddle? for I know that I have no wisdom, small or great. What then can he mean when he says that I am the wisest of men? And yet he is a god, and cannot lie; that would be against his nature. After long consideration, I thought of a method of trying the question. I reflected that if I could only find a man

wiser than myself, then I might go to the god with a refutation in my hand.
I should say to him, 'Here is a man who is wiser than I am; but you said
that I was the wisest.' Accordingly I went to one who had the reputation of
wisdom, and observed him—his name I need not mention; he was a
politician whom I selected for examination—and the result was as follows:
When I began to talk with him, I could not help thinking that he was not
really wise, although he was thought wise by many, and still wiser by
himself; and thereupon I tried to explain to him that he thought himself
wise, but was not really wise; and the consequence was that he hated me,
and his enmity was shared by several who were present and heard me. So
I left him, saying to myself, as I went away: Well, although I do not
suppose that either of us knows anything really beautiful and good, I am
better off than he is,—for he knows nothing, and thinks that he knows;
I neither know nor think that I know. In this latter particular, then, I
seem to have slightly the advantage of him. Then I went to another who
had still higher pretensions to wisdom, and my conclusion was exactly the
same. Whereupon I made another enemy of him, and of many others
besides him. . . .

This inquisition has led to my having many enemies of the worst and
most dangerous kind, and has given occasion also to many calumnies. And
I am called wise, for my hearers always imagine that I myself possess the
wisdom which I find wanting in others: but the truth is, O men of Athens,
that God only is wise, and by his answer he intends to show that the wisdom of men is worth little or nothing; he is not speaking of Socrates, he is
only using my name by way of illustration, as if he said, He, O men, is the
wisest, who, like Socrates, knows that his wisdom is in truth worth nothing.
And so I go about the world, obedient to the god, and search and make
enquiry into the wisdom of any one, whether citizen or stranger, who
appears to be wise; and if he is not wise, then in vindication of the oracle
I show him that he is not wise, and my occupation quite absorbs me, and
I have no time to give either to any public matter of interest or to any
concern of my own, but I am in utter poverty by reason of my devotion
to the god.

There is another thing:—young men of the richer classes, who have not
much to do, come about me of their own accord; they like to hear the
pretenders examined, and they often imitate me, and proceed to examine
others; there are plently of persons, as they quickly discover, who think
they know something, but really know little or nothing; and then those
who are examined by them instead of being angry with themselves are
angry with me: This confounded Socrates, they say; this villainous mis-
leader of youth—and then if somebody asks them, Why, what evil does he
practise or teach? they do not know, and cannot tell; but in order that they
may not appear to be at a loss, they repeat the ready-made charges which
are used against all philosophers about teaching things up in the clouds

and under the earth, and having no gods and making the worse appear the better cause. . . .

Turning to the formal charges against him, Socrates dismisses them almost contemptuously, returning to the main charges as he sees them and his life-long "argument" with his city and its citizenry.

And now, Athenians, I am not going to argue for my own sake, as you may think, but for yours, that you may not sin against the God by con-demning me, who am his gift to you. For if you kill me you will not easily find a successor to me, who, if I may use such a ludicrous figure of speech, am a sort of gadfly, given to the state by God; and the state is a great and noble steed who is tardy in his motions owing to his very size, and requires to be stirred into life. I am that gadfly which God has attached to the state, and all day long and in all places am always fastening upon you, arousing and persuading and reproaching you. You will not easily find another like me, and therefore I would advise you to spare me. I dare say that you may feel out of temper (like a person who is suddenly awakened from sleep), and you think that you might easily strike me dead as Anytus advises, and then you would sleep on for the remainder of your lives, unless God in his care of you sent you another gadfly. When I say I am given to you by God, the proof of my mission is this:—if I had been like other men, I should not have neglected all my own concerns or patiently seen the neglect of them during all these years, and have been doing yours, coming to you individually like a father or elder brother, exhorting you to regard virtue; such conduct, I say, would be unlike human nature. If I had gained anything, or if my exhortations had been paid, there would have been some sense in my doing so; but now, as you will perceive, not even the impudence of my accusers dares to say that I have ever exacted or sought pay of any one; of that they have no witness. And I have a sufficient witness to the truth of what I say—my poverty. . . .

The jury returns the verdict of guilty.

There are many reasons why I am not grieved, O men of Athens, at the vote of condemnation. I expected it, and am only surprised that the votes are so nearly equal; for I had thought that the majority against me would have been far larger; but now, had thirty votes gone over to the other side, I should have been acquitted. And I may say, I think, that I have escaped Meletus. I may say more; for without the assistance of Anytus and Lycon, any one may see that he would not have had a fifth part of the votes, as the law requires, in which case he would have incurred a fine of a thousand drachmae.

And so he proposes death as the penalty. . . .

Some one will say: Yes, Socrates, but cannot you hold your tongue, and then you may go into a foreign city, and no one will interfere with you? Now I have great difficulty in making you understand my answer to this. For if I tell you that to do as you say would be a disobedience to the God, and therefore that I cannot hold my tongue, you will not believe that I am serious; and if I say again that daily to discourse about virtue, and of those other things about which you hear me examining myself and others, is the greatest good of man, and that the unexamined life is not worth living, you are still less likely to believe me. Yet I say what is true, although a thing of which it is hard for me to persuade you. Also, I have never been accustomed to think that I deserve to suffer any harm. Had I money I might have estimated the offence at what I was able to pay, and not have been much the worse. But I have none, and therefore I must ask you to proportion the fine to my means. Well, perhaps I could afford a mina, and therefore I propose that penalty: Plato, Crito, Critobulus, and Apollodorus, my friends here, bid me say thirty minae, and they will be the sureties. Let thirty minae be the penalty; for which sum they will be ample security to you. . . .

Socrates is condemned to death.

And now, O men who have condemned me, I would fain prophesy to you; for I am about to die, and in the hour of death men are gifted with prophetic power. And I prophesy to you who are my murderers, that immediately after my departure punishment far heavier than you have inflicted on me will surely await you. Me you have killed because you wanted to escape the accuser, and not to give an account of your lives. But that will not be as you suppose: far otherwise. For I say that there will be more accusers of you than there are now; accusers whom hitherto I have restrained: and as they are younger they will be more inconsiderate with you, and you will be more offended at them. If you think that by killing men you can prevent some one from censuring your evil lives, you are mistaken; that is not a way of escape which is either possible or honourable; the easiest and the noblest way is not to be disabling others, but to be improving yourselves. This is the prophecy which I utter before my departure to the judges who have condemned me.

Friends, who would have acquitted me, I would like also to talk with you about the thing which has come to pass, while the magistrates are busy, and before I go to the place at which I must die. Stay then a little, for we may as well talk with one another while there is time. You are my friends, and I should like to show you the meaning of this event which has happened to me. O my judges—for you I may truly call judges—I should like to tell you of a wonderful circumstance. Hitherto the divine faculty of which the internal oracle [2] is the source has constantly been in the habit of opposing me even about trifles, if I was going to make a slip or error in any matter; and now as you see there has come upon me that which may be thought, and is generally believed to be, the last and worst evil. But the oracle made no sign of opposition, either when I was leaving my house in the morning, or when I was on my way to the court, or while I was speaking, at anything which I was going to say; and yet I have often been stopped in the middle of a speech, but now in nothing I either said or did touching the matter in hand has the oracle opposed me. What do I take to be the explanation of this silence? I will tell you. It is an intimation that what has happened to me is a good, and that those of us who think that death is an evil are in error. For the customary sign would surely have opposed me had I been going to evil and not to good. . . .

Wherefore, O judges, be of good cheer about death, and know of a certainty, that no evil can happen to a good man, either in life or after death. He and his are not neglected by the gods; nor has my own approaching end happened by mere chance. But I see clearly that the time had arrived when it was better for me to die and be released from trouble; wherefore the oracle gave no sign. For which reason, also, I am not angry with my condemners, or with my accusers; they have done me no harm, although they did not mean to do me any good; and for this I may gently blame them.

Still I have a favour to ask them. When my sons are grown up, I would ask you, O my friends, to punish them; and I would have you trouble them, as I have troubled you, if they seem to care about riches, or anything, more than about virtue; or if they pretend to be something when they are really nothing,—then reprove them, as I have reproved you, for not caring about that for which they ought to care, and thinking that they are something when they are really nothing. And if you do this, both I and my sons will have received justice at your hands.

The hour of departure has arrived, and we go our ways—I to die, and you to live. Which is better God only knows.

[2] This was Socrates' famous "daimon," more than a conscience, less perhaps than a separate "in-dwelling" god, but, as he claimed, at least a guiding voice.—ED.

Socrates: A Modern Perspective
MOSES HADAS AND MORTON SMITH

Which Socrates are we to choose? Is it even possible to reconstruct the real man from either the idealized, "gospel"-like account of Plato or the malicious parody of Aristophanes, or from both together? Two distinguished American professors, Moses Hadas (d. 1966) and Morton Smith, do not think so. They state their case in the following selection from their book Heroes and Gods, Spiritual Biographies in Antiquity.

AS SURELY AS the figure of Achilles is the paradigm for heroic epic, so surely is Socrates the paradigm for aretalogy.[3] He is manifestly the point of departure for the development of the genre after his time, but he is also the culmination of antecedent development. It is likely that the historical Achilles (assuming there was one) was both more and less than Homer's image of him, but even if he was exactly as the image represents him, without it he could never have served posterity as a paradigm. Nor could Socrates have served posterity except through the image Plato fashioned. It is not, strictly speaking, a developed aretalogy that Plato presents; that is to say, he does not provide a single systematic account of a career that can be used as a sacred text. Indeed, Plato's treatment made it impossible for others to elaborate the image plausibly or to reduce it to a sacred text. But the whole image, full and consistent and unmistakable, is presupposed in every Platonic dialogue which contributes to it. Undoubtedly the historical Socrates was an extraordinarily gifted and devoted teacher, and his image does undoubtedly reflect the historical figure, but the image clearly transcends the man, and the image is the conscious product of Plato's art.

Because of Plato, and only Plato, Socrates' position in the tradition of western civilization is unique. Other fifth-century Greeks have won admiration bordering on adulation for high achievement in various fields, but only Socrates is completely without flaw; the perfect image leaves no opening for impugning his wisdom or temperance or courage or whole-hearted devotion to his mission. We might expect that a dim figure out of the imperfectly recorded past, an Orpheus or Pythagoras or even Empedocles, might be idealized, but Socrates lived in the bright and merciless light of a century that could ostracize Aristides, deny prizes to Sophocles,

[3] The worship of, or reverence for, nobility or virtue; from the Greek *areté,* "virtue."—ED.

throw Pericles out of office. Perhaps the nearest approach to Plato's
idealization of Socrates is Thucydides' idealization of Pericles; some critics
have thought that Thucydides' main motive in writing his history was to
glorify Pericles. But Thucydides never claimed for Pericles the kind of
potency that Plato suggests for Socrates, and on the basis of Thucydides'
own history the world has accepted Pericles as a farseeing but not pre-
ternaturally gifted or wholly successful statesman. Only in the case of
Socrates has the idealized image effaced the reality.

What makes Plato's share in the idealization obvious is the existence of
parallel accounts of Socrates that are less reverent. Plato's reports are indeed the fullest: the larger part of his extensive writings purports to be
an exposition of Socrates' thought. But there are other witnesses. . . . In
the *Clouds* of Aristophanes, Socrates is the central figure, and the boot is
on a different foot, for it was produced in 423, when Socrates was not
yet fifty and therefore in the prime of his career but not yet shielded by
the extraordinary eminence later bestowed upon him. Nor was Aristophanes' comedy the only caricature of Socrates. Also in 423 a comic
Socrates figured in a play of Amipsias and two years later in one of
Eupolis. These poets, it must be remembered, were dealing with a personality that was familiar to them and also, perhaps more important, to
their audiences.

The caricature, certainly Aristophanes' and presumably the others' also,
is of course grossly unfair: Socrates did not meddle with natural science
or receive pay for his teaching, as the *Clouds* alleges he did: the most
carping critic could not question his probity. The very absurdity of the
charges and the topsy-turvy carnival atmosphere of the festival eliminated
the possibility of rancor; in the *Symposium*, of which the fictive date is a
decade after the presentation of the *Clouds*, Plato represents Aristophanes
and Socrates as consorting on the friendliest of terms. And yet it is plain
that Aristophanes' large audience was not outraged by the frivolous treatment of a saint, and in the *Apology*, which Socrates is presumed to have
pronounced at his defense twenty-five years later, the point is made that
the caricature had seriously prejudiced the public against Socrates. To some
degree, then, the caricature is a significant corrective to later idealization. . . .

Really to know where the truth lies, . . . we should have his actual
words or a public record of his deeds, but Socrates wrote nothing and was
not, like Pericles, a statesman. The image is therefore not subject to correction on the basis of his own works. Aristophanes also deals harshly
with Euripides, but we have Euripides' own plays to read, so that the
caricature tells us more of Aristophanes than it does of Euripides. Isocrates
wrote an encomium of Evagoras and Xenophon of Agesilaus, but the praise
of these statesmen carries its own corrective. Of Socrates we know, or
think we know, much more than of those others—what he looked like,

how he dressed and walked and talked, and most of all, what he thought
and taught. . . .

Actually the only significant datum in the inventory which is beyond
dispute is that Socrates was condemned to death in 399 B.C. and accepted
his penalty when he might have evaded it. The magnanimity of this act
no one can belittle; it is enough to purify and enhance even a questionable
career, and it is certainly enough to sanctify a Socrates. For Plato it clearly
marked a decisive turn, as he himself records in his autobiographical
Seventh Epistle. For him it undoubtedly crystallized the image of Socrates
that fills the early dialogues. . . . All of Plato's earlier dialogues, and the
more plainly in the degree of their earliness, are as much concerned with
the personality of Socrates as with his teachings. His pre-eminence in
reason, his devotion to his mission, his selfless concern for the spiritual
welfare of his fellow men, the purity of his life, even his social gifts, are
made prominent. The *Apology,* quite possibly the earliest of the Socratic
pieces, is concerned with the man and his personal program, not his
doctrines. Here he is made to present, without coyness or swagger or
unction, his own concept of his mission to sting men, like a gadfly, to self-
examination and to serve as midwife to their travail with ideas. The
Apology also illustrates the devotion of his disciples to Socrates and the
surprisingly large proportion of his jurors who were willing to acquit him.
Again, in the short early dialogues, which are mainly concerned with questioning common misconceptions of such abstract nouns as "piety" or
"friendship," it is the man as defined by his program, not the abstract
doctrine, that is being presented. In the great central group—*Protagoras,
Gorgias, Symposium, Republic*—the proportion of doctrinal content is
larger, but the doctrine requires the personality of Socrates to make it
plausible. The moral significance of education may emerge from the rather
piratical dialectic in the *Protagoras,* but the argument takes on special
meaning from Socrates' wise and tender treatment of the eager and youthful disciple who is enamored of Protagoras' reputation. That it is a worse
thing for a man to inflict than to receive an injury and that a good man
is incapable of being injured is the kind of doctrine which absolutely requires that its promulgator be a saint, as Socrates is pictured in the *Gorgias;*
on the lips of a lesser man it would be nothing more than a rhetorical
paradox. A great weight of individual prestige must similarly be built up
to enable a man to enunciate the grand scheme of the *Republic,* and the
occasional playfulness of the tone only emphasizes the stature of the individual who enunciates it. People too earth-bound to recognize such
stature, like Thrasymachus in Book I, can only find the whole proceeding
absurd. And only from a man whose special stature was recognized could
the vision of Er be accepted as other than an old wives' tale.

In the *Symposium* more than in other dialogues the individuality of
Socrates is underscored. It is not a trivial matter, for establishing the

character of Socrates, that he could be welcome at a party of the fashion-able wits of Athens, could get himself respectably groomed for the occasion, and engage in banter with his fellow guests without compromising his spiritual ascendancy one whit. We hear incidentally of his absolute bravery in battle and his disregard of self in the service of a friend, of his extraordinary physical vitality that enabled him to stand all night pondering some thought while his fellow soldiers bivouacked around him to watch the spectacle, of how he could lose himself in some doorway in a trance and so make himself late for his appointment until he had thought through whatever was on his mind. The subject of the *Symposium* is love, and love had been conceived of, in the series of speeches praising it, in a range from gross homosexuality to romantic attachment, to a cosmic principle of attraction and repulsion, to Socrates' own concept . . . of an ascent to union with the highest goodness and beauty. . .

But it is in the *Phaedo* that Socrates comes nearest to being translated to a higher order of being. In prison, during the hours preceding his death, Socrates discourses to his devoted followers on the most timely and time-less of all questions, the immortality of the soul. The *Phaedo* is the most spiritual and the most eloquent of all dialogues; the account of Socrates' last moments is surely the second most compelling passion in all literature. If Plato's object was to inculcate a belief in immortality, there are of course sound practical reasons for giving the spokesman of the doctrine extraordinary prestige. In such an issue it is the personality of the teacher rather than the cogency of his arguments that is most persuasive. . . .

But the saintliness with which Socrates is endowed in the *Phaedo* seems more than a mere device to promote belief in the immortality of the soul. If belief is being inculcated, it is belief in Socrates, not in immortality. Only an occasional reader of the *Phaedo* could rehearse its arguments for immortality years or months after he had laid the book down; the saintli-ness of Socrates he can never forget. It is his image of Socrates rather than any specific doctrine that Plato wished to crystallize and perpetuate. From the tenor of all his writing it is clear that Plato believed that the welfare of society depended upon leadership by specially endowed and dedicated men. Ordinary men following a prescribed code would not do. Indeed, Plato conceived of his own effectiveness as teacher in much the same way; in the autobiographical *Seventh Epistle* he tells us that no one could claim to have apprehended his teachings merely from study of his writings: long personal contact with a master spirit is essential.

In the centuries after Plato the images of certain saintly figures who, like Socrates, had selflessly devoted themselves to the spiritual improve-ment of the community and had accepted the suffering, sometimes the martyrdom, these efforts entailed, played a considerable role in the develop-ment of religious ideas and practices. In some cases the image may have masked a character negligible or dishonest, and the men who created and exploited the image may have done so for selfish motives; but in some cases, surely, the man behind the image was a devoted teacher whose disciples embroidered his career in good faith into a kind of hagiology [4] that they then used for moral edification. Whatever the motivation, there can be little doubt that the prime model for the spiritual hero was Socrates. . . .

Suggestions for Further Reading

BECAUSE THE STRIKING figure of Socrates exists in a powerful literary and philosophic tradition and yet has almost no historical foundation, there is a nearly irresistible urge to create a "historical Socrates," which has produced a number of biographical or semibiographical works on him. The preeminent modern account is A. E. Taylor, *Socrates* (New York: Anchor, 1953 [1933]), in which the great British Platonist argues that the striking figure of Socrates as derived from Plato's dialogues is essentially an accurate historical account. The book is clear and readable as well as authoritative. An almost equally good account is Jean Brun, *Socrates,* tr. Douglas Scott (New York: Walker, 1962), in which the author, writing for young people, simplifies and sorts out the leading elements in the traditional view of Socrates—i.e. the Delphic dictum "Know thyself," Socrates' "in-dwelling Daimon," and the Socratic irony. At the other extreme are Alban D. Winspear and Tom Silverberg, *Who Was Socrates?* (New York: Russell and Russell, 1960 [1939]), and Norman Gulley, *The Philosophy of Socrates* (London and New York: Macmillan and St. Martin's, 1968). Winspear and Silverberg argue—not entirely convincingly—for a complete revision of the tradition and make Socrates evolve in the course of his career from a democratic liberal to an aristocratic conservative. And Gulley argues for the rejection of Plato's view of Socrates as a skeptic and agnostic in favor of a more constructive role for Socrates in ancient philosophy. Laszlo Versényi, *Socratic Humanism* (New Haven, Conn.: Yale University Press, 1963), while not going as far as Gulley, does advocate a separation between the often paired Socrates and Plato in favor of tying Socrates more closely to the sophists, especially Protagoras and Gorgias. Students should find especially inter-

---

[4] Veneration of a saint or saints.—ED.

esting Alexander Eliot, *Socrates, A Fresh Appraisal of the Most Celebrated Case in History* (New York: Crown, 1967). It is less a fresh appraisal than a popular and extremely readable review of Socrates' background, life, and the evidence brought to his trial. The second part of the book is what the author calls "a free synthesis" of all the Platonic dialogues touching on the trial and death of Socrates—essentially a new, dramatic dialogue account in fresh, modern English.

Of somewhat larger scope is the important scholarly work of Victor Ehrenberg, *The People of Aristophanes, A Sociology of Old Attic Comedy* (New York: Schocken, 1962 [1943]), a study not only of the characters in the plays but also of the audiences; see especially ch. 10, on religion and education, for Socrates. Of larger scope still is T. B. L. Webster, *Athenian Culture and Society* (Berkeley and Los Angeles: University of California Press, 1973), a superb analysis of the linkage between the culture of Athens and its society—the background to an understanding of the place of Socrates in that society and culture. For this sort of analysis, students may prefer Rex Warner, *Men of Athens* (New York: Viking, 1972), a brilliant popularization which sees Socrates as the end product as well as the victim of fifth-century Athenian culture.

The standard work on the system of Athenian government is A. H. M. Jones, *Athenian Democracy* (Oxford, England: Oxford University Press, 1957), which should be updated by reference to W. R. Connor, *The New Politicians of Fifth Century Athens* (Princeton, N.J.: Princeton University Press, 1971).

"The Problem" of Alexander the Great

If Alexander had simply been a successful conqueror, no matter how stupefying his conquests, there would really be no "Alexander problem." But, from his own lifetime, there lingered about Alexander the sense that there was something more to him, that he was "up to something," that he had great, even revolutionary, plans. The conviction of manifest destiny that Alexander himself felt so strongly contributed to this, as did his instinct for the unusual, the cryptic, the dramatic in political and religious, as well as in strategic and military, decisions. But most of all, his death at age thirty-three, in the year 323 B.C.—his conquests barely completed and his schemes for the future only hinted at or imperfectly forecast—led the ancient writers to speculate about the questions, "What if Alexander had lived on?" "What plans would his imperial imagination have conceived?" and to sift and resift every scrap of information available—and to invent a few that were not!

The problem of the ancient sources themselves has added greatly to the difficulty of interpretation. And this is surely ironic. Alexander's own sense of his destiny made him unusually sensitive to the need for keeping records of his deeds. A careful log or diary was maintained, but it exists today only in the most useless fragments, if indeed the "fragments" in question even came from that record. Alexander's staff included at least two scholar-secretaries to keep records. One was Callisthenes, the nephew of Alexander's old friend and tutor Aristotle. The other was

67

the scientist-philosopher Aristobulus. Callisthenes subsequently fell
out with Alexander and was either executed or disgraced, and, while
nothing of his work remains, it was clearly the basis for a strongly
anti-Alexander tradition that flourished particularly in the old states, like
Athens, of the Greek homeland. But the records of Aristobulus, who
was apparently much closer to Alexander and much more favorable to
him, are also lost. Ptolemy, one of Alexander's most trusted generals
and later the founder of the Hellenistic monarchy in Egypt, wrote a
detailed memoir, but this did not survive either.

Later ancient writers like Diodorus and Plutarch, Curtius and
Justin did know these sources and used them. But of the accounts
of Alexander surviving from antiquity, the best one is that of the
Greek writer Arrian, of the second century—thus over four hundred
years removed from his sources! Furthermore, while Arrian's account is
our fullest and most detailed and is based scrupulously on his sources,
it is terribly prosaic: we miss precisely what we most want to have,
some sense of the "why" of Alexander. In spite of Arrian's devotion to
his subject, he tends to tell the story—mainly the military side of it at that
—without significant comment. And where we would like to have
him analyze, he moralizes instead.

Modern scholars have continued to be fascinated by the puzzle of
what Alexander was "up to," and none more than William W. Tarn
(d. 1957). Tarn was one of those brilliant English "amateurs" of
independent means and equally independent views who have contributed
so uniquely to scholarship in a score of fields. He was a lawyer by
profession, but he devoted most of his scholarly life—more than half a
century—to Greek history. Tarn practically invented Hellenistic
scholarship, that is, the study of the post-Alexandrian period in the history
of Greek civilization. He authored numerous books and studies, beginning
with his "Notes on Hellenism in Bactria and India," which appeared in
the *Journal of Hellenic Studies* for 1902, through his first important
book, *Antigonos Gonatas* (1913), to *Hellenistic Civilization* (1928),
Hellenistic Military and Naval Developments (1930), *The Greeks
in Bactria and India* (1938), and chapters in the first edition of the
Cambridge Ancient History (1924–1929).

Since the springboard of the Hellenistic age was Alexander, Tarn
devoted special attention to him. He adopted the stance of a scholar-
lawyer, in a sense, taking Alexander as his "client" and setting out to
make a case for the defense. And Alexander was badly in need of such
defense. The trend of modern scholarship before Tarn had been
to view Alexander as an archtyrant, arbitrary and megalomaniac,
a drunken murderer, and the oppressor of Greek political freedom
and philosophic independence—a view derived ultimately from the
Callisthenes tradition of antiquity.

Tarn was brilliantly successful in turning opinion around in his defense of Alexander, so much so that the "traditional" view of Alexander today is still essentially that created by Tarn. His authority has been so great that it has even affected the way in which we interpret the ancient sources themselves, whether they seem to be "for" or "against" Tarn's case.

The Ancient Sources:
Arrian, Eratosthenes, and Plutarch

*In the first selection of this chapter, we present the five "proof texts"
on which Tarn built his defense of Alexander: one from Arrian, one from
Eratosthenes (preserved in Strabo), and three from Plutarch.*

This passage, from The Life of Alexander the Great *by Arrian,
took place near the end of Alexander's incredible journey of conquest.
In 324 B.C. Alexander assembled his Macedonian troops at Opis in
Mesopotamia and announced that he proposed to discharge and send home,
with lavish rewards, all those who were disabled or overage. But, instead
of gratitude, a smoldering resentment surfaced, and the entire Macedonian
force began to clamor to be sent home. Arrian attributes the resentment
to Alexander's "orientalizing," his adoption of Persian dress and customs,
and his attempt to incorporate Persians and other peoples in his army.
This had offended the Macedonians' stubborn pride and sense of
exclusiveness, and they now threatened a mutiny. Alexander was furious.
After having the ringleaders arrested, he addressed the Macedonians
in a passionate, blistering speech, reminding them of their own accomplishments, as well as his, and of what he had done for them. Alexander's
speech had a profound effect upon the Macedonians, as did the plans,
immediately put into effect, for reorganizing the army in the event that
they defected. But instead of deserting, the Macedonians repented.*

ALEXANDER, THE MOMENT he heard of this change of heart, hastened out
to meet them, and he was so touched by their grovelling repentance and
their bitter lamentations that the tears came into his eyes. While they continued to beg for his pity, he stepped forward as if to speak, but was anticipated by one Callines, an officer of the mounted Hetaeri, distinguished
both by age and rank. "My lord," he cried, "what hurts us is that you
have made Persians your kinsmen—Persians are called 'Alexander's kinsmen'—Persians kiss you. But no Macedonian has yet had a taste of this
honour."

"Every man of you," Alexander replied, "I regard as my kinsman, and
from now on that is what I shall call you."

Thereupon Callines came up to him and kissed him, and all the others
who wished to do so kissed him too. Then they picked up their weapons

and returned to their quarters singing the song of victory at the top of their voices.

To mark the restoration of harmony, Alexander offered sacrifice to the gods he was accustomed to honour, and gave a public banquet which he himself attended, sitting among the Macedonians, all of whom were present. Next them the Persians had their places, and next to the Persians distinguished foreigners of other nations; Alexander and his friends dipped their wine from the same bowl and poured the same libations, following the lead of the Greek seers and the Magi. The chief object of his prayers was that Persians and Macedonians might rule together in harmony as an imperial power. It is said that 9,000 people attended the banquet; they unanimously drank the same toast, and followed it by the paean of victory.

After this all Macedonians—about 10,000 all told—who were too old for service or in any way unfit, got their discharge at their own request.

Eratosthenes of Cyrene, who lived about 200 B.C., was head of the great Library of Alexandria and one of the most learned men of antiquity. But his works exist only in fragments and in citations in the writings of others, such as the following, from The Geography *by the Greek scientist Strabo, of the first century B.C.*

Now, towards the end of his treatise—after withholding praise from those who divide the whole multitude of mankind into two groups, namely, Greeks and Barbarians, and also from those who advised Alexander to treat the Greeks as friends but the Barbarians as enemies—Eratosthenes goes on to say that it would be better to make such divisions according to good qualities and bad qualities; for not only are many of the Greeks bad, but many of the Barbarians are refined—Indians and Arians, for example, and, further, Romans and Carthaginians, who carry on their governments so admirably. And this, he says, is the reason why Alexander, disregarding his advisers, welcomed as many as he could of the men of fair repute and did them favours—just as if those who have made such a division, placing some people in the category of censure, others in that of praise, did so for any other reason than that in some people there prevail the law-abiding and the political instinct, and the qualities associated with education and powers of speech, whereas in other people the opposite characteristics prevail! And so Alexander, not disregarding his advisers, but rather accepting their opinion, did what was consistent with, not contrary to, their advice; for he had regard to the real intent of those who gave him counsel.

Two of the Plutarch passages are from his essay "On the Fortune of Alexander," which is one of the pieces comprising the collection known as the Moralia.

Moreover, the much-admired *Republic* of Zeno, the founder of the Stoic sect, may be summed up in this one main principle: that all the inhabitants of this world of ours should not live differentiated by their respective rules of justice into separate cities and communities, but that we should consider all men to be of one community and one polity, and that we should have a common life and an order common to us all, even as a herd that feeds together and shares the pasturage of a common field. This Zeno wrote, giving shape to a dream or, as it were, shadowy picture of a well-ordered and philosophic commonwealth; but it was Alexander who gave effect to the idea. For Alexander did not follow Aristotle's advice to treat the Greeks as if he were their leader, and other peoples as if he were their master; to have regard for the Greeks as for friends and kindred, but to conduct himself toward other peoples as though they were plants or animals; for to do so would have been to cumber his leadership with numerous battles and banishments and festering seditions. But, as he believed that he came as a heaven-sent governor to all, and as a mediator for the whole world, those whom he could not persuade to unite with him, he conquered by force of arms, and he brought together into one body all men everywhere, uniting and mixing in one great loving-cup, as it were, men's lives, their characters, their marriages, their very habits of life. He bade them all consider as their fatherland the whole inhabited earth, as their stronghold and protection his camp, as akin to them all good men, and as foreigners only the wicked; they should not distinguish between Grecian and foreigner by Grecian cloak and targe, or scimitar and jacket; but the distinguishing mark of the Grecian should be seen in virtue, and that of the foreigner in iniquity; clothing and food, marriage and manner of life they should regard as common to all, being blended into one by ties of blood and children.

After dwelling on the wisdom of Alexander in affecting a mixed Graeco-Macedonian and Persian costume, Plutarch continues.

For he did not overrun Asia like a robber nor was he minded to tear and rend it, as if it were booty and plunder bestowed by unexpected good fortune. . . . But Alexander desired to render all upon earth subject to one law of reason and one form of government and to reveal all men as one people, and to this purpose he made himself conform. But if the deity that sent down Alexander's soul into this world of ours had not recalled him quickly, one law would govern all mankind, and they all would look toward one rule of justice as though toward a common source of light. But as it is, that part of the world which has not looked upon Alexander has remained without sunlight.

*The passage from the famous "Life of Alexander" in Plutarch's Lives
deals with an incident early in Alexander's career, after his conquest of
Egypt—his journey across the desert to the oracle of Ammon at Siwah.*

When Alexander had passed through the desert and was come to the place
of the oracle, the prophet of Ammon gave him salutation from the god as
from a father; whereupon Alexander asked him whether any of the
murderers of his father had escaped him.[1] To this the prophet answered
by bidding him be guarded in his speech, since his was not a mortal father.
Alexander therefore changed the form of his question, and asked whether
the murderers of Philip had all been punished; and then, regarding his own
empire, he asked whether it was given to him to become lord and master
of all mankind. The god gave answer that this was given to him, and that
Philip was fully avenged. Then Alexander made splendid offerings to the
god and gave his priests large gifts of money. . . . We are told, also, that
he listened to the teachings of Psammon [2] the philosopher in Egypt, and
accepted most readily this utterance of his, namely, that all mankind are
under the kingship of God, since in every case that which gets the mastery
and rules is divine. Still more philosophical, however, was his own opinion
and utterance on this head, namely that although God was indeed a common father of all mankind, still, He made peculiarly His own the noblest
and best of them.

Alexander the Great
and the Unity of Mankind
W. W. TARN

*We turn now to the thesis that W. W. Tarn built in defense of Alexander.
He had begun to develop his characteristic view in a number of journal
articles and anticipated it in fairly complete form in his contributions
to the 1927 edition of the* Cambridge Ancient History. *He was later*

[1] Alexander had come to the throne of Macedonia upon the murder of his father,
Philip II, in 336 B.C.—ED.
[2] This is the only reference in antiquity to such a person.—ED.

to state it most completely in his monumental two-volume Alexander
the Great *(Cambridge: Cambridge University Press, 1948). But
the most succinct statement of the Tarn thesis is that contained in his
Raleigh Lecture on History, read before the British Academy in 1933.
It is entitled "Alexander the Great and the Unity of Mankind."*

WHAT I AM going to talk about is one of the great revolutions in human
thought. Greeks of the classical period, speaking very roughly, divided
mankind into two classes, Greeks and non-Greeks; the latter they called
barbarians and usually regarded as inferior people, though occasionally
some one, like Herodotus or Xenophon, might suggest that certain barbarians possessed qualities which deserved consideration, like the wisdom
of the Egyptians or the courage of the Persians. But in the third century B.C.
and later we meet with a body of opinion which may be called univer-
salist; all mankind was one and all men were brothers, or anyhow ought
to be. Who was the pioneer who brought about this tremendous revolution
in some men's way of thinking? Most writers have had no doubt on that
point; the man to whom the credit was due was Zeno, the founder of the
Stoic philosophy. But there are several passages in Greek writers which, *if*
they are to be believed, show that the first man actually to think of it was
not Zeno but Alexander. This matter has never really been examined;
some writers just pass it over, which means, I suppose, that they do not
consider the passages in question historical; others have definitely said
that it is merely a case of our secondary authorities attributing to Alexander
ideas taken from Stoicism. I want to consider to-day whether the passages in question are or are not historical and worthy of credence; that is,
whether Alexander was or was not the first to believe in, and to contemplate, the unity of mankind. This will entail, among other things, some
examination of the concept which Greeks called Homonoia, a word which
meant more than its Latin translation, Concord, means to us; it is more
like Unity and Concord, a being of one mind together, or if we like the
phrase, a union of hearts; ultimately it was to become almost a symbol of
the world's longing for something better than constant war. For convenience
of discussion I shall keep the Greek term Homonoia.

Before coming to the ideas attributed to Alexander, I must sketch very
briefly the background against which the new thought arose, whoever was
its author; and I ought to say that I am primarily talking throughout of
theory, not of practice. It may be possible to find, in the fifth century, or
earlier, an occasional phrase which looks like a groping after something
better than the hard-and-fast division of Greeks and barbarians; but this
comes to very little and had no importance for history, because anything
of the sort was strangled by the idealist philosophies. Plato and Aristotle
left no doubt about their views. Plato said that all barbarians were enemies

by nature; it was proper to wage war upon them, even to the point of enslaving or extirpating them. Aristotle said that all barbarians were slaves by nature, especially those of Asia; they had not the qualities which entitled them to be free men, and it was proper to treat them as slaves. His model State cared for nothing but its own citizens; it was a small aristocracy of Greek citizens ruling over a barbarian peasantry who cultivated the land for their masters and had no share in the State—a thing he had seen in some cities of Asia Minor. Certainly neither Plato nor Aristotle was quite consistent; Plato might treat an Egyptian priest as the repository of wisdom, Aristotle might suggest that the constitution of Carthage was worth studying; but their main position was clear enough, as was the impression Alexander would get from his tutor Aristotle.

There were, of course, other voices. Xenophon, when he wanted to portray an ideal shepherd of the people, chose a Persian king as shepherd of the Persian people. And there were the early Cynics. But the Cynics had no thought of any union or fellowship between Greek and barbarian; they were not constructive thinkers, but merely embodied protests against the vices and follies of civilization. When Diogenes called himself a cosmopolite, a horrible word which he coined and which was not used again for centuries, what he meant was, not that he was a citizen of some imaginary world-state—a thing he never thought about—but that he was not a citizen of any Greek city; it was pure negation. And the one piece of Cynic construction, the ideal figure of Heracles, labouring to free Greece from monsters, was merely shepherd of a *Greek* herd till after Alexander, when it took colour and content from the Stoics and became the ideal benefactor of humanity. All that Xenophon or the Cynics could supply was the figure of an ideal shepherd, not of the human herd, but of some national herd.

More important was Aristotle's older contemporary Isocrates, because of his conception of Homonoia. The Greek world, whatever its practice, never doubted that in theory unity in a city was very desirable; but though the word Homonoia was already in common use among Greeks, it chiefly meant absence of faction-fights, and this rather negative meaning lasted in the cities throughout the Hellenistic period, as can be seen in the numerous decrees in honour of the judicial commissions sent from one city to another, which are praised because they tried to compose internal discord. There was hardly a trace as yet of the more positive sense which Homonoia was to acquire later—a mental attitude which should make war or faction impossible because the parties were at one; and Isocrates extended the application of the word without changing its meaning. He took up a suggestion of the sophist Gorgias and proposed to treat the whole Greek world as one and the futile wars between city and city as faction fights—to apply Homonoia to the Greek race. For this purpose he utilized Plato's idea that the barbarian was a natural enemy, and decided that the way to unite Greeks was to attack Persia; "I come," he said, "to advocate two things: war against the barbarian, Homonoia between ourselves." But somebody had to do the uniting; and Isocrates bethought him of the Cynic Heracles, benefactor of the Greek race, and urged King Philip of Macedonia, a descendant of Heracles, to play the part. But if Philip was to be Heracles and bring about the Homonoia of the Greek world, the way was being prepared for two important ideas of a later time; the essential quality of the king must be that love of man, φιλανθρωπία,[3] which had led Heracles to perform his labours, and the essential business of the king was to promote Homonoia; so far this only applied to Greeks, but if its meaning were to deepen it would still be the king's business. The actual result of all this, the League of Corinth [4] under Philip's presidency, was not quite what Isocrates had dreamt of.

This then was the background against which Alexander appeared. The business of a Macedonian king was to be a benefactor of Greeks to the extent of preventing inter-city warfare; he was to promote Homonoia among Greeks and utilize their enmity to barbarians as a bond of union; but barbarians themselves were still enemies and slaves by nature, a view which Aristotle emphasized when he advised his pupil to treat Greeks as free men, but barbarians as slaves.

I now come to the things Alexander is supposed to have said or thought; and the gulf between them and the background I have sketched is so deep that one cannot blame those who have refused to believe that he ever said or thought anything of the sort. There are five passages which need consideration: one in Arrian; one from Eratosthenes, preserved by Strabo; and three from Plutarch, one of which, from its resemblance to the Strabo passage, has been supposed by one of the acutest critics of our time to be taken in substance from Eratosthenes,[5] and as such I shall treat it. The passage in Arrian says that, after the mutiny of the Macedonians at Opis and their reconciliation to Alexander, he gave a banquet to Macedonians and Persians, at which he prayed for Homonoia and partnership in rule between these two peoples. What Eratosthenes says amounts to this. Aristotle told Alexander to treat Greeks as friends, but barbarians like animals; but Alexander knew better, and preferred to divide men into good and bad without regard to their race, and thus carried out Aristotle's real intention. For Alexander believed that he had a mission from the deity to harmonize men generally and be the reconciler of the world, mixing men's lives and customs as in a loving cup, and treating the good as his kin, the bad as strangers; for he thought that the good man was the real Greek and the bad man the real barbarian. Of the two Plutarch passages, the first says that his intention was to bring about, as between mankind generally, Homonoia and peace and fellowship and make them all one people; and the other,

---

[3] Literally "philanthropy."—ED.
[4] The league Philip formed after defeating the Greek states at Chaeronea in 338 B.C.—ED.
[5] The reference is to the German scholar E. Schwarz.—ED.

which for the moment I will quote without its context, makes him say that
God is the common father of all men.

It is obvious that, wherever all this comes from, we are dealing with a
great revolution in thought. It amounts to this, that there is a natural
brotherhood of all men, though bad men do not share in it; that Homonoia
is no longer to be confined to the relations between Greek and Greek, but
is to unite Greek and barbarian; and that Alexander's aim was to substitute
peace for war, and reconcile the enmities of mankind by bringing them all—
all that is whom his arm could reach, the peoples of his empire—to be of
one mind together: as men were one in blood, so they should become one
in heart and spirit. That such a revolution in thought did happen is un-
questioned; the question is, was Alexander really its author, or are the
thoughts attributed to him those of Zeno or somebody else? . . .

*"To try to answer that question," Tarn follows with a long and complex
analysis of Homonoia and kingship in Graeco-Roman history, leading
to the universalism of the late Roman empire.*

The belief that it was the business of kings to promote Homonoia among
their subjects without distinction of race thus travelled down the line of
kingship for centuries; but the line, you will remember, had no beginning,
for nobody will suppose that it began with writers so obscure as Diotogenes
and Pseudo-Ecphantus. It must clearly have been connected with some
particular king at the start, and that king has to be later than Isocrates and
Philip and earlier than Diotogenes and Demetrius. It would seem that only
one king is possible; we should have to postulate Alexander at the beginning of the line, even if there were not a definite tradition that it *was* he.
This means that Plutarch's statement, that Alxeander's purpose was to
bring about Homonoia between men generally—that is, those men whom
his arm could reach—must be taken to be true, unless some explicit reason
be found for disbelieving it; and I therefore now turn to the Stoics, in order
to test the view that the ideas attributed to him were really taken from
Stoicism. . . . We have seen that it was the business of kings to bring
about Homonoia; but this was not the business of a Stoic, because to him
Homonoia had already been brought about by the Deity, and it existed in
all completeness; all that was necessary was that men should see it. . . .
This is the point I want to make, the irreconcilable opposition between
Stoicism and the theory of kingship, between the belief that unity and concord existed and you must try and get men to see it, and the belief that
unity and concord did not exist and that it was the business of the rulers
of the earth to try and bring them to pass. . . . Consequently, when
Eratosthenes says that Alexander aspired to be the harmonizer and recon-

ciler of the world, and when Plutarch attributes to him the intention of bringing about fellowship and Homonoia between men generally—those men whom his arm reached—then, wherever these ideas came from, they were not Stoic; between them and Stoicism there was a gulf which nothing could bridge. This does not by itself prove that Alexander held these ideas; what it does do is to put out of court the only alternative which has ever been seriously proposed, and to leave the matter where I left it when considering the theory of kingship, that is, that there is a strong presumption that Alexander *was* their author. . . .

Before leaving Stoicism, I must return for a moment to Zeno's distinction of the worthy and the unworthy; for Alexander, as we saw, is said to have divided men into good and bad, and to have excluded the bad from the general kinship of mankind and called them the true barbarians. Might not *this* distinction, at any rate, have been taken from Stoicism and attributed to him? The reasons against this seem conclusive, apart from the difficulty of discarding a statement made by so sound and scientific a critic as Eratosthenes. First, no Stoic ever equated the unworthy class with barbarians; for to him there were no barbarians.

. . . Secondly, while the unworthy in Zeno, as in Aristotle, are the majority of mankind, Alexander's "bad men" are not; they are, as Eratosthenes says, merely that small residue everywhere which cannot be civilized. One sees this clearly in a story never questioned, his prayer at Opis, when he prayed that the Macedonian and Persian races (without exceptions made) might be united in Homonoia. And thirdly, we know where the idea comes from: Aristotle had criticized some who said that good men were really free and bad men were really slaves (whom he himself equated with barbarians), and Alexander is in turn criticizing Aristotle; as indeed Eratosthenes says, though he does not quote this passage of Aristotle. The matter is not important, except for the general question of the credibility of Eratosthenes, and may conceivably only represent that period in Alexander's thought when he was outgrowing Aristotle; it does not conflict, as does Zeno's conception of the unworthy, with a general belief in the unity of mankind. . . .

There is just one question still to be asked; whence did Zeno get his universalism? Plutarch says that behind Zeno's dream lay Alexander's reality; and no one doubts that Alexander was Zeno's inspiration, but the question is, in what form? Most writers have taken Plutarch to mean Alexander's *empire;* but to me this explains nothing at all. One man conquers a large number of races and brings them under one despotic rule; how can another man deduce from this that distinctions of race are immaterial and that the universe is a harmony in which men are brothers? It would be like the fight between the polar bear and the parallelepiped. The Persian kings had conquered and ruled as large an empire as Alexander, including many Greek cities; why did Darius never inspire any one with similar theories? It does seem to me that what Plutarch really means is not Alexander's empire but Alexander's ideas; after all, the frequent references in antiquity to Alexander as a philosopher, one at least of which is contemporary, must mean *something*. Zeno's inspiration, then, was Alexander's idea of the unity of mankind; and what Zeno himself did was to carry this idea to one of its two logical conclusions. Judging by his prayer at Opis for the Homonoia of Macedonians and Persians, Alexander, had he lived, would have worked through national groups, as was inevitable in an empire like his, which comprised many different states and subject peoples; Theophrastus,[6] who followed him, included national groups in his chain of progress towards world-relationship. But Zeno abolished all distinctions of race, all the apparatus of national groups and particular states, and made his world-state a theoretic whole. His scheme was an inspiration to many; but in historical fact it was, and remained, unrealizable. But Alexander's way, or what I think was his way, led to the Roman Empire being called one people. I am not going to bring in modern examples of these two different lines of approach to world-unity, but I want to say one thing about the Roman Empire. It has been said that Stoic ideas came near to realization in the empire of Hadrian and the Antonines, but it is quite clear, the moment it be considered, that this was not the case; that empire was a huge national state, which stood in the line of kingship and was a partial realization of the ideas of Alexander. When a Stoic *did* sit on the imperial throne, he was at once compelled to make terms with the national state; to Marcus Aurelius, the Stoic world-state was no theoretic unity, but was to comprise the various particular states as a city comprises houses. And there is still a living reality in what he said about himself: "As a man I am a citizen of the world-state, but as the particular man Marcus Aurelius I am a citizen of Rome."

I may now sum up. We have followed down the line of kingship the theory that it was the business of a king to promote Homonoia among his subjects—all his subjects without distinction of race; and we have seen that this theory ought to be connected at the start with some king, who must be later than Philip and earlier than Demetrius; and there is a definite tradition which connects the origin of the theory with Alexander. We have further seen that the intention to promote Homonoia among mankind, attributed in the tradition to Alexander, is certainly not a projection backwards from Stoicism, or apparently from anything else, while it is needed to explain certain things said by Theophrastus and done by Alexarchus.[7] Lastly, we have seen the idea of the kinship or brotherhood of mankind appearing suddenly in Theophrastus and Alexarchus; their common source can be no one but Alexander, and again tradition supports this. Only one conclusion from all this seems possible: the things which, in the tradition, Alexander is supposed to have thought and said are, in substance, true. He did say that all men were sons of God, that is brothers, but that God

---

[6] The philosopher-scientist who followed Aristotle as head of his school.—ED.

[7] A minor Macedonian princeling, following Alexander, who set up his small state apparently on the model of Alexander's ideas.—ED.

made the best ones peculiarly his own; he did aspire to be the harmonizer and reconciler of the world—that part of the world which his arm reached; he did have the intention of uniting the peoples of his empire in fellowship and concord and making them of one mind together; and when, as a beginning, he prayed at Opis for partnership in rule and Homonoia between Macedonians and Persians, he meant what he said—not partnership in rule only, but true unity between them. I am only talking of theory, not of actions; but what this means is that he was the pioneer of one of the supreme revolutions in the world's outlook, the first man known to us who contemplated the brotherhood of man or the unity of mankind, whichever phrase we like to use. I do not claim to have given you exact proof of this; it is one of those difficult borderlands of history where one does not get proofs which could be put to a jury. But there is a very strong presumption indeed that it is true. Alexander, for the things he *did,* was called The Great; but if what I have said to-day be right, I do not think we shall doubt that this idea of his—call it a purpose, call it a dream, call it what you will— was the greatest thing about him.

Tarn and the Alexander Ideal
RICHARD A. TODD

Tarn's case for Alexander was brilliant and persuasive. But a new generation of scholars has begun to question both the defense and the defender. Nor is this a matter of superficial revisionism. It is much more fundamental. Tarn's case just will not hold up: the underpinnings of his sources will not support it. And the case is not helped by the fact that, in pursuit of his defense, Tarn often mistranslated key passages in his sources, misdirected or distorted their sense, and grafted his own idealism upon his ideal Alexander.

Ernst Badian, probably Tarn's most effective critic among this generation's scholars, has called the Alexander of Tarn's vision a "phantom" that "has haunted the pages of scholarship" for "a quarter of a century." [8]

[8] Ernst Badian, "Alexander the Great and the Unity of Mankind," *Historia,* 7 (1958), 425.

The criticism of Tarn has for the most part been presented in heavily documented, detailed, and technical works well beyond the skill of most nonspecialists. There is, however, a balanced and thoughtful summary of this growing body of criticism in the essay "W. W. Tarn and the Alexander Ideal" by the young American classical historian Richard A. Todd.

IN ADDITION to many learned books and articles, the great Hellenistic historian, Sir William Woodthorpe Tarn, also wrote a tale for his daughter, *The Treasure of the Isle of Mist.* When in this story the reformed villain Jeconiah asks for a fairy-tale to learn, the doctor in charge of his case advises, "If you can't find a fairy-tale, try him with a history book; he'll never know the difference." A certain scholar has recently said nearly as much about one of Tarn's own history books:

> Tarn was the most distinguished exponent . . . of an attitude that has made the serious study of Alexander's reign from the point of view of political history not only impossible but (to many students) almost inconceivable. . . . It is not the business of the historian to envelop a successful military leader in an aureole of romantic idealisation. . . .[9]

It is true that the vivid imagination and the high idealism present in Tarn's fairy-tale are the very qualities in his historical works that have contributed most to their success and which have at the same time detracted somewhat from the stature of his writings as examples of sound scholarship. There are other qualities of Tarn's mind, however, which carry him far beyond the mere historical romancer. One of these is what F. E. Adcock calls "the judgment and acumen of his legal training."

Tarn was not a "professional" historian. That is, he never took a degree in history nor found it necessary to become a college or university instructor. After Eton he studied Greek philosophy at Trinity College, Cambridge, and then went into law. It was only after the breakdown of his health in 1905 (at the age of 36) that he decided to devote his life to the study of Hellenistic history. . . .

We fancy we can see the lawyer behind the technique and style of Tarn the historian—he masters the evidence and, making every fact obey his command, marshals all in defence of his proposition with the zeal of one who knows his cause is just. Even the more minute questions of Hellenistic history, the oarage of the Greek warship, for example, or the wife of Philip V, call forth the same vigor and conviction as do the larger ones. A friend once remarked to C. Bradford Welles that reading Tarn was "like

[9] E. Badian, "The Death of Parmenio," *Transactions of the American Philological Association,* XCI (1960), 324.

walking over glass solidified on the surface, through which you can see and feel the hot and molten masses below." His intense partisanship, though it often arrayed an army of scholars against him, is one of the most attractive features of his writing, for when he touches one of the many insignificant and unrelated facts of which Hellenistic history is principally made, it becomes important and alive, as does every individual resurrected by him. How successful a lawyer Tarn might have become had he persisted in that career is evident from his famous defence of Alexander the Great.[10] So brilliant was the case he made out for Alexander's innocence that only recently have scholars [11] dared to revive the old charges of tyranny, megalomania, and unprincipled murder, for which, indeed, there has always been ample evidence, though that could be variously interpreted. . . .

That Tarn should be best known for his portrait of Alexander the Great is probably just, for his Alexander seems to lie at the heart of his thinking; the image is reflected throughout his works. The examination of this motif, therefore, should tell us a great deal about Tarn the historian. This selection from the concluding pages of volume I of *Alexander the Great* is the climax of his vision:

> Aristotle's State had still cared nothing for humanity outside its own borders; the stranger must still be a serf or an enemy. Alexander changed all that. When he declared that all men were alike sons of one Father, and when at Opis he prayed that Macedonians and Persians might be partners in the commonwealth and that the people of his world might live in harmony and in unity of heart and mind, he proclaimed for the first time the unity and brotherhood of mankind. . . . Above all, Alexander inspired Zeno's vision of a world in which all men should be members one of another, citizens of one State without distinction of race or institutions, subject only to and in harmony with the Common Law immanent in the Universe, and united in one social life not by compulsion but only by their own willing consent, or (as he put it) by Love. . . .[12]

It may be Tarn's admiration for Alexander that has warped his estimate of Alexander's opponent, the Persian king Darius. Tarn's verdict on Darius, "He may have possessed the domestic virtues; otherwise he was a poor type of despot, cowardly and inefficient," [13] is a clever statement of the Macedonian point of view, but it fails to allow for the bias of our Greek sources, at best hostile to Darius, at their worst merely repeating the propaganda with which Alexander encouraged his troops.

[10] In *Proceedings of the British Academy* for 1933 and *Alexander the Great* (2 vols.; Cambridge, 1948).

[11] Principally E. Badian: *Historia, 1958; Classical Quarterly,* VIII (1958), 156; *TAPhA,* XCI (1960), 324ff.

[12] *Alexander the Great,* I, 147-148.

[13] *Ibid.,* 58.

How central the vision of Alexander is to Tarn's thought may be seen from the frequency with which he measures other historical figures by Alexander standards, turning up brotherhood and unity in the most surprising places. There is probably some justice in his view of the Macedonian king, Antigonos Gonatas,[14] whom Tarn believes to have been the first king to regard himself as the servant of his people, for he was a close friend of Zeno the Stoic, and very well may have said to his son, "Do you not understand, boy, that *our* kingship is a noble servitude?"

But flashes of the idealized Alexander image are seen also in other less likely rulers, the Greek kings of Bactria and India, for instance, who, after Alexander, maintained themselves in power in the East for some two centuries—by the usual royal methods, most scholars have thought. Tarn's judgment is different. The rule of the second-century (B.C.) king, Demetrius, he believes to have been

> a partnership of Greek and Indian; he was not to be a Greek king of Indian subjects, but an Indian king no less than a Greek one, head of both races. . . . It has already been shown that Demetrius was consciously copying Alexander; but in this matter his inspiration was not the Alexander who had cut his blood-stained way to the Beas but the Alexander who had imagined something better, the man who had prayed at Opis for a joint rule of the Macedonian and the Persian, the man whom Eratosthenes had called "reconciler of the world," and who had dreamt of a union of peoples in a human brotherhood.[15]

Knowing little of Demetrius of Bactria, we might give him the benefit of the doubt, but the evidence is really quite fanciful which Tarn uses in his attempt to put the Egyptian king Ptolemy IV, Philopator, in the Alexander tradition—the king Polybius describes as "absorbed in unworthy intrigues, and senseless and continuous drunkennesses. . . ." In a very questionable manner, dreams of brotherhood are deduced from Philopator's Dionysus worship:

> He must have learned from his tutor Eratosthenes that other races beside Greeks were of the human brotherhood; and very possibly, deceived by the current identification of Dionysus' name Sabazius with the Jewish Sabaoth, he thought of uniting Jews and Greeks in Dionysus worship as Ptolemy I had tried to unite Greeks and Egyptians in the worship of Sarapis; and as Sarapis, being Osiris-Apis, could also be equated with Dionysus, Philopator may have dreamt a dream, no unworthy one, of a universal religion which, while promising immortality to its initiates, should reconcile the three chief races in his composite empire. . . .[16]

14 *Antigonos Gonatas* (Oxford, 1913), 256.
15 *The Greeks in Bactria and India* (2nd ed.; Cambridge, 1951), 181.
16 *Cambridge Ancient History*, VII, 727.

Finally, none other than the last Cleopatra has been made Alexander's heir:

> In her relations with the native Egyptians she seems to stand close to Alexander; and in some way she had won their confidence. One reason may have been that she could speak to them in their own language, a thing unique among monarchs of Macedonian blood; but much more important, probably, was her sympathetic attitude toward the native religion, which had laid its spell upon her. Alexander had sacrificed to Apis, but she went further; she began her reign by going to Upper Egypt, to the very center of the old disaffection, and in person at the head of her fleet and of the burghers and priests of Thebes and Hermonthis, escorted a new Buchis bull to his home. . . .[17]

A reading of Tarn's fairy-tale, *The Treasure of the Isle of Mist,* helps us to understand why he chooses to find in the Hellenistic world so much good will among kings, for the treasure which the girl Fiona (his own daughter) seeks and finds is not a material one, but rather an apprehension of his own high idealism. It is the discovery that fame is a battered trumpet, that Aphrodite's girdle gives unpopularity with beauty, that the iron sceptre means both kingly power and exile, and that better than all of these, or any other treasure, is the joy of forgiving one's enemies. Finally, the girl discovers, this act of forgiveness can change the old sinner Jeconiah into a marvel of childlike virtue. That the author of such a book should look for brotherhood and unity wherever he might hope to find it —in the ancient as well as in the modern world—is not surprising.

Does Tarn's idealism mean also optimism? In other words, does he see the course of history as the story of progress, like Macaulay, or does he see brotherhood and unity as rarely occurring, heroic but hopeless ideals lost on a selfish world—more like Carlyle, whose appreciation for the hero in history he certainly shares? The closest approach to an answer to this question will be found in the last sentences of his Alexander book. Alexander's ideal, in the hero's own day, is described as only a "hopeless dream," but its apprehension by later generations shows it not entirely futile:

> There is certainly a line of descent from his prayer at Opis, through the Stoics and one portion of the Christian ideal, to that brotherhood of all men which was proclaimed, though only proclaimed, in the French Revolution. The torch Alexander lit for long only smouldered; perhaps it still only smoulders to-day; but it never has been, and never can be, quite put out.[18]

But this was written in 1926. A later note to this passage (probably about 1948) shows more hesitancy. "I have left the latter part of this

[17] *Ibid.,* X, 36.
[18] *Alexander the Great,* I, 148.

paragraph substantially as written in 1926. Since then we have seen new and monstrous births, and are still moving in a world not realised; and I do not know how to rewrite it." The prospect for realization of Tarn's ideal of brotherhood can hardly have brightened the remaining years of his life.

Tarn's defence of Alexander was brilliant, but the case is once again going against him. If the present trend continues, Alexander seems likely to fall from his recent place near heaven to the lowest circle of hell. The critics are probably more right than wrong. The realities of power politics in the ancient world left little scope for the kind of idealism that Tarn wished to find. This admission, however, hardly detracts from the magnitude of his achievement. More than any other historian it is he who has clothed with flesh the dry bones of Hellenistic history.

Suggestions for Further Reading

AS IS OFTEN THE CASE, the classical sources for the biography of Alexander are among the most lively and entertaining works about him, especially Plutarch and Arrian. Plutarch's Life of Alexander from his *Parallel Lives of Noble Greeks and Romans* (available in several editions) is, like the rest of the biographical sketches in this famous book, a gossipy and charming account, containing most of the familiar anecdotes associated with Alexander. Arrian's work, the most substantial of the ancient sources, despite a certain stuffiness and lack of analytical daring, is solidly based on more contemporary sources now long lost—particularly Ptolemy's journal and the work of Aristobulus. And it contains the best and most detailed account of Alexander's conquests. See the excellent modern translation by Aubrey de Sélincourt, *Arrian's Life of Alexander the Great* (Harmondsworth, England: Penguin, 1958).

The views of W. W. Tarn summarized in the excerpted passage above from his Raleigh Lecture on History, "Alexander the Great and the Unity of Mankind," are spelled out in greater detail in the chapters he wrote on Alexander and his age—chs. 12–15 of the *Cambridge Ancient History*, vol. 6 (Cambridge, England: Cambridge University Press, 1927), and in his larger *Alexander the Great*, 2 vols. (Cambridge, England: Cambridge

University Press, 1948), based on the account in *Cambridge Ancient History* but expanded and updated.

Tarn's most bitter critic is Ernst Badian, who chose to challenge Tarn in particular for the views expressed in his Raleigh Lecture. Badian's article, with the same title, "Alexander the Great and the Unity of Mankind," appeared in *Historia*, 7 (1958), 425–444, and is reprinted in *Alexander the Great, the Main Problems*, ed. G. T. Griffith (New York: Barnes and Noble, 1966). This article is highly specialized, closely reasoned, and contains long passages in Greek; but it is very important and, despite the difficulties of the text, the argument can be clearly followed even by the nonspecialist. Peter Green, *Alexander the Great* (New York: Praeger, 1970), is a modern general account of Alexander's career in the same critical tradition as Badian. Two other modern works that deal more with the conquests than the conqueror are Peter Bamm, *Alexander the Great, Power as Destiny*, tr. J. M. Brownjohn (New York: McGraw-Hill, 1968), and Sir Mortimer Wheeler, *Flames over Persepolis, Turning Point in History* (New York: Morrow, 1968), the latter of particular interest because of Wheeler's expert knowledge of Near Eastern and Indian archaeology. The most balanced and readable modern general account of Alexander is still probably A. R. Burn, *Alexander the Great and the Hellenistic Empire* (London: The English Universities Press, 1947).

Finally, Alexander is the subject of two first-rate historical novels by Mary Renault, *Fire from Heaven* (New York: Pantheon, 1969) and *The Persian Boy* (New York: Pantheon, 1972), the first carrying the story through Alexander's childhood to his accession to the throne of Macedonia, the second recounting his conquests as narrated by the Persian boy-eunuch Bagoas, Alexander's companion and lover. Renault has also produced a nonfiction account, fully as readable as her novels, and based on the meticulous research she prepared for them, *The Nature of Alexander* (New York: Pantheon, 1975).

Julius Caesar:
The Colossus that
Bestrode the Narrow World

Unlike Alexander, who conquered the world "as a boy" and was dead at thirty-three, Julius Caesar reached a mature age without achieving astonishing success. He did have considerable experience as a political faction leader, but in the judgment of most of his contemporaries he was not likely to be a world conqueror of Alexander's stamp. And yet, in 49 B.C., when Caesar was fifty years old, a series of events began to unfold that would make him one of the great conquerors of world history and set him alongside Alexander in the estimation of scholar and schoolboy alike.

For the past ten years, Caesar had been building a military reputation with his successful campaigns in Gaul, Britain, and along the Rhine frontier, but always with an eye on events in the city of Rome and the Roman senate, where he had a personal interest in the fierce contest among cliques and factions that dominated senatorial politics in the last years of the Roman Republic. As the year 49 B.C. approached, Caesar's proconsular authority in Gaul was running out. He demanded that he be permitted to stand *in absentia* for the consulship for the following year—neither an unprecedented nor unreasonable demand. Caesar attempted to negotiate with his old ally, the great general Pompey, perhaps to prolong their alliance. But Pompey, his own military reputation threatened by Caesar's growing prestige, and relentlessly pressured by Caesar's enemies in the senate, refused him and joined with the senate in demanding that

Caesar surrender his military command and return to Rome as a private citizen to stand for the consulship. But to do so would have meant his death or proscription. Thus, in January of 49 B.C., Caesar took the fateful step into open revolution, leading a token force across the Rubicon, the little stream that separated his Gallic province from peninsular Italy.

For nearly a century the Roman constitution had been progressively subverted by a succession of extralegal expedients to legitimize the authority of one strong man after another, one faction after another—whether the prolonged consulships of Marius, the perpetual dictatorship of Sulla, or the triumviral authority that Caesar himself had held with Pompey and Crassus. Such practices, as well as a pervasive disenchantment with the self-serving senatorial oligarchy, had created broad support in Rome and in Italy for a policy of change, even revolutionary change. Caesar's popular reputation attracted that support as he marched south toward Rome. Even Pompey's legions in Spain declared for Caesar. Pompey and his remaining allies fled to Greece, where they were pursued by Caesar under vast emergency authority readily granted by an overawed senate, and were defeated at Pharsalus. In the next four years, Caesar moved through Asia Minor and Syria, Egypt, North Africa, and Spain and encircled the Mediterranean with his conquests, giving the final rough form to the greatest empire of antiquity.

It was at this point that the plot to assassinate Caesar was formed and carried out on the Ides of March of the year 44 B.C.

Caesar and Alexander beg for comparison, despite the many dissimilarities in their lives. Plutarch, the greatest of ancient biographers, paired them in his *Parallel Lives of Noble Greeks and Romans,* and almost every other ancient writer who speculates upon the meaning of Caesar's career suggests comparison with Alexander. The obvious basis for the comparison is, of course, the military parallel and the fact that Caesar, like Alexander, seized his time and wrenched it so violently that the direction of world events was fundamentally changed. But equally important, both men were cut off before their schemes for a civil order could be realized. There was about Caesar, as about Alexander, an aura of things to come, of unfulfilled dreams even more astounding than his conquests. Thus the question again intrigues us, "What would Caesar have accomplished had he lived on?"

In one important respect Caesar differs radically from Alexander—in our sources of information about him. As we saw in the last chapter, all the contemporary works that dealt with the career of Alexander have been lost, and the best surviving account of him was written some four hundred years after he died. Not so with Caesar. He lived during the most heavily documented period in ancient history, a time when we know more about the people and events at the center of the world's stage than we will know again for more than a thousand years. We have Caesar's own considerable volume of writings. We have the works of his

great senatorial contemporary Cicero. We have the writings of poets
and essayists and narrative historians. But despite the abundance of
material and the wealth of detail about Julius Caesar, a clear and con-
vincing picture of the man—what he was and what he might have
become—eludes us, precisely because, as Shakespeare's Cassius says in
Julius Caesar, ". . . he doth bestride the narrow world like a colossus,"
because his dominating personality, his overweening amibition, and his
striking accomplishments made it nearly impossible for his contemporaries
to be objective about him. His own writings are propagandistic, and
the writings of Cicero, his often bitter and vindictive opponent, and
Sallust, his partisan, are obviously biased. The accounts of both Pollio
and Livy exist only in epitomes or in traces in others' works. For our
best account of Caesar, we must reach down into the imperial period that
followed his own brilliant "golden age of Latin literature," to one of
the writers of "the silver age," the biographer Suetonius.

The Life of Caesar
SUETONIUS

The choice of Suetonius is a good one on a number of counts. Although he has been charged with a journalistic style and mentality and with too great a fondness for scandal, rumor, and portent, the late imperial Historia Augusta, *for what it is worth, refers to him as having written* vere, *"truly," and a great modern Roman historian calls him "far and away the best authority" on Caesar.[1] Unlike his contemporary Plutarch, Suetonius was not a moralist using biography as a source of example. Nor was he a deliberate partisan: the factionalism of Caesar's age was long dead. Suetonius was interested only in writing a plain, straightforward account of the men and events that were his subject. And, like Arrian, he turned to archival sources for his information. The book in which his biography of Caesar appears,* The Lives of the Twelve Caesars, *was begun when Suetonius was still in the imperial civil service of the Emperor Hadrian. It is clear that he had access to archival records, now long lost, as well as to literary sources, and that he followed his sources carefully. His biography of Caesar was apparently a part of the book done before Suetonius left the imperial service in about A.D. 120 and thus is especially well documented with records and sources.*

And yet, in an important sense, Suetonius was the captive of those very sources he followed so scrupulously. For even though Suetonius was more than a century removed from his sources, the hostility toward Caesar that these records expressed is clearly reflected in Suetonius's writing. Despite his fascination and admiration for Caesar, Suetonius's basic assessment is that Caesar's arrogance and his flaunting of the republican tradition led to his murder: "He abused his powers and was justly slain."

Even after the Civil War and the furious activity of the years 48–44 B.C., Suetonius tells us, Caesar was full of plans for beautifying the city of Rome, opening libraries, draining the Pomptine marshes, building new highways, constructing a canal through the Isthmus of Corinth, and waging war against both the Dacians and the Parthians.

[1] Sir Ronald Syme, in a review of Matthias Gelzer's *Caesar der Politiker und Staatsmann* in *Journal of Roman Studies,* 34 (1944), 95.

ALL THESE ENTERPRISES and plans were cut short by his death. But before I speak of that, it will not be amiss to describe briefly his personal appearance, his dress, his mode of life, and his character, as well as his conduct in civil and military life.

He is said to have been tall of stature, with a fair complexion, shapely limbs, a somewhat full face, and keen black eyes; sound of health, except that towards the end he was subject to sudden fainting fits and to nightmare as well. He was twice attacked by the falling sickness during his campaigns. He was somewhat overnice in the care of his person, not only keeping the hair of his head closely cut and his face smoothly shaved, but, as some have charged, even having superfluous hair plucked out. His baldness was a disfigurement which troubled him greatly, since he found that it was often the subject of the gibes of his detractors. Because of it he used to comb forward his scanty locks from the crown of his head, and of all the honors voted him by the Senate and people there was none which he received or made use of more gladly than the privilege of wearing a laurel wreath at all times. . . .

It is admitted by all that he was much addicted to women, as well as very extravagant in his intrigues with them, and that he seduced many illustrious women, among them Postumia, wife of Servius Sulpicius, Lollia, wife of Aulus Gabinius, Tertulla, wife of Marcus Crassus, and even Gnaeus Pompey's wife Mucia. . . .

He had love affairs with Queens, too, including Eunoe the Moor, wife of Bogudes, on whom, as well as on her husband, he bestowed many splendid presents, as Naso writes. But his greatest favorite was Cleopatra, with whom he often feasted until daybreak, and he would have gone through Egypt with her in her state-barge almost to Aethiopia, had not his soldiers refused to follow him. Finally he called her to Rome and did not let her leave until he had laden her with high honors and rich gifts, and he allowed her to give his name to the child which she bore. . . .

That he drank very little wine not even his enemies denied. There is a saying of Marcus Cato that Caesar was the only man who undertook to overthrow the state when sober. Even in the matter of food Gaius Oppius tells us that he was so indifferent, that once when his host served stale oil instead of fresh, and the other guests would have none of it, Caesar partook even more plentifully than usual, that he might not seem to charge his host with carelessness or lack of manners.

But his abstinence did not extend to pecuniary advantages, either when in command of armies or when in civil office. For we have the testimony of some writers that when he was Proconsul in Spain, he not only begged money from the allies, to help pay his debts, but also attacked and sacked some towns of the Lusitanians, although they did not refuse his terms and opened their gates to him on his arrival. In Gaul he pillaged shrines and temples of the Gods filled with offerings, and oftener sacked towns for the sake of plunder than for any fault. . . .

He was highly skilled in arms and horsemanship, and of incredible powers of endurance. On the march he headed his army, sometimes on horseback, but oftener on foot, bareheaded both in the heat of the sun and in rain. He covered great distances with incredible speed, making a hundred miles a day in a hired carriage and with little baggage, swimming the rivers which barred his path or crossing them on inflated skins, and very often arriving before the messengers sent to announce his coming. . . .

He joined battle, not only after planning his movements in advance but on a sudden opportunity, often immediately at the end of a march, and sometimes in the foulest weather, when one would least expect him to make a move. It was not until his later years that he became slower to engage, through a conviction that the oftener he had been victor, the less he ought to tempt fate, and that he could not possibly gain as much by success as he might lose by a defeat. He never put his enemy to flight without also driving him from his camp, thus giving him no respite in his panic. When the issue was doubtful, he used to send away the horses, and his own among the first, to impose upon his troops the greater necessity of standing their ground by taking away that aid to flight. . . .

When his army gave way, he often rallied it single-handed, planting himself in the way of the fleeing men, laying hold of them one by one, even seizing them by the throat and turning them to face the enemy; that, too, when they were in such a panic that an eagle-bearer made a pass at him with the point as he tried to stop him, while another left the standard in Caesar's hand when he would hold him back. . . .

At Alexandria, while assaulting a bridge, he was forced by a sudden sally of the enemy to take to a small skiff. When many others threw themselves into the same boat, he plunged into the sea, and after swimming for two hundred paces, got away to the nearest ship, holding up his left hand all the way, so as not to wet some papers which he was carrying, and dragging his cloak after him with his teeth, to keep the enemy from getting it as a trophy.

He valued his soldiers neither for their personal character nor their fortune, but solely for their prowess, and he treated them with equal strictness and indulgence. . . .

He certainly showed admirable self-restraint and mercy, both in his conduct of the civil war and in the hour of victory. While Pompey threatened to treat as enemies those who did not take up arms for the government, Caesar gave out that those who were neutral and of neither party should be numbered with his friends. He freely allowed all those whom he had made Centurions [2] on Pompey's recommendation to go over to his rival. . . . At the battle of Pharsalus he cried out, "Spare your fellow citizens," and afterwards allowed each of his men to save any one man he pleased of the opposite party. . . .

---

[2] Centurions were "company grade" officers in the Roman legion.—ED.

Yet after all, his other actions and words so far outweigh all his good qualities that it is thought he abused his power and was justly slain. For not only did he accept excessive honors, such as an uninterrupted consulship, the dictatorship for life, and the censorship of public morals, as well as the forename Imperator,[3] the surname of Father of his Country, a statue among those of the Kings,[4] and a raised couch in the orchestra of the theater. He also allowed honors to be bestowed on him which were too great for mortal man: a golden throne in the House and on the judgment seat; a chariot and litter in the procession at the circus; temples, altars, and statues beside those of the Gods; a special priest, an additional college of the Luperci, and the calling of one of the months by his name. In fact, there were no honors which he did not receive or confer at pleasure.

He held his third and fourth consulships in name only, content with the power of the dictatorship conferred on him at the same time as the consulships. Moreover, in both years he substituted two Consuls for himself for the last three months, in the meantime holding no elections except for Tribunes and plebeian Aediles, and appointing Praefects instead of the Praetors, to manage the affairs of the city during his absence. When one of the Consuls suddenly died the day before the Kalends of January, he gave the vacant office for a few hours to a man who asked for it. With the same disregard of law and precedent he named magistrates for several years to come, bestowed the emblems of consular rank on ten ex-Praetors, and admitted to the House men who had been given citizenship, and in some cases even half-civilized Gauls. He assigned the charge of the mint and of the public revenues to his own slaves, and gave the oversight and command of the three legions which he had left at Alexandria to a favorite boy of his called Rufio, son of one of his freedmen.

No less arrogant were his public utterances, which Titus Ampius records: that the Republic was a name only, without substance or reality; that Sulla did not know his A. B. C. when he laid down his dictatorship; that men ought now to be more circumspect in addressing him, and to regard his word as law. So far did he go in his presumption, that when a soothsayer once announced to him the direful omen that a victim offered for sacrifice was without a heart, he said: "The entrails will be more favorable when I please. It ought not to be taken as a miracle if a beast have no heart."

But it was the following action in particular that roused deadly hatred against him. When the Senate approached him in a body with many highly honorary decrees, he received them before the temple of Venus Genetrix without rising. Some think that when he attempted to get up, he was held back by Cornelius Balbus; others, that he made no such move at all, but

---

[3] The title *Imperator,* synonymous with conqueror, was that by which troops would hail a victorious commander. It first assumed a permanent and royal character through Caesar's use of it as a prenomen.

[4] Statues of each of the seven Kings of Rome were in the Capitol, to which an eighth was added in honor of Brutus, who expelled the last. The statue of Julius was afterwards raised near them.

on the contrary frowned angrily on Gaius Trebatius when he suggested that he should rise. This action of his seemed the more intolerable, because when he himself in one of his triumphal processions rode past the benches of the Tribunes, he was so incensed because one of their number, Pontius Aquila by name, did not rise, that he cried: "Come then, Aquila, mighty Tribune, and take from me the Republic," and for several days afterwards, he would promise a favor to no one without adding, "That is, if Pontius Aquila will give me leave."

To an insult which so plainly showed his contempt for the Senate he added an act of even greater insolence. After the sacred rites of the Latin Festival, as he was returning to the city, amid the extravagant and unprecedented demonstrations of the populace, some one in the press placed on his statue a laurel wreath with a white fillet tied to it. When Epidius Marullus and Caesetius Flavus, Tribunes of the Commons, gave orders that the ribbon be removed from the crown and the man taken off to prison, Caesar sharply rebuked and deposed them, either offended that the hint at regal power had been received with so little favor, or, as was said, that he had been robbed of the glory of refusing it. But from that time on he could not rid himself of the odium of having aspired to the title of monarch, although he replied to the Commons, when they hailed him as King, "I am Caesar and not King." At the Lupercalia, when the Consul Antony several times attempted to place a crown upon his head as he spoke from the rostra, he put it aside and at last sent it to the Capitol, to be offered to Jupiter Optimus Maximus. Nay, more, the report had spread in various quarters that he intended to move to Ilium or Alexandria, taking with him the resources of the state, draining Italy by levies, and leaving it and the charge of the city to his friends; also that at the next meeting of the Senate Lucius Cotta would announce as the decision of the Fifteen,[5] that inasmuch as it was written in the books of fate that the Parthians could be conquered only by a King, Caesar should be given that title. . . .

More than sixty joined the conspiracy against him, led by Gaius Cassius and Marcus and Decimus Brutus. At first they hesitated whether to form two divisions at the elections in the Campus Martius, so that while some hurled him from the bridge as he summoned the tribes to vote, the rest might wait below and slay him; or to set upon him in the Sacred Way or at the entrance to the theater. When, however, a meeting of the Senate was called for the Ides of March in the Hall of Pompey, they readily gave that time and place the preference.

Now Caesar's approaching murder was foretold to him by unmistakable signs: . . . when he was offering sacrifice, the soothsayer Spurinna warned him to beware of danger, which would come not later than the Ides of March. . . .

Both for these reasons and because of poor health he hesitated for a long

---

[5] The college of fifteen priests who inspected and expounded the Sybilline books.

time whether to stay at home and put off what he had planned to do in the Senate. But at last, urged by Decimus Brutus not to disappoint the full meeting, which had for some time been waiting for him, he went forth almost at the end of the fifth hour. When a note revealing the plot was handed him by some one on the way, he put it with others which he held in his left hand, intending to read them presently. Then, after many victims had been slain, and he could not get favorable omens, he entered the House in defiance of portents, laughing at Spurinna and calling him a false prophet, because the Ides of March were come without bringing him harm. Spurinna replied that they had of a truth come, but they had not gone.

As he took his seat, the conspirators gathered about him as if to pay their respects, and straightway Tillius Cimber, who had assumed the lead, came nearer as though to ask something. When Caesar with a gesture put him off to another time, Cimber caught his toga by both shoulders. As Caesar cried, "Why, this is violence!" one of the Cascas stabbed him from one side just below the throat. Caesar caught Casca's arm and ran it through with his stylus, but as he tried to leap to his feet, he was stopped by another wound. When he saw that he was beset on every side by drawn daggers, he muffled his head in his robe, and at the same time drew down its lap to his feet with his left hand, in order to fall more decently, with the lower part of his body also covered. And in this wise he was stabbed with three and twenty wounds, uttering not a word, but merely a groan at the first stroke, though some have written that when Marcus Brutus rushed at him, he said in Greek, "You too, my child?" All the conspirators made off, and he lay there lifeless for some time, until finally three common slaves put him on a litter and carried him home, with one arm hanging down.

The Heroic Image of Caesar
THEODOR MOMMSEN

Theodor Mommsen (1817–1903) was awarded the Nobel Prize for Literature in 1902, largely for the literary achievement of his monumental, multivolume The History of Rome. *The Nobel citation called him the "greatest . . . master of historical narrative" of his age—a considerable claim in an era that had produced Ranke and Burckhardt, Guizot,*

Grote, Carlyle, and Macaulay. Still, the assertion may be true. Mommsen,
a prolific writer, had gained an immense and well-deserved authority,
and his massive The History of Rome *was profoundly influential. It was*
Mommsen who at last placed the study of ancient history on a scientific
and critical foundation. And he began and directed the first great critical
collection of ancient Latin inscriptions.

Like W. W. Tarn, Theodor Mommsen was trained both in classics and
in law. His first academic appointment was as professor of law at Leipzig.
Then in 1858 he was appointed to the chair of ancient history at the
University of Berlin. Throughout his long life, Mommsen was not only
a professor but a passionate political activist. He was involved in the
Revolution of 1848 and lost his academic post at Leipzig because of it.
In the 1870s he was a prominent member of the Prussian Parliament,
frequently clashing with Otto von Bismarck. Like many great historians,
Mommsen read the past in terms of present politics. Thus his view of
Caesar and the late Roman Republic was colored by his profound
disillusionment with German political liberalism and an equally profound
hatred for Junker conservatism. Julius Caesar became for Mommsen
the archetypal strong man who had swept away the broken pieces of a
ruined oligarchy and set the rule of the beneficent Roman Empire firmly
on its base. While Mommsen has been rightly criticized for the extrava-
gance of his opinions both on Caesar and on the late Roman Republic,
his views, though never quite accepted as the "standard" interpretation,
did exert a strong influence on modern scholarship until fairly recently.

Here, from The History of Rome, *is Mommsen's evaluation of*
Julius Caesar. The prose is old fashioned and florid and the judgments
are dated, but there is still some power left in the sweep of Mommsen's
portrayal of his "perfect man."

THE NEW MONARCH of Rome, the first ruler over the whole domain of
Romano-Hellenic civilization, Gaius Julius Caesar, was in his fifty-sixth
year . . . when the battle at Thapsus [46 B.C.], the last link in a long
chain of momentous victories, placed the decision as to the future of the
world in his hands. Few men have had their elasticity so thoroughly put
to the proof as Caesar—the sole creative genius produced by Rome, and
the last produced by the ancient world, which accordingly moved on in the
path that he marked out for it until its sun went down. Sprung from one
of the oldest noble families of Latium—which traced back its lineage to
the heroes of the Iliad and the kings of Rome, and in fact to the Venus-
Aphrodite common to both nations—he spent the years of his boyhood
and early manhood as the genteel youth of that epoch were wont to spend
them. He had tasted the sweetness as well as the bitterness of the cup of
fashionable life, had recited and declaimed, had practised literature and

made verses in his idle hours, had prosecuted love-intrigues of every sort, and got himself initiated into all the mysteries of shaving, curls, and ruffles pertaining to the toilette-wisdom of the day, as well as into the still more mysterious art of always borrowing and never paying. But the flexible steel of that nature was proof against even these dissipated and flighty courses; Caesar retained both his bodily vigour and his elasticity of mind and of heart unimpaired. In fencing and in riding he was a match for any of his soldiers, and his swimming saved his life at Alexandria; the incredible rapidity of his journeys, which usually for the sake of gaining time were performed by night—a thorough contrast to the procession-like slowness with which Pompeius moved from one place to another—was the astonishment of his contemporaries and not the least among the causes of his success. The mind was like the body. His remarkable power of intuition revealed itself in the precision and practicability of all his arrangements, even where he gave orders without having seen with his own eyes. His memory was matchless, and it was easy for him to carry on several occupations simultaneously with equal self-possession. . . .

Casear was thoroughly a realist and a man of sense; and whatever he undertook and achieved was pervaded and guided by the cool sobriety which constitutes the most marked peculiarity of his genius. To this he owed the power of living energetically in the present, undisturbed either by recollection or by expectation; to this he owed the capacity of acting at any moment with collected vigour, and of applying his whole genius even to the smallest and most incidental enterprise; to this he owed the many-sided power with which he grasped and mastered whatever understanding can comprehend and will can compel; to this he owed the self-possessed ease with which he arranged his periods as well as projected his campaigns; to this he owed the "marvellous serenity" which remained steadily with him through good and evil days; to this he owed the complete independence, which admitted of no control by favourite or by mistress, or even by friend. It resulted, moreover, from this clearness of judgment that Caesar never formed to himself illusions regarding the power of fate and the ability of man; in his case the friendly veil was lifted up, which conceals from man the inadequacy of his working. Prudently as he laid his plans and considered all possibilities, the feeling was never absent from his breast that in all things fortune, that is to say accident, must bestow success; and with this may be connected the circumstance that he so often played a desperate game with destiny, and in particular again and again hazarded his person with daring indifference. As indeed occasionally men of predominant sagacity betake themselves to a pure game of hazard, so there was in Caesar's rationalism a point at which it came in some measure into contact with mysticism.

Gifts such as these could not fail to produce a statesman. From early youth, accordingly, Caesar was a statesman in the deepest sense of the term, and his aim was the highest which man is allowed to propose to himself—the political, military, intellectual, and moral regeneration of his own deeply decayed nation, and of the still more deeply decayed Hellenic nation intimately akin to his own. The hard school of thirty years' experience changed his views as to the means by which this aim was to be reached; his aim itself remained the same in the times of his hopeless humiliation and of his unlimited plenitude of power, in the times when as demagogue and conspirator he stole towards it by paths of darkness, and in those when, as joint possessor of the supreme power and then as monarch, he worked at his task in the full light of day before the eyes of the world. . . . According to his original plan he had purposed to reach his object, like Pericles and Gaius Gracchus, without force of arms, and throughout eighteen years he had as leader of the popular party moved exclusively amid political plans and intrigues—until, reluctantly convinced of the necessity for a military support, he, when already forty years of age, put himself at the head of an army [59 B.C.]. . . .

The most remarkable peculiarity of his action as a statesman was its perfect harmony. In reality all the conditions for this most difficult of all human functions were united in Caesar. A thorough realist, he never allowed the images of the past or venerable tradition to disturb him; for him nothing was of value in politics but the living present and the law of reason, just as in his character of grammarian he set aside historical and antiquarian research and recognized nothing but on the one hand the living *usus loquendi* and on the other hand the rule of symmetry. A born ruler, he governed the minds of men as the wind drives the clouds, and compelled the most heterogeneous natures to place themselves at his service—the plain citizen and the rough subaltern, the genteel matrons of Rome and the fair princesses of Egypt and Mauretania, the brilliant cavalry-officer and the calculating banker. His talent for organization was marvellous; no statesman has ever compelled alliances, no general has ever collected an army out of unyielding and refractory elements with such decision, and kept them together with such firmness, as Caesar displayed in constraining and upholding his coalitions and his legions; never did regent judge his instruments and assign each to the place appropriate for him with so acute an eye.

He was monarch; but he never played the king. Even when absolute lord of Rome, he retained the deportment of the party-leader; perfectly pliant and smooth, easy and charming in conversation, complaisant towards every one, it seemed as if he wished to be nothing but the first among his peers. Caesar entirely avoided the blunder into which so many men otherwise on an equality with him have fallen, of carrying into politics the military tone of command; however much occasion his disagreeable relations with the senate gave for it, he never resorted to outrages. . . . Caesar was monarch; but he was never seized with the giddiness of the tyrant. He is perhaps the only one among the mighty ones of the earth, who in great matters and little never acted according to inclination or caprice, but always without exception according to his duty as ruler, and who, when he looked back on his life, found doubtless erroneous calculations to deplore, but no false step of passion to regret. There is nothing in the history of Caesar's life, which even on a small scale can be compared with those poetico-sensual ebullitions—such as the murder of Kleitos or the burning or Persepolis—which the history of his great predecessor in the east records. He is, in fine, perhaps the only one of those mighty ones, who has preserved to the end of his career the statesman's tact of discriminating between the possible and the impossible, and has not broken down in the task which for greatly gifted natures is the most difficult of all—the task of recognizing, when on the pinnacle of success, its natural limits. What was possible he performed, and never left the possible good undone for the sake of the impossible better, never disdained at least to mitigate by palliatives evils that were incurable. But where he recognized that fate had spoken, he always obeyed. . . .

Such was this unique man, whom it seems so easy and yet is so infinitely difficult to describe. His whole nature is transparent clearness; and tradition preserves more copious and more vivid information about him than about any of his peers in the ancient world. Of such a personage our conceptions may well vary in point of shallowness or depth, but they cannot be, strictly speaking, different; to every not utterly perverted inquirer the grand figure has exhibited the same essential features, and yet no one has succeeded in reproducing it to the life. The secret lies in its perfection. In his character as a man as well as in his place in history, Caesar occupies a position where the great contrasts of existence meet and balance each other. Of mighty creative power and yet at the same time of the most penetrating judgment; no longer a youth and not yet an old man; of the highest energy of will and the highest capacity of execution; filled with republican ideals and at the same time born to be a king; a Roman in the deepest essence of his nature, and yet called to reconcile and combine in himself as well as in the outer world the Roman and the Hellenic types of culture—Caesar was the entire and perfect man.

Caesar the Politician
RONALD SYME

*The long-time Oxford professor Sir Ronald Syme is probably our leading
ancient historian today. His most important book, and possibly the
outstanding work in Roman history in this generation,[6] is* The Roman
Revolution. *Syme worked on this book through the late 1930s, against
the backdrop of events taking place in Mommsen's Germany, but the
vision of one-man rule was not quite as alluring to him as it had been to
Mommsen. Syme's view of Caesar, however, was not only affected by
the rise of Hitler and the political drift toward World War II. He had
before him an impressive accumulation of scholarly research on the
darker side of the Caesarian monarchy. Eduard Meyer's* Caesars Monarchie
und das Principat des Pompejus *(1919) argues that Caesar aspired
to the establishment of a Hellenistic monarchy in Rome. The second
volume of Jerome Carcopino's* Histoire Romaine *(1936) deals with
Caesar and maintains that, since his youth, Caesar's ambition was
directed toward monarchy.*

Syme also read the important work of Matthias Gelzer—Die Nobilität
der Römischen Republik *(1912) and* Caesar der Politiker und
Staatsmann *(1921)—which prompted him to examine some of the same
ground, the social and political setting in which Caesar lived and
died. Syme, like Gelzer, was especially interested in the senatorial
oligarchy. The "Roman Revolution" of his title, he argues, occurred
when this oligarchy lost its power to a new social group composed of
people from all parts of Italy, even the provinces. And he saw Caesar as
the political genius who began the revolution that he could not then control.*

*Syme insists that Caesar be judged—as he was murdered— "for what
he was, not for what he might become," be that an oriental despot
or a Hellenistic monarch. What Caesar was was a Roman aristocrat
whose brilliance and luck enabled him to surpass his fellow aristocrats.
The key event leading to his assassination was not his arrogance, which was
common to his class and station, and not even his high-handedness
in subverting the republic; it was the Caesarian dictatorship, prolonged
first for ten years and then, in January of 44 B.C., for life, that was
intolerable to the senatorial nobility and the cause of his murder.*

The following, from The Roman Revolution, *is Syme's analysis of
Caesar.*

[6] Cf. the review, for example, of Michael Ginsburg in *American Historical Review*, 46 (1940), 108.

THE CONQUEST of Gaul, the war against Pompeius and the establishment of the Dictatorship of Caesar are events that move in a harmony so swift and sure as to appear pre-ordained; and history has sometimes been written as though Caesar set the tune from the beginning, in the knowledge that monarchy was the panacea for the world's ills, and with the design to achieve it by armed force. Such a view is too simple to be historical.

Caesar strove to avert any resort to open war. Both before and after the outbreak of hostilities he sought to negotiate with Pompeius. Had Pompeius listened and consented to an interview, their old *amicitia* might have been repaired. With the nominal primacy of Pompeius recognized, Caesar and his adherents would capture the government—and perhaps reform the State. Caesar's enemies were afraid of that—and so was Pompeius. After long wavering Pompeius chose at last to save the oligarchy. Further, the proconsul's proposals as conveyed to the Senate were moderate and may not be dismissed as mere manoeuvres for position or for time to bring up his armies. Caesar knew how small was the party willing to provoke a war. As the artful motion of a Caesarian tribune had revealed, an overwhelming majority in the Senate, nearly four hundred against twenty-two, wished both dynasts to lay down their extraordinary commands. A rash and factious minority prevailed.

The precise legal points at issue in Caesar's claim to stand for the consulate in absence and retain his province until the end of the year 49 B.C. are still matters of controversy. If they were ever clear, debate and misrepresentation soon clouded truth and equity. The nature of the political crisis is less obscure. Caesar and his associates in power had thwarted or suspended the constitution for their own ends many times in the past. Exceptions had been made before in favour of other dynasts; and Caesar asserted both legal and moral rights to preferential treatment. In the last resort his rank, prestige and honour, summed up in the Latin word *dignitas,* were all at stake: to Caesar, as he claimed, "his *dignitas* had ever been dearer than life itself." Sooner than surrender it, Caesar appealed to arms. A constitutional pretext was provided by the violence of his adversaries: Caesar stood in defence of the rights of the tribunes and the liberties of the Roman People. But that was not the plea which Caesar himself valued most—it was his personal honour.

His enemies appeared to have triumphed. They had driven a wedge between the two dynasts, winning over to their side the power and prestige of Pompeius. They would be able to deal with Pompeius later. It might not come to open war; and Pompeius was still in their control so long as he was not at the head of an army in the field. Upon Caesar they had thrust the choice between civil war and political extinction. . . .

Caesar was constrained to appeal to his army for protection. At last the enemies of Caesar had succeeded in ensnaring Pompeius and in working the constitution against the craftiest politician of the day: he was declared a public enemy if he did not lay down his command before a certain day. By invoking constitutional sanctions against Caesar, a small faction misrepresented the true wishes of a vast majority in the Senate, in Rome, and in Italy. They pretended that the issue lay between a rebellious proconsul and legitimate authority. Such venturesome expedients are commonly the work of hot blood and muddled heads. The error was double and damning. Disillusion followed swiftly. Even Cato was dismayed. It had confidently been expected that the solid and respectable classes in the towns of Italy would rally in defence of the authority of the Senate and the liberties of the Roman People, that all the land would rise as one man against the invader. Nothing of the kind happened. Italy was apathetic to the war-cry of the Republic in danger, sceptical about its champions. . . .

Caesar, it is true, had only a legion to hand: the bulk of his army was still far away. But he swept down the eastern coast of Italy, gathering troops, momentum and confidence as he went. Within two months of the crossing of the Rubicon he was master of Italy. Pompeius made his escape across the Adriatic carrying with him several legions and a large number of senators, a grievous burden of revenge and recrimination. The enemies of Caesar had counted upon capitulation or a short and easy war.

They had lost the first round. Then a second blow, quite beyond calculation: before the summer was out the generals of Pompeius in Spain were outmanoeuvred and overcome. Yet even so, until the legions joined battle on the plain of Pharsalus, the odds lay heavily against Caesar. Fortune, the devotion of his veteran legionaries and the divided counsels of his adversaries secured the crowning victory. But three years more of fighting were needed to stamp out the last and bitter resistance of the Pompeian cause in Africa and in Spain.

"They would have it thus," said Caesar as he gazed upon the Roman dead at Pharsalus, half in patriot grief for the havoc of civil war, half in impatience and resentment. They had cheated Caesar of the true glory of a Roman aristocrat—to contend with his peers for primacy, not to destroy them. His enemies had the laugh of him in death. Even Pharsalus was not the end. His former ally, the great Pompeius, glorious from victories in all quarters of the world, lay unburied on an Egyptian beach, slain by a renegade Roman, the hireling of a foreign king. Dead, too, and killed by Romans, were Caesar's rivals and enemies, many illustrious consulars. Ahenobarbus fought and fell at Pharsalus, and Q. Metellus Scipio ended worthy of his ancestors; while Cato chose to fall by his own hand rather than witness the domination of Caesar and the destruction of the Free State.

That was the nemesis of ambition and glory, to be thwarted in the end. After such wreckage, the task of rebuilding confronted him, stern and thankless. Without the sincere and patriotic co-operation of the governing class, the attempt would be all in vain, the mere creation of arbitrary power, doomed to perish in violence. . . .

Under these unfavourable auspices, a Sulla but for *clementia,* a Gracchus but lacking a revolutionary programme, Caesar established his Dictatorship. His rule began as the triumph of a faction in civil war: he made it his task to transcend faction, and in so doing wrought his own destruction. A champion of the People, he had to curb the People's rights, as Sulla had done. To rule, he needed the support of the *nobiles,* yet he had to curtail their privileges and repress their dangerous ambitions.

In name and function Caesar's office was to set the State in order again (*rei publicae constituendae*). Despite odious memories of Sulla, the choice of the Dictatorship was recommended by its comprehensive powers and freedom from the tribunician veto. Caesar knew that secret enemies would soon direct that deadly weapon against one who had used it with such dexterity in the past and who more recently claimed to be asserting the rights of the tribunes, the liberty of the Roman People. He was not mistaken. Yet he required special powers: after a civil war the need was patent. The Dictator's task might well demand several years. In 46 B.C. his powers were prolonged to a tenure of ten years, an ominous sign. A gleam of hope that the emergency period would be quite short flickered up for a moment, to wane at once and perish utterly. In January 44 B.C. Caesar was voted the Dictatorship for life. About the same time decrees of the Senate ordained that an oath of allegiance should be taken in his name. Was this the measure of his ordering of the Roman State? Was this a *res publica constituta*?

It was disquieting. Little had been done to repair the ravages of civil war and promote social regeneration. For that there was sore need, as both his adherents and his former adversaries pointed out. From Pompeius, from Cato and from the oligarchy, no hope of reform. But Caesar seemed different: he had consistently advocated the cause of the oppressed, whether Roman, Italian or provincial. He had shown that he was not afraid of vested interests. But Caesar was not a revolutionary. . . .

[He] postponed decision about the permanent ordering of the State. It was too difficult. Instead, he would set out for the wars again, to Macedonia and to the eastern frontier of the Empire. At Rome he was hampered: abroad he might enjoy his conscious mastery of men and events, as before in Gaul. Easy victories—but not the urgent needs of the Roman People.

About Caesar's ultimate designs there can be opinion, but no certainty. The acts and projects of his Dictatorship do not reveal them. For the rest, the evidence is partisan—or posthumous. No statement of unrealized intentions is a safe guide to history, for it is unverifiable and therefore the most attractive form of misrepresentation. The enemies of Caesar spread rumours to discredit the living Dictator: Caesar dead became a god and a myth, passing from the realm of history into literature and legend, declamation and propaganda. . . .

Yet speculation cannot be debarred from playing round the high and momentous theme of the last designs of Caesar the Dictator. It has been supposed and contended that Caesar either desired to establish or had actually inaugurated an institution unheard of in Rome and unimagined there—monarchic rule, despotic and absolute, based upon worship of the ruler, after the pattern of the monarchies of the Hellenistic East. Thus may Caesar be represented as the heir in all things of Alexander the Macedonian and as the anticipator of Caracalla, a king and a god incarnate, levelling class and nation, ruling a subject, united and uniform world by right divine.

This extreme simplification of long and diverse ages of history seems to suggest that Caesar alone of contemporary Roman statesmen possessed either a wide vision of the future or a singular and elementary blindness to the present. But this is only a Caesar of myth or rational construction. . . .

If Caesar must be judged, it is by facts and not by alleged intentions. As his acts and his writings reveal him, Caesar stands out as a realist and an opportunist. In the short time at his disposal he can hardly have made plans for a long future or laid the foundation of a consistent government. Whatever it might be, it would owe more to the needs of the moment than to alien or theoretical models. More important the business in hand; it was expedited in swift and arbitrary fashion. Caesar made plans and decisions in the company of his intimates and secretaries: the Senate voted but did not deliberate. As the Dictator was on the point of departing in the spring of 44 B.C. for several years of campaigning in the Balkans and the East, he tied up magistracies and provincial commands in advance by placing them, according to the traditional Roman way, in the hands of loyal partisans, or of reconciled Pompeians whose good sense should guarantee peace. For that period, at least, a salutary pause from political activity: with the lapse of time the situation might become clearer in one way or another. . . .

At the moment it was intolerable: the autocrat became impatient, annoyed by covert opposition, petty criticism and laudations of dead Cato. That he was unpopular he well knew. "For all his genius, Caesar could not see a way out," as one of his friends was subsequently to remark. And there was no going back. To Caesar's clear mind and love of rapid decision, this brought a tragic sense of impotence and frustration—he had been all things and it was no good. He had surpassed the good fortune of Sulla Felix and the glory of Pompeius Magnus. In vain—reckless ambition had ruined the Roman State and baffled itself in the end. Of the melancholy that descended upon Caesar there stands the best of testimony—"my life has been long enough, whether reckoned in years or in renown." The words were remembered. The most eloquent of his contemporaries did not disdain to plagiarize them.

The question of ultimate intentions becomes irrelevant. Caesar was slain for what he was, not for what he might become. . . .

It is not necessary to believe that Caesar planned to establish at Rome a "Hellenistic Monarchy," whatever meaning may attach to that phrase. The Dictatorship was enough. The rule of the *nobiles,* he could see, was an anachronism in a world-empire; and so was the power of the Roman plebs when all Italy enjoyed the franchise. Caesar in truth was more conservative and Roman than many have fancied; and no Roman conceived of government save through an oligarchy. But Caesar was being forced into an autocratic position. It meant the lasting domination of one man instead of the rule of the law, the constitution and the Senate; it announced the triumph soon or late of new forces and new ideas, the elevation of the army and the provinces, the depression of the traditional governing class. Caesar's autocracy appeared to be much more than a temporary expedient to liquidate the heritage of the Civil War and reinvigorate the organs of the Roman State. It was going to last—and the Roman aristocracy was not to be permitted to govern and exploit the Empire in its own fashion. The tragedies of history do not arise from the conflict of conventional right and wrong. They are more august and more complex. Caesar and Brutus each had right on his side. . . .

Without a party a statesman is nothing. He sometimes forgets that awkward fact. If the leader or principal agent of a faction goes beyond the wishes of his allies and emancipates himself from control, he may have to be dropped or suppressed. . . .

When Caesar took the Dictatorship for life and the sworn allegiance of senators, it seemed clear that he had escaped from the shackles of party to supreme and personal rule. For this reason, certain of the most prominent of his adherents combined with Republicans and Pompeians to remove their leader. The Caesarian party thus split by the assassination of the Dictator none the less survived, joined for a few months with Republicans in a new and precarious front of security and vested interests led by the Dictator's political deputy until a new leader, emerging unexpected, at first tore it in pieces again, but ultimately, after conquering the last of his rivals, converted the old Caesarian party into a national government in a transformed State. The composition and vicissitudes of that party, though less dramatic in unity of theme than the careers and exploits of the successive leaders, will yet help to recall the ineffable complexities of authentic history.

Suggestions for Further Reading

AS IN THE CASE of Alexander, the ancient sources for the life of Julius
Caesar are among the liveliest and most entertaining accounts of him.
Students are encouraged to read the rest of Suetonius' sketch beyond what
is excerpted in this chapter. They are also encouraged to read Plutarch's
Life of Caesar, which, as we have noted, he wrote to be compared with his
Life of Alexander. Plutarch and Suetonius between them give us most of
the anecdotal matter commonly associated with Caesar. We have in addition, as also noted above, the considerable volume of Caesar's own writings
in several attractive modern editions, *The Gallic War*, tr. and ed. Moses
Hadas (New York: Modern Library, 1957), tr. J. Warrington (New
York: Heritage, 1955), and tr. S. A. Handford (Baltimore: Penguin,
1965); and *The Civil War*, ed. and tr. Jane F. Mitchell (Baltimore: Penguin, 1967). We also have references to Caesar scattered throughout the
works of such contemporaries as Cicero and Sallust.

Caesar has always been a fascinating figure, and there are an impossibly
large number of biographies of him. Two recent ones can be especially
recommended to students. Probably the best brief biography is J. P. V. D.
Balsdon, *Julius Caesar and Rome* (London: The English Universities
Press, 1967), an authoritative work by an established authority, another
in the excellent "Teach Yourself History Library" series. Students may
prefer the somewhat larger and more lavish Michael Grant, *Caesar* (London: Weidenfeld and Nicolson, 1974), in the "Great Lives" series; it is
interesting and readable as well as authoritative, another book by one of
the best modern popularizers of ancient history.

There are also many books dealing with Caesar's era and the late
Roman republic. One of the best of these, and one that combines the account of the man and the era, is Matthias Gelzer, *Caesar, Politician and
Statesman*, tr. Peter Needham (Cambridge, Mass.: Harvard University
Press, 1968). Despite its relentlessly prosaic quality, it is an important
interpretive work by a great German scholar, stressing Caesar as a political
figure of genius and paralleling the views of Sir Ronald Syme, which are
represented in this chapter. A somewhat broader account, still considered
a standard work by many authorities, is that of F. E. Adcock in chs. 15–17
in vol. 9 of the *Cambridge Ancient History* (Cambridge, England: Cambridge University Press, 1932). Also recommended are R. E. Smith, *The
Failure of the Roman Republic* (Cambridge, England: Cambridge University Press, 1955); the somewhat more detailed Erich S. Gruen, *The*

Last Generation of the Roman Republic (Berkeley: University of California Press, 1974); and the now famous small study by Lily Ross Taylor, *Party Politics in the Age of Caesar* (Berkeley: University of California Press, 1975 [1949]).

Finally, two special studies are recommended, the attractive small book by F. E. Adcock, *Caesar as Man of Letters* (Cambridge, England: Cambridge University Press, 1956), and Gen. John F. C. Fuller, *Julius Caesar: Man, Soldier, and Tyrant* (New Brunswick, N.J.: Rutgers University Press, 1965), a lively, opinionated, and somewhat debunking book by a great military historian about Caesar as a less-than-brilliant general.

Augustine:
The Thinking Man's Saint

The historian Edward Gibbon capsulized the rise of Christianity in
this dramatic sentence: "A pure and humble religion gently insinuated
itself into the minds of men, grew up in silence and obscurity, derived
new vigor from opposition, and finally erected the triumphant banner of
the Cross on the ruins of the Capitol." [1] While modern historians may
quarrel with one aspect or another of Gibbon's views, most agree
that by the mid-fourth century Christianity was the dominant spiritual
force in the Roman Empire. The public policy of persecution had been
replaced by toleration and then endorsement; and since Constantine
every emperor, save the much maligned Julian "the Apostate"
(361–363), had been at least nominally Christian. The church as an
institution had taken form, and its officials were people of importance,
from one end of the empire to the other. It was at long last both
fashionable and profitable to be Christian; and men of position and
substance adopted the faith.

It is thus not surprising that a bright, well-educated, and ambitious
young man of the late fourth century should have been attracted to
Christianity. What is unusual is that he wrote a sensitive, detailed account
of the experience of his conversion, entitled the *Confessions.* This work
is all the more valuable, for the man who wrote it went on to become
the most important theologian of the early church and one of the most
influential thinkers in human history—St. Augustine.

[1] *Decline and Fall of the Roman Empire,* Ch. XV.1.

The Confessions
ST. AUGUSTINE

The Confessions *is a remarkable book. A modern critic has called
it ". . . one of the truest, frankest, and most heart-lifting autobiographies
ever written."* [2] *For us, however, its "heart-lifting" inspirational quality—
and surely it was written to impart just that quality—will be of less
interest than its fascinating revelation of the process by which a tough-
minded intellectual, examining his own life, was brought not only to
embrace Christianity but to make it the very center of his being. No
document has ever laid open that process more candidly or more
searchingly than the* Confessions.

*Aurelius Augustinus was born at Tagaste in Roman North Africa
in 354, of a not-uneducated pagan father and a devoutly Christian mother.
Signs of intellectual precocity led his father to send the boy to school at
an early age and at considerable financial sacrifice. He was trained first
at the nearby town of Madaura and then at the great city of Carthage,
the capital and the intellectual and trade center of Roman Africa.
Augustine was studying to be a professional rhetorician. And neither
the program nor its aims—the study of eloquence for the sake of
persuasion—had changed in centuries. When he finished his schooling,
Augustine became a teacher of rhetoric. He also became a member
of the Manicheans, a sect particularly strong in North Africa that
taught a form of radical dualism as its principal spiritual-intellectual
doctrine. Though he remained a Manichean for some nine years,
Augustine was also attracted to astrology; he was impressed with Cicero's
urbane, academic skepticism; he studied Aristotle and Plato and the
fashionable Neoplatonism; and he sampled and rejected the Christian
Bible. Without fully realizing it, his search for belief was beginning.*

*By this time Augustine had become a teacher in his native Tagaste,
had taken a wife, and had fathered a son. He then obtained a teaching
position in Carthage and was becoming a well-known rhetorician and
philosopher when, in 383 at the age of twenty-nine, he went to teach in
Rome. Within a year, he heard of a position as master of rhetoric to
the great city of Milan, which in these declining years of the Roman
empire had come to overshadow the old capital as the center of imperial
government in the West. It was an important position; Augustine
competed for it, delivering a public oration, and was awarded the post.*

[2] Stewart Perowne, *The End of the Roman World* (New York: Crowell, 1967),
p. 143.

It was in Milan that Augustine came under the influence of one of the most powerful figures in the early church, St. Ambrose, the Bishop of Milan, who, as Augustine says, "received me as a father." The process of conversion was under way. But it was to be neither an easy nor a painless process. For such a man as Augustine had hard intellectual questions to ask of any faith.

Let St. Augustine himself continue the story.

I BEGAN TO love him at first not as a teacher of the truth (for I had quite despaired of finding it in your Church) but simply as a man who was kind and generous to me. I used to listen eagerly when he preached to the people, but my intention was not what it should have been; I was, as it were, putting his eloquence on trial to see whether it came up to his reputation, or whether its flow was greater or less than I had been told. So I hung intently on his words, but I was not interested in what he was really saying and stood aside from this in contempt. I was much pleased by the charm of his style, which, although it was more learned, was still, so far as the manner of delivery was concerned, not so warm and winning as the style of Faustus.[3] With regard to the actual matter there was, of course, no comparison. Faustus was merely roving around among Manichaean fallacies, while Ambrose was healthily teaching salvation. But salvation is far from sinners of the kind that I was then. Yet, though I did not realize it, I was drawing gradually nearer.

For although my concern was not to learn what he said but only to hear how he said it (this empty interest being all that remained to me, now that I had despaired of man's being able to find his way to you), nevertheless, together with the language, which I admired, the subject matter also, to which I was indifferent, began to enter into my mind. Indeed I could not separate the one from the other. And as I opened my heart in order to recognize how eloquently he was speaking it occurred to me at the same time (though this idea came gradually) how truly he was speaking. . . .

By this time my mother had joined me. Her piety had given her strength and she had followed me over land and sea, confident in you throughout all dangers. In the perils of the sea it was she who put the fresh heart into the sailors although as a rule it is for the sailors to reassure the passengers who are inexperienced on the high seas. But she promised them that they would get safely to land because you had promised this to her in a vision. She found me in grave danger indeed, my danger being that of despairing of ever discovering the truth. I told her that, though I was not yet a

---

[3] A famous Manichean preacher. Augustine had eagerly anticipated hearing him but was disappointed when he did. From this point his break with Manicheanism began.—ED.

Catholic Christian, I was certainly no longer a Manichaean; but she showed no great signs of delight, as though at some unexpected piece of news, because she already felt at ease regarding that particular aspect of my misery; she bewailed me as one dead, certainly, but as one who would be raised up again by you; she was in her mind laying me before you on the bier so that you might say to the widow's son: *"Young man, I say unto thee, Arise,"* and he should revive and begin to speak and you should give him to his mother. So her heart was shaken by no storm of exultation when she heard that what she had daily begged you with her tears should happen had in so large a part taken place—that I was now rescued from falsehood, even though I had not yet attained the truth. She was indeed quite certain that you, who had promised her the whole, would give her the part that remained, and she replied to me very calmly and with a heart full of confidence that she believed in Christ that, before she departed from this life, she would see me a true Catholic. . . .

I was not yet groaning in prayer for you to help me. My mind was intent on inquiry and restless in dispute. I considered Ambrose himself, who was honored by people of such importance, a lucky man by worldly standards; only his celibacy seemed to me rather a burden to bear. But I could neither guess nor tell from my own experience what hope he had within him, what were his struggles against the temptations of his exalted position, what solace he found in adversity; nor could I tell of that hidden mouth of his (the mouth of his heart), what joys it tasted in the rumination of your bread. And he on his side did not know of the turmoil in which I was or the deep pit of danger before my feet. I was not able to ask him the questions I wanted to ask in the way I wanted to ask them, because I was prevented from having an intimate conversation with him by the crowds of people, all of whom had some business with him and to whose infirmities he was a servant. And for the very short periods of time when he was not with them, he was either refreshing his body with necessary food or his mind with reading. When he was reading, his eyes went over the pages and his heart looked into the sense, but voice and tongue were resting. Often when we came to him (for no one was forbidden to come in, and it was not customary for visitors even to be announced) we found him reading, always to himself and never otherwise; we would sit in silence for a long time, not venturing to interrupt him in his intense concentration on his task, and then we would go away again. We guessed that in the very small time which he was able to set aside for mental refreshment he wanted to be free from the disturbance of other people's business and would not like to have his attention distracted. . . . But I needed to find him with plenty of time to spare if I was to pour out to him the full flood of agitation boiling up inside me, and I could never find him like this. Yet every Sunday I listened to him rightly preaching to the people the word of truth, and I became more and more sure that all those knots of cunning calumny which, in their attacks on the holy books, my deceivers had tied could be unraveled. In particular I discovered that the phrase "man, created by Thee, after Thine own image" was not understood by your spiritual children, whom you have made to be born again by grace through the Catholic mother, in such a way as to mean that you are bounded by the shape of a human body. And although I had not the faintest or most shadowy notion about what a spiritual substance could be, nevertheless with a kind of pleasant shame I blushed to think of how for all these years I had been barking not against the Catholic faith but against figments of carnal imaginations. . . .

. . . So I was both confounded and converted, and I was glad, my God, that your only Church, the body of your only son—that Church in which the name of Christ had been put upon me as an infant[4]—was not flavored with this childish nonsense and did not, in her healthy doctrine, maintain the view that you, the Creator of all things, could be, in the form of a human body, packed into a definite space which, however mighty and large, must still be bounded on all sides. . . . But it was the same with me as with a man who, having once had a bad doctor, is afraid of trusting himself even to a good one. So it was with the health of my soul which could not possibly be cured except by believing, but refused to be cured for fear of believing something false. So I resisted your hands, for it was you who prepared the medicines of faith and applied them to the diseases of the world and gave them such potency. . . .

And I, as I looked back over my life, was quite amazed to think of how long a time had passed since my nineteenth year, when I had first become inflamed with a passion for wisdom and had resolved that, when once I found it, I would leave behind me all the empty hopes and deceitful frenzies of vain desires. And now I was in my thirtieth year, still sticking in the same mud, still greedy for the enjoyment of things present, which fled from me and wasted me away, and all the time saying: "I shall find it tomorrow. See, it will become quite clear and I shall grasp it. Now Faustus will come and explain everything. What great men the Academics are! Is it true that no certainty can possibly be comprehended for the direction of our lives? No, it cannot be. We must look into things more carefully and not give up hope. And now see, those things in the Scriptures which used to seem absurd are not absurd; they can be understood in a different and perfectly good way. I shall take my stand where my parents placed me as a child until I can see the truth plainly. But where shall I look for it? And when shall I look for it? Ambrose has no spare time; nor have I time for reading. And where can I find the books? From where can I get them and when can I get them? Can I borrow them from anybody? I must arrange fixed periods of time and set aside certain hours for the health of my soul.

---

4 Though he had not been baptized as a child, he had apparently been at least nominally Christian, through his mother's influence—ED.

A great hope has dawned. The Catholic faith does not teach the things I thought it did and vainly accused it of teaching. The learned men of that faith think it quite wrong to believe that God is bounded within the shape of a human body. Why then do I hesitate to knock, so that the rest may be laid open to me? My pupils take up all my time in the morning. But what do I do for the rest of the day? Why not do this? But, if I do, how shall I find time to call on influential friends whose support will be useful to me? When shall I prepare the lessons for which my pupils pay? When shall I have time to relax and to refresh my mind from all my preoccupations? . . . As I became more unhappy, so you drew closer to me. Your right hand was ready, it was ready to drag me out of the mud and to wash me; but I did not know. And there was nothing to call me back from that deeper gulf of carnal pleasure, except the fear of death and of judgment to come, and this, whatever the opinions I held from time to time, never left my mind. . . .

Now my evil abominable youth was a thing of the past. I was growing into manhood, and the older I was the more discreditable was the emptiness of my mind. I was unable to form an idea of any kind of substance other than what my eyes are accustomed to see. I did not think of you, God, in the shape of a human body. From the moment when I began to have any knowledge of wisdom I always avoided that idea, and I was glad that I had found the same view held in the faith of our spiritual mother, your Catholic Church. But how else I was to think of you, I did not know. . . .

As to me, I would certainly say and I firmly believed that you—our Lord, the true God, who made not only our souls but our bodies, and not only our souls and bodies but all men and all things—were undefilable and unalterable and in no way to be changed, and yet I still could not understand clearly and distinctly what was the cause of evil. Whatever it might be, however, I did realize that my inquiry must not be carried out along lines which would lead me to believe that the immutable God was mutable; if I did that, I should become myself the very evil which I was looking for. And so I pursued the inquiry without anxiety, being quite certain that what the Manichees said was not true. I had turned against them with my whole heart, because I saw that in their inquiries into the origin of evil they were full of evil themselves; for they preferred to believe that your substance could suffer evil rather than that their substance could do evil. . . . So I thought of your creation as finite and as filled with you, who were infinite. And I said: "Here is God, and here is what God has created; and God is good and is most mightily and incomparably better than all these. Yet He, being good, created them good, and see how He surrounds them and fills them. Where, then, is evil? Where did it come from and how did it creep in here? What is its root and seed? Or does it simply not exist? In that case why do we fear and take precautions against something that does not exist? Or if there is no point in our fears, then our fears themselves are an evil which goads and tortures the heart for no good reason—and all the worse an evil if there is nothing to be afraid of and we are still afraid. Therefore, either there is evil which we fear or else the fact that we do fear is evil. Where then does evil come from, seeing that God is good and made all things good? Certainly it was the greater and supreme Good who made these lesser goods, yet still all are good, both the creator and his creation. Where then did evil come from? Or was there some evil element in the material of creation, and did God shape and form it, yet still leave in it something which He did not change into good? But why? Being omnipotent, did He lack the power to change and transform the whole so that no trace of evil should remain? Indeed why should He choose to use such material for making anything? Would He not rather, with this same omnipotence, cause it not to exist at all? Could it exist against His will? Or, supposing it was eternal, why for so long through all the infinite spaces of time past did He allow it to exist and then so much later decide to make something out of it? Or, if He did suddenly decide on some action, would not the omnipotent prefer to act in such a way that this evil material should cease to exist, and that He alone should be, the whole, true, supreme, and infinite Good? Or, since it was not good that He who was good should frame and create something not good, then why did He not take away and reduce to nothing the material that was evil and then Himself provide good material from which to create all things? For He would not be omnipotent if He could not create something good without having to rely on material which He had not Himself created."

These were the kind of thoughts [5] which I turned over and over in my unhappy heart, a heart overburdened with those biting cares that came from my fear of death and my failure to discover the truth. Yet the faith of your Christ, our Lord and Saviour, professed in the Catholic Church, remained steadfastly fixed in my heart, even though it was on many points still unformed and swerving from the right rule of doctrine. But, nevertheless, my mind did not abandon it, but rather drank more and more deeply of it every day.

By this time too I had rejected the fallacious forecasts and impious ravings of the astrologers. . . .

But then, after reading these books of the Platonists which taught me to seek for a truth which was incorporeal, I came to see your *invisible things, understood by those things which are made.* I fell back again from this point, but still I had an apprehension of what, through the darkness

---

[5] The long and complex foregoing discussion of "the problem of evil" relates, on the one hand, to Augustine's rejection of Manicheanism, which explained evil by identifying it with matter, and, on the other, to his own important speculations on the problem of free will and predestination.—ED.

of my mind, I was not able to contemplate; I was certain that you are and that you are infinite, yet not in the sense of being diffused through space whether infinite or finite: that you truly are, and are always the same, not in any part or by any motion different or otherwise: also that all other things are from you, as is proved most certainly by the mere fact that they exist. On all these points I was perfectly certain, but I was still too weak to be able to enjoy you. I talked away as if I were a finished scholar; but, if I had not sought the way to you in Christ our Saviour, what would have been finished would have been my soul. For I had begun to want to have the reputation of a wise man; my punishment was within me, but I did not weep; I was merely puffed up with my knowledge. Where was that charity which builds from the foundation of humility, the foundation which is Christ Jesus? Humility was not a subject which those books would ever have taught me. Yet I believe that you wanted me to come upon these books before I made a study of your Scriptures. You wanted the impression made by them on me to be printed in my memory, so that when later I had become, as it were, tamed by your books (your fingers dressing my wounds), I should be able to see clearly what the difference is between presumption and confession, between those who see their goal without seeing how to get there and those who see the way which leads to that happy country which is there for us not only to perceive but to live in. For if I had been first trained in your Scriptures and by my familiarity with them had found you growing sweet to me, and had then afterward come upon these books of the Platonists, it is possible that they might have swept me away from the solid basis of piety; or, even if I had held firmly to that healthy disposition which I had imbibed, I might have thought that the same disposition could be acquired by someone who had read only the Platonic books.[6]

So I most greedily seized upon the venerable writings of your spirit and in particular the works of the apostle Paul. In the past it had sometimes seemed to me that he contradicted himself and that what he said conflicted with the testimonies of the law and the prophets; but all these difficulties had now disappeared; I saw one and the same face of pure eloquence and learned *to rejoice with trembling*. Having begun, I discovered that everything in the Platonists which I had found true was expressed here, but it was expressed to the glory of your grace. . . .

Augustine, convinced now on the intellectual plane, retires to a garden with his friend Alypius, who had accompanied him from Africa—and the controversy "in my heart" begins.

[6] This is a reference to the Neoplatonic writings that Augustine had again taken up with renewed interest. These works had long been esteemed by the Christians as being an aid to faith. Notice that they are so regarded by Augustine.—ED.

So went the controversy in my heart—about self, and self against self. And Alypius stayed close by me, waiting silently to see how this strange agitation of mine would end.

And now from my hidden depths my searching thought had dragged up and set before the sight of my heart the whole mass of my misery. Then a huge storm rose up within me bringing with it a huge downpour of tears. So that I might pour out all these tears and speak the words that came with them I rose up from Alypius (solitude seemed better for the business of weeping) and went further away so that I might not be embarrassed even by his presence. This was how I felt and he realized it. No doubt I had said something or other, and he could feel the weight of my tears in the sound of my voice. And so I rose to my feet, and he, in a state of utter amazement, remained in the place where we had been sitting. I flung myself down on the ground somehow under a fig tree and gave free rein to my tears; they streamed and flooded from my eyes, an *acceptable sacrifice to Thee*. And I kept saying to you, not perhaps in these words, but with this sense: *"And Thou, O Lord, how long? How long, Lord; wilt Thou be angry forever? Remember not our former iniquities."* For I felt that it was these which were holding me fast. And in my misery I would exclaim: "How long, how long this 'tomorrow and tomorrow'? Why not now? Why not finish this very hour with my uncleanness?"

So I spoke, weeping in the bitter contrition of my heart. Suddenly a voice reaches my ears from a nearby house. It is the voice of a boy or a girl (I don't know which) and in a kind of singsong the words are constantly repeated: "Take it and read it. Take it and read it." At once my face changed, and I began to think carefully of whether the singing of words like these came into any kind of game which children play, and I could not remember that I had ever heard anything like it before. I checked the force of my tears and rose to my feet, being quite certain that I must interpret this as a divine command to me to open the book and read the first passage which I should come upon. For I had heard this about Antony[7]: he had happened to come in when the Gospel was being read, and as though the words read were spoken directly to himself, had received the admonition: *Go, sell that thou hast, and give to the poor, and thou shalt have treasure in heaven, and come and follow me.* And by such an oracle he had been immediately converted to you.

So I went eagerly back to the place where Alypius was sitting, since it was there that I had left the book of the Apostle when I rose to my feet. I snatched up the book, opened it, and read in silence the passage upon which my eyes first fell: *Not in rioting and drunkenness, not in chambering and wantonness, not in strife and envying: but put ye on the Lord Jesus*

[7] The Egyptian desert hermit, St. Anthony. Augustine and his friends had only recently heard the whole miraculous story of St. Anthony from a mutual friend who had visited them. Thus it was much in his mind.—ED.

Christ, and make not provision for the flesh in concupiscence. I had no
wish to read further; there was no need to. For immediately I had reached
the end of this sentence it was as though my heart was filled with a light of
confidence and all the shadows of my doubt were swept away.

A New Look
at the Confessions
PETER BROWN

*What does modern scholarship have to say about this book, which has
fascinated readers for more than fifteen hundred years? There is no better
work for such an examination than the well-received, recent critical
biography of Augustine by the young Oxford scholar Peter Brown.*

   Peter Brown treats the Confessions *as a source for the understanding
of Augustine's inner self, his emotional disposition and intellectual
growth. But Brown also has a synoptic view of the vast scholarship
on this work, as on every writing of Augustine, and that scholarship is
brought to bear in his conclusions about the* Confessions.

WANDERING, TEMPTATIONS, sad thoughts of mortality and the search for
truth: these had always been the stuff of autobiography for fine souls, who
refused to accept superficial security. Pagan philosophers had already
created a tradition of "religious autobiography" in this vein: it will be
continued by Christians in the fourth century, and will reach its climax
in the *Confessions* of S. Augustine.

   Augustine, therefore, did not need to look far to find an audience for
the *Confessions.* It had been created for him quite recently, by the amazing
spread of asceticism in the Latin world. The *Confessions* was a book for
the *servi Dei,* for the "servants of God," it is a classic document of the
tastes of a group of highly sophisticated men, the *spiritales,* the "men of
the spirit." It told such men just what they wanted to know about—the
course of a notable conversion; it asked of its readers what they made a

habit of asking for themselves—the support of their prayers. It even contained moving appeals to the men who might join this new élite: to the austere Manichee and the pagan Platonist, still standing aloof from the crowded basilicas of the Christians. . . .

The *Confessions* is very much the book of a man who had come to regard his past as a training for his present career. Thus, Augustine will select as important, incidents and problems that immediately betray the new bishop of Hippo. He had come to believe that the understanding and exposition of the Scriptures was the heart of a bishop's life. His relations with the Scriptures, therefore, come to form a constant theme throughout the *Confessions*. His conversion to the Manichees, for instance, is now diagnosed, not in terms of a philosophical preoccupation with the origin of evil, but as a failure to accept the Bible. We see Ambrose through the eyes of a fellow-professional: we meet him as a preacher and exegete, facing the Christian people in the basilica, not as the connoisseur of Plotinus.[8] Augustine remembered how, in his early days in Milan, he had seen the distant figure of Ambrose as a bishop, from the outside only. Now a bishop himself, he will ensure that he will not be seen in this way: he will tell his readers exactly how he still had to struggle with his own temptations; and in the last three books of the *Confessions,* as he meditates on the opening lines of the book of *Genesis,* he will carry his readers with him into his thoughts as he, also, sat in his study, as he had once seen Ambrose sit, wrapt in the silent contemplation of an open page. . . .

The *Confessions,* therefore, is not a book of reminiscences. They are an anxious turning to the past. The note of urgency is unmistakable. "Allow me, I beseech You, grant me to wind round and round in my present memory the spirals of my errors. . . ."

It is also a poignant book. In it, one constantly senses the tension between the "then" of the young man and the "now" of the bishop. The past can come very close: its powerful and complex emotions have only recently passed away; we can still feel their contours through the thin layer of new feeling that has grown over them. . . .

Augustine had been forced to come to terms with himself. The writing of the *Confessions* was an act of therapy. The many attempts to explain the book in terms of a single, external provocation, or of a single, philosophical *idée fixe,* ignore the life that runs through it. In this attempt to find himself, every single fibre in Augustine's middle age grew together with every other, to make the *Confessions* what it is. . . .

The *Confessions* are a masterpiece of strictly intellectual autobiography. Augustine communicates such a sense of intense personal involvement in the ideas he is handling, that we are made to forget that it is an exceptionally difficult book. Augustine paid his audience of *spiritales* the great (perhaps the unmerited) compliment of talking to them, as if they were as

8 The third-century Alexandrian scholar who really created Neoplatonism. He was a great favorite of St. Ambrose.

steeped in Neo-Platonic philosophy as himself. His Manichaean phase, for instance, is discussed in terms of ideas on which the Platonists regarded themselves as far in advance of the average thought of their age, the ideas of a "spiritual" reality, and of the omnipresence of God. . . .

It is often said that the *Confessions* is not an "autobiography" in the modern sense. This is true, but not particularly helpful. Because, for a Late Roman man, it is precisely this intense, autobiographical vein in the *Confessions,* that sets it apart from the intellectual tradition to which Augustine belonged.

It is more important to realize that the *Confessions* is an autobiography in which the author has imposed a drastic, fully-conscious choice of what is significant. The *Confessions* are, quite succinctly, the story of Augustine's "heart," or of his "feelings"—his *affectus.* An intellectual event, such as the reading of a new book, is registered only, as it were, from the inside, in terms of the sheer excitement of the experience, of its impact on Augustine's feelings: of the *Hortensius* of Cicero, for instance, he would never say "it changed my views" but, so characteristically, "it changed my way of feeling"—*mutavit affectum meum.*

The emotional tone of the *Confessions* strikes any modern reader. The book owes its lasting appeal to the way in which Augustine, in his middle-age, had dared to open himself up to the feelings of his youth. Yet, such a tone was not inevitable. Augustine's intense awareness of the vital role of "feeling" in his past life had come to grow upon him. . . .

Seeing that Augustine wrote his *Confessions* "remembering my wicked ways, thinking them over again in bitterness," it is amazing how little of this bitterness he has allowed to colour his past feelings. They are not made pale by regret: it is plainly the autobiography of a man who, even as a schoolboy, had known what it was to be moved only by "delight," to be bored by duty, who had enjoyed fully what he had enjoyed: " 'One and one is two, two and two is four,' this was a hateful jingle to me: and the greatest treat of all, that sweet illusion—the Wooden Horse full of armed men, Troy burning and the very ghost of Creusa.". . .

Augustine analyses his past feelings with ferocious honesty. They were too important to him to be falsified by sentimental stereotypes. It is not that he had abandoned strong feeling: he merely believed it possible to transform feelings, to direct them more profitably. This involved scrutinizing them intently. . . .

The *Confessions* are one of the few books of Augustine's, where the title is significant. *Confessio* meant, for Augustine, "accusation of oneself; praise of God." In this one word, he had summed up his attitude to the human condition: it was the new key with which he hoped, in middle age, to unlock the riddle of evil.

The Age of Augustine:
The Pagan-Christian Tradition
M. L. W. LAISTNER

*While the searing, intensely personal conversion experience of Augustine
was clearly unique—and would have been unique for such a man in
any age—both Augustine and the church he finally came to embrace
were the end products of a long and complex accommodation that
we must examine in order to set both the man and the institution in
the age to which they belonged.*

*The earliest converts to Christianity were, if not "slaves and
outcasts," at least humble men, like its earliest preachers, the "weak and
simple apostles." But Christianity did not remain simple. In the course
of the second and third centuries—perhaps even earlier—the flourishing
new cult attracted in increasing numbers men who were the products
of the schools of rhetoric and philosophy that had been established
in every city of the empire. As it fought its way to recognition, Christianity
had to answer the philosophic questions posed by both its antagonists
and its converts. In this inherent conflict between the fanatic spiritualism
of early Christianity and the logical rationalism of the classical
philosophic tradition lay one of the gravest problems the early church
had to face. The problem manifested itself in the form of doctrinal
disputes so bitter and prolonged that they threatened the very existence
of the church. But out of the debates that roiled about these controversies,
the church gradually developed its doctrine. And in the process, the
disparate elements of the pagan intellectual tradition and the Christian
spiritual tradition were reconciled. Augustine played a major role in
that process, combining in himself the disparate elements of the
accommodation.*

*To put the age of Augustine in perspective, we turn to the work of
the great modern Anglo-American scholar M. L. W. Laistner (d. 1959).
Laistner devoted most of his impressive scholarship to the problem of the
transmission of the classical intellectual tradition to the Middle Ages.
Augustine and the age of Augustine were crucial to that process. The
following selection is from the last and one of the best of Laistner's
books,* Thought and Letters in Western Europe A.D. 500 to 900.

THE POLICY OF religious toleration adopted by Constantine and Licinius radically altered the position of the Christian minorities in the Empire. The communities of the Faithful, which for three centuries had been either illicit organizations, or, even when tolerated by the highest authority, were without legal status, now came into the category of permitted associations. The Christians, who hitherto had always been liable to suffer individually or in groups because of occasional outbursts of popular hostility in the several provinces of the Roman world, and in whose lives for sixty years (251–311) a precarious toleration had alternated with rigorous persecution by the imperial Government, could now live in and by their faith without let or hindrance. Moreover, if religious differences provoked disturbances of the peace, the Christians could, if wronged, claim the redress under the law that was the right of all citizens, whatever their religious beliefs. Within less than a decade from 313 the Church had secured from the emperor the right to corporate ownership of property, and like other lawful associations, could receive testamentary bequests. As a result the wealth of the Church grew with remarkable swiftness. Even if nothing further had developed from these changes they would have been noteworthy enough; actually the fourth century witnessed a transformation which deserves to be called revolutionary. With the exception of Julian, all the emperors from Constantine I were Christian rulers. The adherents of a religion which was not only permitted but fostered by the imperial family increased with such rapidity that at the death of Theodosius I in A.D. 395 the Christians in the Empire were in a marked majority. . . .

Long before 313 the ecclesiastical organization had travelled a long way from the simple system of the primitive Church. The democratic election of elders by each congregation had been gradually superseded, as a purely parochial arrangement no longer sufficed for a steadily expanding body, by a monarchic method of government which developed side by side with the growth of a more elaborate hierarchy. In the fourth century this evolution became more rapid than before. The Church which waxed so quickly in size and authority began to derive inspiration from the civil law of the Empire for her own purposes. From this and from the decisions of councils and synods, over and above the authority of the Bible and tradition handed down from Apostolic times, there developed, slowly but steadily, the impressive body of canon law. So, too, in the matter of administration: the organization of the temporal State seems to have served as a model for the ecclesiastical. . . .

The transmutation of a despised cult into a State religion was not effected without moral and spiritual loss. All too often worldliness and love of the good things of this life contrasted glaringly with the lofty ethics of the primitive Christian communities, even as they gave the lie to the efficacy of the Church's teaching whose moral standards had not been lowered. Not less painful is the effect produced by contemplating the disunion and often rancorous quarrels in the Christian body as a whole, and their concomitant religious intolerance. . . .

The attitude of Christian thinkers to pagan education and literature, which brought in its train the problem how best to instruct the children of Christians, is a question of some complexity. . . . When Christianity early in the fourth century became "a lawful religion," there would indeed have been no danger or illegality in the establishment of specifically Christian schools; but there were nevertheless in practice very real difficulties to overcome, especially in the western half of the Empire. Although the Latin Church by then could boast of Tertullian, Cyprian, Victorinus of Pettau, Arnobius, and Lactantius, their writings were not suitable as school-books. There were no treatises on grammar, rhetoric, or any of the liberal arts save those by pagan authors; and, while there was no danger to orthodoxy in declensions, conjugations, and, in short, the rules of idiomatic language and composition, the illustrations from literature which were sown broadcast through the more popular text-books of grammar and rhetoric were from infidel prose writers and poets. At every turn the Christian boy or youth was familiarized with pagan mythology, and with aspects of pagan literature and thought which the leaders of the Church were bound to disapprove. Thus there existed a dilemma from which there was no escape for those who were willing to seek a compromise.

The extreme attitude in the earlier period is well exemplified by Tertullian who fiercely attacked pagan letters. His famous aphorism, "the philosophers are the patriarchs of the heretics," illustrates the danger to which, in his view, well-to-do Christians were exposed if they were subjected to the higher education of the day. He would have liked, too, to forbid Christians to teach the literature of the heathen; yet he was bound to advise sending children to school. This could only mean handing them over to the *litterator* or *grammaticus,* in other words, giving them the same education as their pagan contemporaries. How far the safeguard which he advocates, that the young should first have received some religious instruction at home, was effective, it would be rash to surmise. And in at least one passage Tertullian admits that the study of philosophy might have some value and that ignorance can be more dangerous than knowledge. . . .

Both Jerome and Augustine had pondered more deeply on educational theory and practice, and on the place of non-Christian literature in a scheme of Christian education. Both men had enjoyed the best secular education available in their day, Jerome in Rome, Augustine at Madaura and in Carthage, whose schools were reputed amongst the best in the Empire. Both again were experienced teachers. . . .

Augustine, like Jerome, had passed with distinction through the schools of the *grammaticus* and *rhetor;* but unlike his older contemporary, he was himself for a decade a teacher of rhetoric in Africa, in Rome, and finally in Milan. From several of his works it is possible to ascertain with some distinctness his earlier and his later views on the education of a Christian. He himself has recorded the profound impression left upon his youthful mind—he was nineteen years old at the time—by the study of Cicero's *Hortensius.* The purpose of this treatise, which has not survived, was to serve as an introduction to the study of philosophy (and, more particularly, to Cicero's own works in this field), and at the same time to combat prevailing misconceptions about the value of philosophical speculations. The effect of its perusal on the young Augustine was far-reaching. It was an antidote to the one-sided rhetorical training which had hitherto fallen to his lot. It started that deep admiration for Cicero which remained with him to the end of his life. It gave a new direction to his intellectual activity by leading him to some interest in science and to a study of philosophy, particularly Neoplatonism. The steadily deepening understanding which came to him from constant application to these subjects ultimately caused him to reject the Manichaean heresy to which he had adhered for a few years. The treatise, *De ordine,* composed in 386 at Cassiciacum near Milan, a retreat to which he had withdrawn with a few friends after his conversion to the orthodox Faith, is a dialogue having as its theme the order existing in the Universe, and the position and significance of evil therein. The existence of order and method throughout the Universe is illustrated incidentally from divers human examples, amongst others from the liberal arts. As one would expect from a Ciceronian and an ex-teacher, his attitude is liberal and even enthusiastic. . . .

But Augustine's most elaborate contribution to educational theory is the long treatise, *De doctrina Christiana.* . . .

There are many passages in the *De doctrina Christiana* which show Augustine striving for some mean between practical necessity and orthodoxy. He deserves all credit for being the first to write a comprehensive guide for the education of the Christian teacher; a book, moreover, which became a standard work in the Middle Ages. At the same time those parts which deal with the liberal arts, in which the standard of attainment regarded as needful is still elementary, reflect the low level to which the intellectual life of the later Empire had declined. One may also wonder whether, if he had completed his encyclopedia of the liberal arts, the treatment of each subject and the standard aimed at would have been more exacting; and whether such a work would have been able to displace the older pagan treatises in the monasteries and Christian schools of the earlier Middle Ages. In Books II and III Augustine is fain to admit the need of the liberal arts but, like other Christian thinkers before him, he urges that their study should cease as early as possible; and science—he is thinking particularly of astronomy—is dangerous because it may lead the student to belief in astrology which was so prevalent during the later Empire. In Book IV, written a year before the *Retractations,* he tries to prove that there is no necessity for profane literature in training the Christian preacher or orator, because the Scriptures provide all necessary material for illustration. . . . [But] what did Augustine himself do in composing Book IV of the *De doctrina Christiana?* He adapted Cicero's *Orator* to Christian needs, even as the first Latin treatise on Christian ethics, Ambrose's *De officiis,* was modelled on Cicero's dialogue of the same name. Augustine took his illustrations from Christian authors, but the framework of the whole is closely modelled on the *Orator.* Thus the love and admiration for Rome's greatest orator was never quenched in Augustine's heart. And the noble and impressive chapters which conclude the *De doctrina Christiana* (IV, 28 and 29) are the utterance not of a narrow doctrinaire but of a man who can recognize and welcome truth wheresoever he may find it.

Suggestions for Further Reading

ST. AUGUSTINE WAS not only an important and influential thinker, he was also a prolific writer, and students are encouraged to read more extensively in his works—certainly to read further in *The Confessions* and at least to try the book generally considered Augustine's most influential work, *The City of God.* Both works are available in a number of editions. For *The City of God,* because of its size and complexity, students may prefer St. Augustine, *The City of God, An Abridged Version,* tr. Gerald G. Walsh, D. B. Zema, Grace Monahan, and D. J. Honan, ed. and intro. V. J. Bourke (New York: Doubleday, 1958). For a further sampling *An Augustine Reader,* ed. John J. O'Meara (New York: Doubleday, 1973) or *Basic Writings of St. Augustine,* ed. Whitney J. Oates, 2 vols. (New York: Random House, 1948) are recommended.

There is a wilderness of interpretive and explanatory writing about Augustine and his thought, most of it recondite in the extreme, but there are some useful aids. The most readily available and one of the most generally useful is *A Companion to the Study of St. Augustine,* ed. Roy W. Battenhouse (New York: Oxford University Press, 1955). A more strictly theological guide of the same sort is Eugène Portalié, *A Guide to the Thought of St. Augustine,* intro. V. J. Bourke, tr. R. J. Bastian (Chicago: Regnery, 1960), the republication and translation of a famous essay from a French dictionary of Catholic theology at the turn of the century.

Equally orthodox but more lively and readable is Etienne Gilson, *The Christian Philosophy of St. Augustine*, tr. L. E. M. Lynch (New York: Random House, 1960), a standard work of interpretation by the greatest Catholic authority on medieval philosophy. More specifically, students can read from a well-selected series of modern critical essays, *Saint Augustine, His Age, Life and Thought* (Cleveland and New York: Meridian, 1969).

Of a more biographical nature is Frederik van der Meer, *Augustine the Bishop* (London and New York: Sheed and Ward, 1961), a classic work dealing in great detail essentially with Augustine as Bishop of Hippo, the city, its people, the area, and the controversies that involved its famous bishop. Three of those controversies—the Manichaean, the Donatist, and the Pelagian—are examined in considerable detail in Gerald Bonner, *St. Augustine of Hippo, Life and Controversies* (Philadelphia: Westminster Press, 1963).

There is no lack of books dealing with the historical setting of Augustine and Augustinianism or with late antiquity and the early Middle Ages. Two of the old standard works are still among the best: Ferdinand Lot, *The End of the Ancient World and the Beginnings of the Middle Ages*, tr. Philip and Mariette Leon (New York: Barnes and Noble, 1953 [1931]), and Samuel Dill, *Roman Society in the Last Century of the Western Empire* (London: Macmillan, 1898). One of the best recent accounts of the rise of Christianity within late Roman antiquity is R. A. Markus, *Christianity in the Roman World* (New York: Scribners, 1974). Finally, students will find useful (if somewhat heavyweight) a fundamental work of reference, A. H. M. Jones, *The Later Roman Empire 284–602, A Social, Economic, and Administrative Survey*, 2 vols. (Norman: University of Oklahoma Press, 1964).

Charlemagne
and the First Europe

The world of late Roman antiquity that had shaped the mind and spirit of
St. Augustine was already, even in his own lifetime, crumbling under
the impact of the Germanic barbarian invasions. His great reflection on
history, *The City of God,* was written in response to the fall of the city
of Rome to the Visigoths in 410, and as he lay dying in the year 430
his own episcopal city of Hippo was under siege by the Vandals. Within
another century, the Roman political order in the west had disappeared
completely, to be replaced by a number of regional barbarian kingdoms
under their German tribal chiefs. The Roman world had entered
irretrievably upon what an earlier generation of historians was fond of
calling "the Dark Ages."

Though the darkness was by no means as pervasive as scholars once
thought, the early Middle Ages were a time of great dislocation,
surely one of the two or three most important periods of transition in the
history of western civilization—for the product of the transition was
nothing less than what some historians have called "the first Europe."

It was a Europe no longer classical and imperial, no longer a vast
free-trade network of cities governed by a centralized system and ruled
by a common law. It was a Europe from which long distance trade had
disappeared, to be replaced by an economic localism. It was a Europe of
equally localized culture, in which the common classical tradition was
maintained by an ever dwindling minority of educated people, with an

131

ever decreasing sophistication. Most, virtually all, of those educated were professional churchmen, for, perhaps most important of all, the first Europe was a Christian Europe.

The great Frankish king Charlemagne (768–814) was, by all accounts and from whatever interpretive viewpoint we choose to see him, the pivotal figure in this first Europe. The Franks were one of the barbarian Germanic tribes that succeeded to the broken pieces of the western empire. By a combination of luck, talent, and timing, they had come to be the leading power among their fellow barbarians. Their position was enhanced by Charlemagne's immediate predecessors, his grandfather Charles Martel and his father, Pepin, who established the claim of his house to the Frankish kingdom. Frankish supremacy was assured by Charlemagne's dramatic conquests, which brought most of continental western Europe—save only Moslem Spain south of the Ebro River, southern Italy, and the barbarian fringes of the Scandinavian North— under his rule.

Charlemagne's imperial rule was epitomized in his resumption of the ancient imperial title. On Christmas day of the year 800, in the church of St. Peter in Rome, Pope Leo III crowned Charlemagne as "Emperor of the Romans." No one had claimed this exalted title in more than three hundred years, and no barbarian king had ever before presumed to such a dignity. Charlemagne continued to bear his other titles, so we are not sure precisely how he himself saw his imperial role—whether it was an "umbrella" title over his many different dominions, a Christian symbol for "the temporal sword," or simply "a feather in his cap." We do know that it involved him in a delicate and complex negotiation with the other "Emperor of the Romans" in Byzantium, whose rights, however remotely exercised, Charlemagne's act had encroached upon. The assumption of the title, moreover, by virtue of the part played by the pope, was inextricably bound up with the larger role of the church in the secular affairs of the West.

We cannot be sure what Charlemagne's plans for his empire were, although he saw to the imperial succession of his son Louis the Pious. We cannot even be certain of the extent to which Charles was able to realize the plans he did have, for the records of the time simply do not tell us.

But however many unanswered questions remain, the records do contain a precious contemporary account of King Charles, written by his devoted friend, the Frankish noble Einhard.

The Emperor Charlemagne
EINHARD

*One of the most obvious signs of the barbarism of early medieval Europe
is the scarcity of records. Even more scarce than documentary records
are the literary accounts—the biographies, the memoirs, the formal
histories—that can give flesh and substance to historical figures. Most,
even the greatest, personages of the early Middle Ages remain simply
names, with only a handful of facts (and often doubtful "facts" at that)
attached to them. Fortunately, this is not the case for Charlemagne.
We might wish that Einhard's account had been longer and more detailed,
or that he had included more information about Charles' public policy,
his political motives, his plans for the empire, and the structure of
his reign. But we are lucky to have what we do. Einhard was sensitive
about his modest literary gifts. Indeed, he could not even conceive of a
formal framework for his account; he simply took Suetonius's biography
of Augustus and substituted his own material in the model. But so
indebted was Einhard to Charles, his "lord and foster father," and so
important were his lord's deeds that he chose to record them rather "than
to suffer the most glorious life of this most excellent king, the greatest of
all the princes of his day, and his illustrious deeds, hard for men of
later times to imitate, to be wrapped in the darkness of oblivion."* [1]

Despite its limitations, Einhard's Life of Charlemagne *is an extraordinarily valuable document. It would have been under any circumstances. But
its value is enhanced because Einhard was an intimate of the king and
his family; he had been raised at Charles' court and later was one of
his most trusted councillors. No one was in a better position than Einhard
to write on Charles the Great.*

*After sketching the background of Charles' dynasty and how the
Carolingians (for this is the name historians have given to the house
of* Carolus Magnus*) succeeded to the Frankish throne, how Charles' father,
Pepin, set aside the last of the weak Merovingians with their "vain title
of king," Einhard describes in some detail the wars of conquest that
earned for Charles the title "Charles the Great"—his pacification of
Aquitaine, his conquest of the Lombards and his assumption of the
Lombard crown, his long wars with the pagan Saxons along the eastern
frontier, his unsuccessful attempt to invade Moslem Spain, his successful*

---

[1] *The Life of Charlemagne by Einhard* (Ann Arbor: University of Michigan
Press, 1960), Preface, p. 16. Translated from the *Monumenta Germaniae* by
Samuel Epes Turner.

*quelling of the revolt of Bavaria, and his wars against the Avars along
the Danube, the Danes, and other border peoples. Then Einhard continues:*

SUCH ARE THE wars, most skilfully planned and successfully fought, which
this most powerful king waged during the forty-seven years of his reign.
He so largely increased the Frank kingdom, which was already great and
strong when he received it at his father's hands, that more than double its
former territory was added to it. The authority of the Franks was formerly
confined to that part of Gaul included between the Rhine and the Loire,
the Ocean and the Balearic Sea; to that part of Germany which is inhabited
by the so-called Eastern Franks, and is bounded by Saxony and the Danube,
the Rhine and the Saale—this stream separates the Thuringians from the
Sorabians; and to the country of the Alemanni and Bavarians. By the wars
above mentioned he first made tributary Aquitania, Gascony, and the
whole of the region of the Pyrenees as far as the River Ebro, which rises
in the land of the Navarrese, flows through the most fertile districts of
Spain, and empties into the Balearic Sea, beneath the walls of the city of
Tortosa. He next reduced and made tributary all Italy from Aosta to
Lower Calabria, where the boundary line runs between the Beneventans
and the Greeks, a territory more than a thousand miles long; then Saxony,
which constitutes no small part of Germany, and is reckoned to be twice
as wide as the country inhabited by the Franks, while about equal to it
in length; in addition, both Pannonias, Dacia beyond the Danube, and
Istria, Liburnia, and Dalmatia, except the cities on the coast, which he
left to the Greek Emperor for friendship's sake, and because of the treaty
that he had made with him. In fine, he vanquished and made tributary
all the wild and barbarous tribes dwelling in Germany between the Rhine
and the Vistula, the Ocean and the Danube, all of which speak very much
the same language, but differ widely from one another in customs and dress.
The chief among them are the Welatabians, the Sorabians, the Abodriti, and
the Bohemians, and he had to make war upon these; but the rest, by far
the larger number, submitted to him of their own accord.

He added to the glory of his reign by gaining the good will of several
kings and nations. . . . His relations with Aaron, King of the Persians,[2]
who ruled over almost the whole of the East, India excepted, were so
friendly that this prince preferred his favor to that of all the kings and
potentates of the earth, and considered that to him alone marks of honor
and munificence were due. Accordingly, when the ambassadors sent by
Charles to visit the most holy sepulchre and place of resurrection of our

---

[2] This was the famous Harun al-Raschid (786–809), not "King of the Persians"
but the Abbasid Caliph of Baghdad, with whom Charles did indeed enjoy good
diplomatic relations. Harun was most likely interested in a possible alliance against
the Byzantine Empire.—ED.

Lord and Savior presented themselves before him with gifts, and made known their master's wishes, he not only granted what was asked, but gave possession of that holy and blessed spot. When they returned, he dispatched his ambassadors with them, and sent magnificent gifts, besides stuffs, perfumes, and other rich products of the Eastern lands. A few years before this, Charles had asked him for an elephant, and he sent the only one that he had. The Emperors of Constantinople, Nicephorus, Michael, and Leo, made advances to Charles, and sought friendship and alliance with him by several embassies; and even when the Greeks suspected him of designing to wrest the empire from them, because of his assumption of the title Emperor, they made a close alliance with him, that he might have no cause of offense. In fact, the power of the Franks was always viewed by the Greeks and Romans with a jealous eye, whence the Greek proverb "Have the Frank for your friend, but not for your neighbor." . . .

He liked foreigners, and was at great pains to take them under his protection. There were often so many of them, both in the palace and the kingdom, that they might reasonably have been considered a nuisance; but he, with his broad humanity, was very little disturbed by such annoyances, because he felt himself compensated for these great inconveniences by the praises of his generosity and the reward of high renown.

Charles was large and strong, and of lofty stature, though not disproportionately tall (his height is well known to have been seven times the length of his foot); the upper part of his head was round, his eyes very large and animated, nose a little long, hair fair, and face laughing and merry. Thus his appearance was always stately and dignified, whether he was standing or sitting; although his neck was thick and somewhat short, and his belly rather prominent; but the symmetry of the rest of his body concealed these defects. His gait was firm, his whole carriage manly, and his voice clear, but not so strong as his size led one to expect. His health was excellent, except during the four years preceding his death, when he was subject to frequent fevers; at the last he even limped a little with one foot. Even in those years he consulted rather his own inclinations than the advice of physicians, who were almost hateful to him, because they wanted him to give up roasts, to which he was accustomed, and to eat boiled meat instead. In accordance with the national custom, he took frequent exercise on horseback and in the chase, accomplishments in which scarcely any people in the world can equal the Franks. He enjoyed the exhalations from natural warm springs, and often practiced swimming, in which he was such an adept that none could surpass him; and hence it was that he built his palace at Aix-la-Chapelle, and lived there constantly during his latter years until his death. He used not only to invite his sons to his bath, but his nobles and friends, and now and then a troop of his retinue or bodyguard, so that a hundred or more persons sometimes bathed with him.

He used to wear the national, that is to say, the Frank, dress—next his skin a linen shirt and linen breeches, and above these a tunic fringed with silk; while hose fastened by bands covered his lower limbs, and shoes his feet, and he protected his shoulders and chest in winter by a close-fitting coat of otter or marten skins. Over all he flung a blue cloak, and he always had a sword girt about him, usually one with a gold or silver hilt and belt; he sometimes carried a jeweled sword, but only on great feastdays or at the reception of ambassadors from foreign nations. He despised foreign costumes, however handsome, and never allowed himself to be robed in them, except twice in Rome, when he donned the Roman tunic, chlamys, and shoes; the first time at the request of Pope Hadrian, the second to gratify Leo, Hadrian's successor. On great feastdays he made use of embroidered clothes and shoes bedecked with precious stones, his cloak was fastened by a golden buckle, and he appeared crowned with a diadem of gold and gems, but on other days his dress varied little from the common dress of the people.

Charles was temperate in eating, and particularly so in drinking, for he abominated drunkenness in anybody, much more in himself and those of his household. . . . Charles had the gift of ready and fluent speech, and could express whatever he had to say with the utmost clearness. He was not satisfied with command of his native language merely, but gave attention to the study of foreign ones, and in particular was such a master of Latin that he could speak it as well as his native tongue; but he could understand Greek better than he could speak it. He was so eloquent, indeed, that he might have passed for a teacher of eloquence. He most zealously cultivated the liberal arts, held those who taught them in great esteem, and conferred great honors upon them. He took lessons in grammar of the deacon Peter of Pisa, at that time an aged man. Another deacon, Albin of Britain, surnamed Alcuin, a man of Saxon extraction, who was the greatest scholar of the day, was his teacher in other branches of learning. The King spent much time and labor with him studying rhetoric, dialectics, and especially astronomy; he learned to reckon, and used to investigate the motions of the heavenly bodies most curiously, with an intelligent scrutiny. He also tried to write, and used to keep tablets and blanks in bed under his pillow, that at leisure hours he might accustom his hand to form the letters; however, as he did not begin his efforts in due season, but late in life, they met with ill success.[3]

He cherished with the greatest fervor and devotion the principles of the Christian religion, which had been instilled into him from infancy. Hence it was that he built the beautiful basilica at Aix-la-Chapelle, which he adorned with gold and silver and lamps, and with rails and doors of solid brass. He had the columns and marbles for this structure brought from Rome and Ravenna, for he could not find such as were suitable elsewhere. . . .

---

[3] What is probably meant here is not that Charles literally could not write but that he could not master the precise and beautiful "book hand," the Carolingian Minuscule, developed by Alcuin for the use of the court copyists.—Ed.

He was very forward in succoring the poor, and in that gratuitous generosity which the Greeks call alms, so much so that he not only made a point of giving in his own country and his own kingdom, but when he discovered that there were Christians living in poverty in Syria, Egypt, and Africa, at Jerusalem, Alexandria, and Carthage, he had compassion on their wants, and used to send money over the seas to them. The reason that he zealously strove to make friends with the kings beyond seas was that he might get help and relief to the Christians living under their rule. He cherished the Church of St. Peter the Apostle at Rome above all other holy and sacred places, and heaped its treasury with a vast wealth of gold, silver, and precious stones. He sent great and countless gifts to the popes, and throughout his whole reign the wish that he had nearest at heart was to re-establish the ancient authority of the city of Rome under his care and by his influence, and to defend and protect the Church of St. Peter, and to beautify and enrich it out of his own store above all other churches. Although he held it in such veneration, he only repaired to Rome to pay his vows and make his supplications four times during the whole forty-seven years that he reigned.

When he made his last journey thither, he had also other ends in view. The Romans had inflicted many injuries upon the Pontiff Leo, tearing out his eyes and cutting out his tongue, so that he had been compelled to call upon the King for help. Charles accordingly went to Rome, to set in order the affairs of the Church, which were in great confusion, and passed the whole winter there. It was then that he received the titles of Emperor and Augustus, to which he at first had such an aversion that he declared that he would not have set foot in the Church the day that they were conferred, although it was a great feastday, if he could have foreseen the design of the Pope. He bore very patiently with the jealousy which the Roman emperors showed upon his assuming these titles, for they took this step very ill; and by dint of frequent embassies and letters, in which he addressed them as brothers, he made their haughtiness yield to his magnanimity, a quality in which he was unquestionably much their superior.

It was after he had received the imperial name that, finding the laws of his people very defective (the Franks have two sets of laws, very different in many particulars [4]), he determined to add what was wanting, to reconcile the discrepancies, and to correct what was vicious and wrongly cited in them. However, he went no further in this matter than to supplement the laws by a few capitularies, and those imperfect ones; but he caused the unwritten laws of all the tribes that came under his rule to be compiled and reduced to writing. He also had the old rude songs that celebrate the deeds and wars of the ancient kings written out for transmission to posterity. He began a grammar of his native language. He gave the months names in his own tongue, in place of the Latin and barbarous names by which they were formerly known among the Franks. . . .

[4] The codes of the two Frankish tribes, the Salian and Ripuarian, that had combined to form the nation.—ED.

Toward the close of his life, when he was broken by ill-health and old age, he summoned Louis, King of Aquitania, his only surviving son by Hildegard, and gathered together all the chief men of the whole kingdom of the Franks in a solemn assembly. He appointed Louis, with their unanimous consent, to rule with himself over the whole kingdom, and constituted him heir to the imperial name; then, placing the diadem upon his son's head, he bade him be proclaimed Emperor and Augustus. This step was hailed by all present with great favor, for it really seemed as if God had prompted him to it for the kingdom's good; it increased the King's dignity, and struck no little terror into foreign nations. After sending his son back to Aquitania, although weak from age he set out to hunt, as usual, near his palace at Aix-la-Chapelle, and passed the rest of the autumn in the chase, returning thither about the first of November. While wintering there, he was seized, in the month of January, with a high fever, and took to his bed. As soon as he was taken sick, he prescribed for himself abstinence from food, as he always used to do in case of fever, thinking that the disease could be driven off, or at least mitigated, by fasting. Besides the fever, he suffered from a pain in the side, which the Greeks call pleurisy; but he still persisted in fasting, and in keeping up his strength only by draughts taken at very long intervals. He died January twenty-eighth, the seventh day from the time that he took to his bed, at nine o'clock in the morning, after partaking of the holy communion, in the seventy-second year of his age and the forty-seventh of his reign.

A New Portrait of the Emperor
HEINRICH FICHTENAU

We turn now from Einhard's contemporary account of Charlemagne to the description by the modern Austrian medievalist Heinrich Fichtenau. It is rather more a reconstruction than a description, for in The Carolingian Empire, The Age of Charlemagne, *Fichtenau goes beyond Einhard's account to the other fragmentary records of Charles' age, as well as to the best of modern Carolingian scholarship. Fichtenau's work is a careful, even conservative, attempt to set Charlemagne securely in his age. The result is a distinguished new portrait of the emperor to set beside that of his adoring friend and subject.*

NO MAN'S STATURE is increased by the accumulation of myths, and nothing is detracted from genuine historical greatness by the consideration of a man's purely human side. In order to analyse an epoch it is necessary to analyse the man who was its centre, who determined its character and who was, at the same time, shaped and determined by it. It is therefore not mere curiosity but an endeavour to fulfil the historian's task if we strive to pierce and get behind the myth that has surrounded the figure of Charles. That myth has been built up over a period of centuries and has tended to conjure up in place of a tangible personality, full of vitality, the figure of a timeless hero.

In the case of Charles—and that alone would justify our beginning with him—we can even form a picture of his bodily physique. The bodily appearance of his contemporaries, although we know their names and their works, remains shadow-like for us to-day. But as far as Charles the Great is concerned, we are not only in possession of his bodily remains but also have an exact description of his appearance. It is true that Charles's biographer Einhard borrowed the terms of his description from Suetonius. Nevertheless it was possible for him to choose from among the numerous biographies of the ancient emperors which he found in Suetonius those expressions which were most applicable to his master. Einhard and his contemporaries were especially struck by Charles's bodily size. Ever since the opening of Charles's tomb in 1861 we have known that his actual height was a full 6 feet 3½ inches. It was therefore not poetic licence when one of the court-poets, describing the royal hunt, remarked: "The king, with his broad shoulders, towers above everybody else." . . .

It is a pity that Einhard fails us when he describes Charles's personality, for his description is entirely conventional. It had to be conventional, for, although emperors may differ in physical build, they must all have the same virtues, namely the imperial virtues without which nobody can be a real emperor. Thus his description of Charles is couched in Aristotelian and Stoic terms, such as *temperantia, patientia,* and *constantia animi.* And in so far as Einhard attributed *magnanimitas* and *liberalitas* to Charles, we can discern a mingling of ancient and Germanic princely ideals. When the hospitality shown to foreign guests resulted in neglect of considerations of public economy, Stoic *magnanimitas* was imperceptibly transformed into Germanic "loftiness of spirit." For Charles "found in the reputation of generosity and in the good fame that followed generous actions a compensation even for grave inconveniences."

The Stoic traits in Einhard's picture of Charles are, however, by no means insignificant. Many of Charles's counsellors must have drawn his attention to the fact that these traits were ideals that had been appropriate to his imperial predecessors and therefore appropriate for him. People must have appealed again and again to his *clementia,* a Stoic concept subsumed under *temperantia,* when it was a question of preventing the execution of conspirators, of liberating hostages, or of returning property that had been confiscated in punishment for an offence. Stoicism was, after all, allied with Christianity. A Christian ruler had to exercise self-control. If he indulged in *crudelitas* and raged against his enemies he was not far from the very opposite of a good king, the *rex iniquus* or tyrant.

Charles endeavoured in more than one sense to live up to the model of Stoic and Christian self-discipline. He could not tolerate drunkards in his palace. Banquets were held only on important feast days. Fasting, however, he deeply loathed. He often complained that it impaired his health. When he was an old man he conducted a long battle with his physicians who never succeeded in making him eat boiled meat in place of the roast to which he was accustomed. The fact that Einhard incorporated such stories in his biography and that a large number of almost humourous anecdotes, such as were collected later by Notker,[5] were recounted by his own contemporaries, shows that there was a very real difference between the late Roman, and especially the Byzantine, conception of the ruler, on one hand, and the Frankish conception, on the other. Charles did not observe in his court the stiff dignity and the ceremonious distance that became an emperor. In this respect he never modelled himself on anyone; he behaved naturally and revealed his true self.

There is no evidence that Charles ever withdrew from the people around him in order to ponder and work out his plans. He always needed the company of people, of his daughters, of his friends, and even of his menial retinue. He not only invited to his banquets everybody who happened to be about; he also gathered people for the hunt and even insisted that his magnates, his learned friends and his bodyguard were to be present when he was having a bath. The author of a poetical description of palace life at Aix-la-Chapelle refers repeatedly to the noisy bustle in the baths. It seems that Charles was happiest among the din of the hunt or in the midst of the building going on at Aix-la-Chapelle.

Charles was the centre of the whole kingdom—not only because it became him as ruler to be the centre, but also because it suited his temperament. Generally receptive, and approaching both science and scholarship with an open mind, he wanted to feel that he was at the centre of everything. It must have been an easy matter for court scholars, like Theodulf of Orléans, to persuade the king that his intellectual faculties were broader than the Nile, larger than the Danube and the Euphrates, and no less powerful than the Ganges. . . . As a rule the courtiers, and Alcuin

---

[5] A late Carolingian monastic chronicler.—ED.

among them, vied with each other in hiding from the king that there was any difference of quality between the achievements of ancient Christian civilization and their own. A new Rome or Athens was expected to arise in Aix-la-Chapelle, and they were anxious to emphasize their superiority over Byzantium, where government was in the hands of females and theology was riddled with errors. Charles required all the fresh naturalness of his temperament in order to prevent himself from sliding from the realm of practical possibilities into the world of fantastic dreams and illusions in which so many Roman emperors had foundered. . . .

At times Charles's affability, so much praised by Einhard, gave way to surprising explosions of temper. . . . Without a reference to such explosions, however, the portrait of Charles's impulsive and impetuous nature would be incomplete. The king's ire, which made his contemporaries tremble, was quite a different matter. It was part of the Germanic, just as it was of the oriental, conception of a ruler and was contrary to the Stoic ideal. At the beginning of the legend of Charlemagne there stands the figure of the "iron Charles" as his enemies saw him approaching—clad from top to toe in iron, and with an iron soul as well. In confusion they shouted: "Oh, the iron! Woe, the iron!" Not only the king's enemies, however, but also his faithful followers stood in fear of him. Charles's grandson Nithard wrote with approval that Charles had governed the nations with "tempered severity." Charles was able to control the warring men and the centrifugal tendencies of his dominions because the fear of his personal severity made evil men as gentle as lambs. He had the power to make the "hearts of both Franks and barbarians" sink. No amount of official propaganda could produce the same effect as the hardness of Charles's determination. The lack of such determination in Louis, his successor, was among the factors that led to the decay of the empire.

This side of Charles's character, although necessary for the preservation of the kingdom, was well beyond the boundaries laid down by the precepts of Stoicism and of Christianity. Charles himself was probably not aware of this. But Einhard, his biographer, who had much sympathy with both these ideals, felt it deeply. . . . Charles thought of himself as a Christian through and through, but he never managed to transcend the limits of the popular piety of the Franks. . . . He supported needy Christians, even outside the borders of the empire. He sent money to Rome and made four pilgrimages to the papal city. Such were the religious works of Charles as related by his biographer, Einhard. The inner life of the Christian, the regeneration of the soul and the new religious attitude which, at the very time when Einhard was writing, Charles's son, Louis the Pious, was labouring to acquire, are not so much as mentioned. The reason why Einhard is silent about such things is scarcely that he could not find the words to describe them in his model, Suetonius. Charles organized the salvation of his soul as he was wont to organize his Empire. It would have been contrary to his nature, and the most difficult task of all, for him to seek the highest levels of spiritual experience in his own heart. His task as a ruler, as he saw it, was to act upon the world.

We must remember, however, that the world upon which he acted bore little resemblance to the sober and dry reality created by modern commerce and technology. Such modern conceptions were shaped much later, mostly under the impression of Calvinism. They were unknown to Charles, who, for instance, first learnt of the pope's mutilation in distant Rome through a dream. He took it to be one of his duties as a ruler to observe the course of the stars with the greatest of attention, for the approach of misfortune for his kingdom could be foretold from the stars more accurately than from anything else. For this reason the emperor devoted more time and labour to the study of astronomy than to any other of the "liberal arts." If the observation of the stars had been a mere hobby, he would surely have interrupted it while he was devastating the Saxon country with his army. . . .

Charles the Great was not one of those men who have to fight against their times and who, misunderstood by their contemporaries, are appreciated only after their death. He embodied all the tendencies of his own age; he was carried forward by them and, at the same time, moved them forward. It is impossible to describe him except in close conjunction with his friends and the magnates of his land. But for the picture to be complete he must also be shown in the midst of his family. He was surrounded by his children, his wives and the retinue of females, whose numbers and conduct seemed so unbecoming to the puritanism of his successor when he first entered the palace. Such conditions were not peculiar to Charles. It was all part and parcel of Frankish tradition. Charles lived as the head of a clan. The servants were, at least for the purposes of everyday life, included in the clan. As part of the family they enjoyed peace and protection and were, together with their master's blood relations, subject to his authority. Within the framework of the old tribal law, the master ruled his household unconditionally. . . .

In the king's palace there was a constant going and coming. Emigrés from England and from Byzantium rubbed shoulders with foreign ambassadors and all manner of public officials. There must have been, nevertheless, a few fixed key positions in the organization. There was little love lost among the occupants of these positions. For the most part, our sources remain silent on this matter. But now and again we catch a glimpse of the situation. The office of the chamberlain was one of these key positions. It was he who received the people who had come to demand an audience. He decided whether and in what order they were to appear before the king. He also received the annual "donations" of the magnates to the royal treasure which was in his custody. Alcuin considered himself happy to count this man among his friends and emphasized again and again how many envious people and evil counsellors were busy in other places trying to ruin the king.

Alcuin wrote repeatedly that, though the king tried to enforce justice, he was surrounded by predatory men. His judgment was probably no less partisan than that of his opponents who maintained that he himself was ruining the king. . . . Charles's own open and generous nature had never been inclined to inquire too closely into the intrigues and corruptions of his trusted friends and servants.

All things considered, there is little difference between the picture we form of Charles's surroundings and the one we have of his ancestors and of other princes of the period. The only difference was that the imperial household, as in fact the empire itself, was greater, more splendid and therefore also more exposed to danger. As long as its power and splendour were increasing, the cracks in the structure remained concealed. It was the achievement of Charles's own powerful personality to have brought about this rise which, without him, might have taken generations to reach its zenith. His efforts were crowned with success because his whole personality was in tune with the progressive forces active among his people. If this had not been the case, no amount of power concentrated in the hands of the king would have suffered to stamp his countenance upon the age. If this is remembered much of the illusion of well-nigh superhuman achievement, that has inspired both the mediaeval legend of Charlemagne and many modern narratives, is dispelled. What remains is quite enough justification for calling Charles historically great.

A More Somber Light
F. L. GANSHOF

Just as Heinrich Fichtenau represents the tradition of Austrian-German scholarship in modern Carolingian studies, the other great tradition, the Belgian-French, is represented by the Belgian scholar François Louis Ganshof—who has been justly called the dean of Carolingian studies. The passage excerpted below is from an address presented to the Mediaeval Academy of America in 1948. It is in the nature of a summary judgment drawn from a lifetime of patient study and reflection, and has not been materially altered by his continued work of the last thirty years. Ganshof does not really dissent from the portrait created by Fichtenau. But he has always had a penchant for analysis rather than interpretation. He therefore strives to go beyond the limitations of Einhard's biography and other contemporary biographical fragments to describe not so much Charlemagne the man as Charlemagne the statesman. The result is a somewhat somber judgment, dwelling more upon his limitations than his accomplishments. For Ganshof is sharply aware that if Fichtenau sees Charlemagne as the universal father figure of the first Europe,[6] it is of a Europe hardly yet born and due for many turns and reverses before it can realize the promise anticipated in the age of Charlemagne.

We begin just before what Ganshof calls the fifth and last period of Charlemagne's reign.

IT WOULD SEEM that by 792, when Charles was fifty years old, he had acquired experience and wisdom; perhaps, also, the advice of certain counsellors had brought him to understand that moderation is necessary to consolidate the results of victory. One of the deep causes of the Saxon revolt of 792–793 had been the reign of terror of 785, caused especially by the *Capitulatio de partibus Saxoniæ,*[7] to secure the Frankish domination and the authority of the Christian religion. One must mention, also, the ruthlessness shown by the clergy in exacting payment of the tithe. In 797 a more gentle rule was introduced in Saxony by the *Capitulare Saxonicum* and the results of this new policy were favorable. In the Danube countries the methods used were less rigorous than formerly in Saxony.

A feature which at this period seems to have developed strongly was Charles' special care concerning the interests of the church and their close association with the interests of the state. In the capitulary, where dispositions made by the Synod of Frankfurt in 794 were promulgated, regulations of purely political or administrative character are next to those concerning the life of the church, e.g., the measures taken to extend the right of exclusive jurisdiction of the church over the clerics, and those aiming to render the discipline of the higher clergy more strict by reestablishing over the bishops, chiefs of the dioceses, the superior hierarchical office of the metropolitan.

In matters of dogma the Synod of Frankfurt, under the presidency of Charlemagne, had agreed with Pope Hadrian to condemn adoptianism, a christological heresy. Contrary to the advice of the pope, the synod had condemned the worship of images, which had been restored to honor by the decision of a so called œcumenical council of the Eastern Church. Charlemagne had already got his theologians to criticize this worship in

---

[6] D. A. Bullough, *"Europae Pater:* Charlemagne and His Achievement in the Light of Recent Scholarship," *English Historical Review,* 85 (1970), 59–105.

[7] "The Capitulary on the Saxon Regions." Capitularies were edicts of the crown which had the effect of law and are among the best evidence we have of Charlemagne's paternalistic style of government.—ED.

the *Libri Carolini*. In spite of his reverence for the Holy See, Charlemagne appears to be, far more than the pope, the real head of the church in the West. When Leo III ascended the pontifical throne in 795, on the death of Hadrian, Charles stated precisely their respective positions in a letter which leaves no doubt on the subject. The pope became more or less the first of his bishops.

Alcuin and a few other clerics had developed an idea linked with ancient traditions. To protect the church against many corrupt practices and dangers, the realization of the will of God on earth required the reestablishment in the West of an imperial power that would protect faith and church. Charlemagne, in their eyes, fulfilled the necessary conditions to be that Roman Christian emperor; to be, indeed, an emperor quite different in their minds from the historical Constantine and Theodosius. Favorable circumstances occurred. A revolution in Rome overthrew Pope Leo III in 799 and created an extremely difficult situation which remained confused even after Charles had had the pope reestablished on his throne. Charlemagne not only admired in Alcuin the theologian and the scholar to whom he had entrusted the task of revising the Latin text of the Bible, but he also had confidence in his judgment and was strongly under his influence. It was, I believe, owing to Alcuin that he went to Rome with the idea of putting order into the affairs of the church; it was under the same influence that he accepted there the imperial dignity. Pope Leo III crowned him emperor on 25 December 800.

To give even a short account of the immediate and later effects of this great event would be irrelevant here. I shall merely mention the fifth and last period of the reign of Charlemagne, which began on the day following the coronation. It is a rather incoherent stage of his career. One notices this when trying to distinguish what changes in Charlemagne's conduct could be attributed to the influence of his newly-acquired dignity.

He certainly appreciated his new position. He intended to make the most of it towards Byzantium and he exercised a political and military pressure on the eastern emperor until that Byzantine prince recognized his imperial title in 812. However, in matters of government Charles's attitude was not constant. In 802, shortly after his return from Italy, he appeared to be fully aware of the eminent character of his imperial power. He stated that it was his duty to see that all western Christians should act according to the will of God; he ordered all his subjects to take a new oath of allegiance, this time in his quality of emperor, and he extended the notion of allegiance. He started legislating in the field of private law; he stipulated that the clergy must obey strictly canonical legislation or the Rule of St. Benedict; he reformed the institution of his enquiring and reforming commissioners, the *missi dominici*, to make it more efficient. In spite of all this, when (806) he settled his succession, the imperial dignity appeared to have lost, in his eyes, much of its importance. Unless it were to lose its meaning entirely, the empire was indivisible. Yet Charles foresaw the partition of his states between his three sons, according to the ancient Frankish custom, and took no dispositions concerning the *imperialis potestas*. Doubtless those things that had influenced him a few years earlier were no longer effective and the Roman tradition and Alcuin's influence no longer dominated him. Everything was as if the imperial dignity had been for Charles a very high distinction but a strictly personal one. In the very last years of his reign, however, he seemed again to attach more importance to this dignity and most likely some new influences had altered his mind. His two older sons, Charles and Pepin, being dead, he himself conferred the title of emperor on his son Louis in 813.

During the end of the reign, with the one exception of the Spanish "march," which was enlarged and reinforced (Barcelona was taken in 801), no new territorial acquisition was made, in spite of military efforts often of considerable importance. The campaigns against the Northern Slavs, against Bohemia, against the Bretons of Armorica, and against the duke of Benevento only resulted in the recognition of a theoretical supremacy. Actually, fearful dangers became apparent. The Danes threatened the boundary of Saxony and their fleets devastated Frisia; the Saracen fleets threatened the Mediterranean coasts. The general impression left by the relation of these events is the weakening of the Carolingian monarchy. This impression increases when one examines internal conditions of the empire. In the state as in the church abuses increased; insecurity grew worse; the authority of the emperor was less and less respected. The capitularies, more and more numerous, constantly renewed warnings, orders, and interdictions which were less and less obeyed. Charles had grown old. Until then, his personal interferences and those which he directly provoked, had made up for the deficiencies of a quite inadequate administrative organization in an empire of extraordinary size. The physical and intellectual capacities of Charles were declining; he stayed almost continuously at Aachen, his favorite residence after 794, and he hardly ever left the place after 808. The strong antidote present before was now missing; all the political and social defects revealing a bad government appeared. When Charlemagne died in Aachen on 28 January 814, at the age of seventy-two, the Frankish state was on the verge of decay.

I have tried to describe and characterize briefly the successive phases of Charlemagne's reign. Is it possible to grasp his personality as a statesman? Perhaps. A primary fact that must be emphasized is that—even compared with others of his time—Charlemagne was not a cultivated man. In spite of his thirst for knowledge and his admiration of culture, he was ignorant of all that is connected with intellectual life and he had little gift for abstraction.

But he had a sense for realities, and especially those of power. He knew how one gains power, how one remains in power and how one reaches the highest degrees of superior and supreme power. His attitude towards the imperial dignity revealed this. The conception of the clerics, and especially of Alcuin, for whom that dignity was an ideal magistrature infinitely above the royal power, was quite inaccessible to him. He knew or rather he felt, that the real basis of his power was solely his double royal authority [8] and he refused to omit evidence of this from his titles after the imperial coronation. For him the imperial dignity magnified and glorified the royal authority; it neither absorbed nor replaced it.

Charles had also the sense of what was practicable. Save for the campaign in Spain in 778, he undertook no tasks out of proportion to his means.

Einhard praises the equanimity of Charlemagne, his *constantia*. This was, indeed, a remarkable aspect of his personality. In the two periods of crisis which shook his reign—in 778 and in 792/793—no danger, no catastrophe, could make him give up the tasks he had undertaken or alter his methods of government. The moderation with which he happened to treat his vanquished enemies at certain times was not in contradiction with the constancy of his character. On the contrary. Equanimity implies a clear view of one's plans and one can therefore understand the variations of Charlemagne's attitude towards the imperial dignity, the full significance of which he never really understood.

To have a clear line of conduct and keep to it is one thing, but it is quite another to follow out a complete and detailed program. Charlemagne had, indeed, certain lines of conduct that he followed persistently. The facts presented are sufficient to show this as regards his foreign policy. It is also true as regards political, administrative, and juridical institutions. Charlemagne wanted to improve their efficiency so as to bring about a more complete fulfillment of his wishes and to achieve greater security for his subjects. But one cannot make out a real program in his actions. He resorted to shifts; he adopted and improved what was already existing. This is true of the institution of the *missi,* true also of the royal court of justice, of the royal vassality and of the "immunity." Occasionally he created something new, but without troubling about a general scheme. His reforms were empiric and at times went through several stages of development: as in the case of the organization of the *placita generalia,*[9] which was roughly outlined at the beginning of the reign but did not assume a definite shape until about the year 802, and also the use of writing in recording administrative and juridical matter, prescribed by a series of distinct decisions relating to particular cases.

One must avoid any attempt to credit Charlemagne with preoccupations proper to other times. Because of his efforts to protect *pauperes liberi homines,*[10] for instance, one cannot attribute to him the inaugura-

[8] As king of the Franks and of the Lombards.—ED.
[9] The General Assembly.—ED.
[10] Impoverished free men.—ED.

tion of a social policy; nor because he promulgated the *capitulare de villis* [11] can one speak of an economic policy. In both cases he acted on the spur of urgent interests then on hand: free men of modest condition supplied soldiers and the royal manors had to be fit to maintain the court. . . .

This sketch of Charles as a statesman would be distorted if stress was not laid upon his religious concerns. It is indeed hard to draw a line between his religious and his political ideas. His will to govern and to extend his power was inseparable from his purpose to spread the Christian religion and let his subjects live according to the will of God. If something of the "clerical" conception of the empire struck him deeply, it was the feeling that he was personally responsible for the progress of God's Kingdom on earth. But always it was he who was concerned. His piousness, his zeal for the Christian religion were no obstacles to his will to power; in religious matters as in others the pope was nothing more than his collaborator.

One is often tempted to turn Charlemagne into a superman, a far-seeing politician with broad and general views, ruling everything from above; one is tempted to see his reign as a whole, with more or less the same characteristics prevailing from beginning to end. This is so true that most of the works concerning him, save for the beginning and the end of his reign, use the geographical or systematic order rather than a chronological one. The distinctions that I have tried to make between the different phases of his reign may, perhaps, help to explain more exactly the development and effect of Charlemagne's power; they may help us to appreciate these more clearly. Perhaps, also, the features that I have noted bring out the human personality in the statesman and lead to the same results. The account I have given and the portrait I have drawn certainly justify the words which the poet ascribed to Charles in the last verse but one of the *Chanson de Roland*: "Deus" dist li Reis, "si penuse est ma vie." ("O Lord," said the king, "how arduous is my life.")

---

[11] The Capitulary on Manors.—ED.

Suggestions for Further Reading

THE ALMOST unique value of Einhard's biography of Charlemagne is dramatized by the scarcity and poor quality of other contemporary sources. Students can become aware of this contrast by looking even briefly at some of these other materials. There is a life of Charlemagne nearly contemporary with Einhard's, authored by a monk of St. Gall—possibly Notker the Stammerer. But unlike the solid and straightforward narrative of Einhard, the monk's account is disjointed and rambling, filled with legendary matter and scraps of the history of his monastery, and almost totally unreliable. It is available in a good modern edition, *Early Lives of Charlemagne by Eginhard and the Monk of St. Gall*, tr. and ed. A. J. Grant (New York: Cooper Square, 1966). Of the same sort are two somewhat later biographies of the brothers Adalard and Wala, abbots of Corbie, by the monk Radbertus of Corbie, although they contain only a few casual bits of information about Charlemagne, despite the fact that the two abbots were Charlemagne's cousins and both had played prominent roles at court: *Charlemagne's Cousins: Contemporary Lives of Adalard and Wala*, tr. and ed. Allen Cabaniss (Syracuse: Syracuse University Press, 1967). The only other narrative source of any value for the reign of Charlemagne is the Royal Frankish Annals, but they are thin and uncommunicative. They can be read as part of *Carolingian Chronicles, Royal Frankish Annals and Nithard's Histories*, tr. Bernhard W. Scholz with Barbara Rogers (Ann Arbor: University of Michigan Press, 1970). Several of these accounts and other sorts of documentary materials relating to Charlemagne's reign have been collected in a convenient and well-edited series of selections, *The Reign of Charlemagne, Documents on Carolingian Government and Administration*, ed. H. R. Loyn and John Percival (New York: St. Martin's, 1975).

Because of the stature and importance of Charlemagne and despite the problem of the sources, scholars continue to write about him. Many of their works are specialized scholarly studies. Some can be read profitably by beginning students, such as the several essays in Heinrich Fichtenau, *The Carolingian Empire*, excerpted above, or some of the articles of F. L. Ganshof collected in *The Carolingians and the Frankish Monarchy, Studies in Carolingian History*, tr. Janet Sondheimer (Ithaca, N.Y.: Cornell University Press, 1971). There are two excellent modern works, both brief and readable, that treat interesting aspects of Charles' reign: Richard E. Sullivan, *Aix-la-Chapelle in the Age of Charlemagne*, "Centers of Civilization Series" (Norman: University of Oklahoma Press, 1963), focuses on the cultural achievements at Charles' capital, and Jacques Boussard, *The Civilization of Charlemagne,* tr. Frances Partridge (New York: McGraw-Hill, 1968), presents a favorable revisionist interpretation of the Carolingian culture. One of the most important and most readable of the works on this period is Donald Bullough, *The Age of Charlemagne* (New York: Putnam, 1965).

Of the several biographies of Charlemagne, the best, as well as the most exciting and readable, is Richard Winston, *Charlemagne: From the Hammer to the Cross* (New York: Vintage, 1954). A somewhat briefer and less colorful biography but by an established authority is James A. Cabaniss, *Charlemagne,* "Rulers and Statesmen of the World" (Boston: Twayne, 1972).

Henri Pirenne, *Mohammed and Charlemagne,* tr. Bernard Miall (New York: Barnes and Noble, 1958 [1939]), is the masterwork of a great medieval historian and the chief entry in an important medieval scholarly controversy which continues to be of some interest to students of Charlemagne's reign. It has to do with the question of when and how the Middle Ages actually began. Pirenne says not until Charlemagne. The controversy and its chief figures are represented in *The Pirenne Thesis, Analysis, Criticism, and Revision,* ed. Alfred F. Havighurst (Boston: Heath, 1958). Students are also referred to two more recent works which indicate that the Pirenne controversy is still alive: Bryce Lyon, *The Origins of the Middle Ages, Pirenne's Challenge to Gibbon* (New York: Norton, 1972), and Robert S. Lopez, *The Birth of Europe* (New York: Lippincott, 1967).

Peter Abelard:
"The Knight of Dialectic"

By the turn of the twelfth century, the Europe of Charlemagne had been transformed. The downward curve of population had steadied and then begun to climb. There were more knights than there were fiefs for them to hold. They had joined the host of William the Bastard, Duke of Normandy, in his chancy adventure against England in the summer of 1066 in return for promises of land, as a decade earlier others had followed the Norman Guiscards and Hautevilles to Sicily. They swelled the armies of Saxon dukes and German kings in their conquests of eastern Europe and of Spanish Christian kings in the *reconquista* of Spain from the Moslems. And they went off to the crusades, the grandest adventure of an expanding Christendom.

Less sanguinary souls had taken to the roads with backpacks and strings of mules. Commerce began to revive, linking together villages and fortresses that would soon become towns and cities. The urban centers swelled with a growing population.

This bulging, booming, changing Europe had need for the skills of the mind. Schools multiplied—there were monastic schools, cathedral schools, guild schools, notarial schools. And men of learning found themselves thrust into the center of things. "The Renaissance of the twelfth century" was at hand, a revolution in learning and teaching, in the subjects to be taught and the methods of teaching them. It was to produce a renewed interest in the Latin classics, revived study of the ancient

Roman civil law and the codification of the law of the church. It was
to bring a flood of Moslem and Jewish and, ultimately, Greek influences
into the processes of Western thought and within a century to create
medieval scholasticism, with the medieval university as its institutional
setting.

One of the most fascinating, controversial, and important figures of
this world of twelfth-century intellectualism was the scholar-teacher-
philosopher-theologian-poet Peter Abelard (1079–1142). Abelard
is remembered principally for the arrogant rationalism he expounded
among the schoolmen of Paris, Laon, Melun, and Corbeil, and particularly
for his logical textbook *Sic et Non;* for his ill-fated romance with Heloise,
the fair niece of Canon Fulbert; and for Fulbert's terrible vengeance
upon him. But modern scholarship has begun to search beyond the inherited
stereotypes of Abelard as the demon lover and the rationalist-out-of-time,
neither of which can satisfactorily account for the astonishing reputation
that Abelard had among his own contemporaries.

The Story of My Misfortunes
PETER ABELARD

*The building of a kind of legendary Abelard began during his own lifetime
and resulted, in part, from the appearance of Abelard's autobiography,
its stark Latin title* Historia suarum calamitatum *somewhat weakly
translated as* The Story of My Misfortunes. *This remarkable and candid
book had a strange beginning. In 1135 a friend, apparently very close
to Abelard—he calls him "most dear brother in Christ and comrade closest
to me in the intimacy of speech"—appealed to him for consolation in
some sorrow of his own. In response, Abelard wrote him "of the sufferings
which have sprung out of my misfortunes" "so that, in comparing your
sorrows with mine, you may discover that yours are in truth nought, or
at the most but of small account, and so shall you come to bear them
more easily."*

*After describing his home in Brittany and how he had given up his
feudal inheritance and gained the permission of his father to pursue studies,
Abelard continues:*

I CAME AT length to Paris, where above all in those days the art of dialectics
was most flourishing, and there did I meet William of Champeaux, my
teacher, a man most distinguished in his science both by his renown and
by his true merit. With him I remained for some time, at first indeed well
liked of him; but later I brought him great grief, because I undertook to
refute certain of his opinions, not infrequently attacking him in disputation,
and now and then in these debates, I was adjudged victor. Now this, to
those among my fellow students who were ranked foremost, seemed all
the more insufferable because of my youth and the brief duration of my
studies.

Out of this sprang the beginning of my misfortunes, which have followed
me even to the present day; the more widely my fame was spread abroad,
the more bitter was the envy that was kindled against me. It was given out
that I, presuming on my gifts far beyond the warranty of my youth, was
aspiring despite my tender years to the leadership of a school; nay, more,
that I was making ready the very place in which I would undertake this
task, the place being none other than the castle of Melun, at that time a

royal seat. My teacher himself had some foreknowledge of this, and tried to remove my school as far as possible from his own. Working in secret, he sought in every way he could before I left his following to bring to nought the school I had planned and the place I had chosen for it. Since, however, in that very place he had many rivals, and some of them men of influence among the great ones of the land, relying on their aid I won to the fulfillment of my wish; the support of many was secured for me by reason of his own unconcealed envy. From this small inception of my school, my fame in the art of dialectics began to spread abroad, so that little by little the renown, not alone of those who had been my fellow students, but of our very teacher himself, grew dim and was like to die out altogether. Thus it came about that, still more confident in myself, I moved my school as soon as I well might to the castle of Corbeil, which is hard by the city of Paris, for there I knew there would be given more frequent chance for my assaults in our battle of disputation. . . .

To him did I return, for I was eager to learn more of rhetoric from his lips; and in the course of our many arguments on various matters, I compelled him by most potent reasoning first to alter his former opinion on the subject of the universals,[1] and finally to abandon it altogether. Now, the basis of this old concept of his regarding the reality of universal ideas was that the same quality formed the essence alike of the abstract whole and of the individuals which were its parts: in other words, that there could be no essential differences among these individuals, all being alike save for such variety as might grow out of the many accidents of existence. Thereafter, however, he corrected this opinion, no longer maintaining that the same quality was the essence of all things, but that, rather, it manifested itself in them through diverse ways. This problem of universals is ever the most vexed one among logicians, to such a degree, indeed, that even Porphyry,[2] writing in his "Isagoge" regarding universals, dared not attempt a final pronouncement thereon, saying rather: "This is the deepest of all problems of its kind." Wherefore it followed that when William had first revised and then finally abandoned altogether his views on this one subject, his lecturing sank into such a state of negligent reasoning that it could scarce be called lecturing on the science of dialectics at all; it was as if all his science had been bound up in this one question of the nature of universals.

Thus it came about that my teaching won such strength and authority that even those who before had clung most vehemently to my former master, and most bitterly attacked my doctrines, now flocked to my school. . . .

While these things were happening, it became needful for me again to

[1] This is a reference to the most famous and fundamental of all medieval learned controversies, the Nominalist-Realist controversy over the nature of reality and "universal" properties. The Nominalists traced their position ultimately to Aristotle; the Realists, to Plato.—ED.

[2] A third-century Neoplatonic philosopher whose works were important in the transmission of medieval Platonism.—ED.

repair to my old home, by reason of my dear mother, Lucia, for after the conversion of my father, Berengarius, to the monastic life, she so ordered her affairs as to do likewise. When all this had been completed, I returned to France,[3] above all in order that I might study theology, since now my oft-mentioned teacher, William, was active in the episcopate of Châlons. In this field of learning Anselm of Laon, who was his teacher therein, had for long years enjoyed the greatest renown.

I sought out, therefore, this same venerable man, whose fame, in truth, was more the result of long-established custom than of the potency of his own talent or intellect. If any one came to him impelled by doubt on any subject, he went away more doubtful still. He was wonderful, indeed, in the eyes of these who only listened to him, but those who asked him questions perforce held him as nought. He had a miraculous flow of words, but they were contemptible in meaning and quite void of reason. When he kindled a fire, he filled his house with smoke and illumined it not at all. He was a tree which seemed noble to those who gazed upon its leaves from afar, but to those who came nearer and examined it more closely was revealed its barrenness. . . .

It was not long before I made this discovery, and stretched myself lazily in the shade of that same tree. I went to his lectures less and less often, a thing which some among his eminent followers took sorely to heart, because they interpreted is as a mark of contempt for so illustrious a teacher. . . .

Challenged by those "eminent followers" of Anselm, Abelard undertakes to lecture on scripture, at their choice, "that most obscure prophecy of Ezekiel," and carries it off brilliantly—at least in his own opinion.

Now this venerable man of whom I have spoken was acutely smitten with envy, and straightway incited, as I have already mentioned, by the insinuations of sundry persons, began to persecute me for my lecturing on the Scriptures no less bitterly than my former master, William, had done for my work in philosophy. . . .

And so, after a few days, I returned to Paris, and there for several years I peacefully directed the school which formerly had been destined for me, nay, even offered to me, but from which I had been driven out. At the very outset of my work there, I set about completing the glosses on Ezekiel which I had begun at Laon. These proved so satisfactory to all who read them that they came to believe me no less adept in lecturing on

[3] Brittany was not yet a part of the royal domain of "France." He means the vicinity of Paris.—ED.

theology than I had proved myself to be in the field of philosophy. . . . Thus, I, who by this time had come to regard myself as the only philosopher remaining in the whole world, and had ceased to fear any further disturbance of my peace, began to loosen the rein on my desires, although hitherto I had always lived in the utmost continence. And the greater progress I made in my lecturing on philosophy or theology, the more I departed alike from the practice of the philosophers and the spirit of the divines in the uncleanness of my life. For it is well known, methinks, that philosophers, and still more those who have devoted their lives to arousing the love of sacred study, have been strong above all else in the beauty of chastity.

Thus did it come to pass that while I was utterly absorbed in pride and sensuality, divine grace, the cure for both diseases, was forced upon me, even though I, forsooth, would fain have shunned it. First was I punished for my sensuality, and then for my pride. . . .

Now there dwelt in that same city of Paris a certain young girl named Héloïse, the niece of a canon who was called Fulbert. Her uncle's love for her was equalled only by his desire that she should have the best education which he could possibly procure for her. Of no mean beauty, she stood out above all by reason of her abundant knowledge of letters. Now this virtue is rare among women, and for that very reason it doubly graced the maiden, and made her the most worthy of renown in the entire kingdom. It was this young girl whom I, after carefully considering all those qualities which are wont to attract lovers, determined to unite with myself in the bonds of love, and indeed the thing seemed to me very easy to be done. So distinguished was my name, and I possessed such advantages of youth and comeliness, that no matter what woman I might favour with my love, I dreaded rejection of none. . . .

Thus, utterly aflame with my passion for this maiden, I sought to discover means whereby I might have daily and familiar speech with her, thereby the more easily to win her consent. For this purpose I persuaded the girl's uncle, with the aid of some of his friends, to take me into his household—for he dwelt hard by my school—in return for the payment of a small sum. My pretext for this was that the care of my own household was a serious handicap to my studies, and likewise burdened me with an expense far greater than I could afford. Now, he was a man keen in avarice, and likewise he was most desirous for his niece that her study of letters should ever go forward, so, for these two reasons, I easily won his consent to the fulfillment of my wish, for he was fairly agape for my money, and at the same time believed that his niece would vastly benefit by my teaching. More even than this, by his own earnest entreaties he fell in with my desires beyond anything I had dared to hope, opening the way for my love; for he entrusted her wholly to my guidance, begging me to give her instruction whensoever I might be free from the duties of my school, no matter whether by day or by night, and to punish her sternly if ever I should find her negligent of her tasks. In all this the man's simplicity was nothing short of astounding to me; I should not have been more smitten with wonder if he had entrusted a tender lamb to the care of a ravenous wolf. . . .

The inevitable ensued. Heloise became pregnant, and the child was born. Abelard proposed marriage, but Heloise was reluctant for fear of damaging his career. They finally agreed upon a secret marriage. Then, to protect her from the fury of her uncle and her family, Abelard sent her to the convent at Argenteuil where she had been educated as a young girl.

When her uncle and his kinsmen heard of this, they were convinced that now I had completely played them false and had rid myself forever of Héloïse by forcing her to become a nun. Violently incensed, they laid a plot against me, and one night, while I, all unsuspecting, was asleep in a secret room in my lodgings, they broke in with the help of one of my servants, whom they had bribed. There they had vengeance on me with a most cruel and most shameful punishment, such as astounded the whole world, for they cut off those parts of my body with which I had done that which was the cause of their sorrow. This done, straightway they fled, but two of them were captured, and suffered the loss of their eyes and their genital organs. One of these two was the aforesaid servant, who, even while he was still in my service, had been led by his avarice to betray me.

When morning came the whole city was assembled before my dwelling. It is difficult, nay, impossible, for words of mine to describe the amazement which bewildered them, the lamentations they uttered, the uproar with which they harassed me, or the grief with which they increased my own suffering. Chiefly the clerics, and above all my scholars, tortured me with their intolerable lamentations and outcries, so that I suffered more intensely from their compassion than from the pain of my wound. In truth I felt the disgrace more than the hurt to my body, and was more afflicted with shame than with pain. My incessant thought was of the renown in which I had so much delighted, now brought low, nay, utterly blotted out, so swiftly by an evil chance. I saw, too, how justly God had punished me in that very part of my body whereby I had sinned. I perceived that there was indeed justice in my betrayal by him whom I had myself already betrayed; and then I thought how eagerly my rivals would seize upon this manifestation of justice, how this disgrace would bring bitter and enduring grief to my kindred and my friends, and how the tale of this amazing outrage would spread to the very ends of the earth. . . .

I must confess that in my misery it was the overwhelming sense of my disgrace rather than any ardour for conversion to the religious life that drove me to seek the seclusion of the monastic cloister. Héloïse had already, at my bidding, taken the veil and entered a convent. Thus it was that we both put on the sacred garb, I in the abbey of St. Denis, and she in the convent of Argenteuil, of which I have already spoken. . . .

But even in the monastery Abelard could be neither silent nor humble. His theological writings—in particular a book on the Trinity—led to his being summoned before a council at Soissons. And though the condemnation of his work was far from unanimous, the book was nevertheless condemned, and Abelard himself was forced to cast it into the flames. He was banished to another monastery, which he was eventually permitted to leave. He sought out a lonely spot in the forest near Troyes in Champagne, built a hut, and formed his own monastic congregation. But even here students came to be taught, and his critics revived their charges, this time led by the most formidable religious figure of the century, the great St. Bernard of Clairvaux. And, though Abelard's account ends before that point, Bernard succeeded in having him condemned by the church. But Abelard died in 1142 before the ban could take effect.

A "Renaissance Man" of the Twelfth Century
CHARLES HOMER HASKINS

The classic modern treatment of Abelard is to be found in Charles Homer Haskins' The Renaissance of the Twelfth Century, *one of the outstanding works of modern medieval scholarship. This book was one of the contributions to the academic controversy in the early part of this century over the status and conception of the Renaissance. That dispute has long been over, but Haskins' charming book survives, as well as his interpretation of Abelard as one of the principal figures in the construction of a medieval Renaissance.*

Haskins begins his account at the point of Abelard's confrontation with St. Bernard. This is where Abelard himself, as we have seen, left off in the history of his own misfortunes.

"VANITY OF VANITIES, saith the preacher," and St. Bernard was first and foremost a preacher, and a fundamentalist preacher at that. Vain above all to him were pride of intellect and absorption in the learning of this world, and his harshest invectives were hurled at the most brilliant intellect of his age, Abaelard, that "scrutinizer of majesty and fabricator of heresies" who "deems himself able by human reason to comprehend God altogether." Between a mystic like Bernard and a rationalist like Abaelard there was no common ground, and for the time being the mystic had the church behind him. With Abaelard we have another type of autobiography, the intellectual, in that long tale of misfortune which he addressed to an unknown friend under the title of *Historia suarum calamitatum*.

Abaelard, it is true, was a monk and an abbot, but he became such by force of circumstances and not from choice. Even when he retires into the forests of Champagne or the depths of Brittany, he has always one eye on Paris and his return thither; indeed, his *Historia calamitatum* seems to have been written to prepare the way for his coming back, to serve an immediate purpose rather than for posterity. It shows nothing of monastic humility or religious vocation, but, on the contrary, is full of arrogance of intellect and joy of combat, even of the lust of the flesh and the lust of the eyes and the pride of life. Its author was a vain man, vain of his penetrating mind and skill in debate, vain of his power to draw away others' students, vain even of his success with the fair sex—so that he "feared no repulse from whatever woman he might deign to honor with his love"—always sure of his own opinions and unsparing of his adversaries. He relies on talent rather than on formal preparation, venturing into the closed field of theology and even improvising lectures on those pitfalls of the unwary, the obscurest parts of the prophet Ezekiel. He was by nature always in opposition, a thorn in the side of intellectual and social conformity. In the classroom he was the bright boy who always knew more than his teachers and delighted to confute them, ridiculing old Anselm of Laon, whose reputation he declared to rest upon mere tradition, unsupported by talent or learning, notable chiefly for a wonderful flow of words without meaning or reason, "a fire which gave forth smoke instead of light," like the barren fig tree of the Gospel or the old oak of Lucan, mere shadow of a great name. In the monastery of Saint-Denis he antagonized the monks by attacking the traditions respecting their founder and patron saint. Always it is he who is right and his many enemies who are wrong. And, as becomes a history of his misfortunes, he pities himself much. Objectively, the facts of Abaelard's autobiography can in the main be verified from his other writings and the statements of contemporaries. Subjectively, the *Historia calamitatum* confirms itself throughout, if we discern between the bursts of self-confidence the intervals of irresolution and despondency in what he tries to present as a consistently planned career. The prolixity and the citations of ancient authority are of the Middle Ages, as are the particular problems with which his mind was occupied, but the personality might turn up in any subsequent epoch— "portrait of a radical by himself"! Yet, just as Heloise's joy in loving belongs to the ages, Abaelard's joy in learning is more specifically of the new renaissance, of which he is the bright particular star. . . .

In Abaelard . . . we have one of the most striking figures of the mediaeval renaissance. Vain and self-conscious, as we have found him in his autobiography, his defects of temperament must not blind us to his great mental gifts. He was daring, original, brilliant, one of the first philosophical minds of the whole Middle Ages. First and foremost a logician, with an unwavering faith in the reasoning process, he fell in with the dialectic preoccupations of his age, and did more than any one else to define the problems and methods of scholasticism, at least in the matter of universals and in his *Sic et non*. The question of universals, the central though not the unique theme of scholastic philosophy, is concerned with the nature of general terms or conceptions, such as man, house, horse. Are these, as the Nominalists asserted, mere names and nothing more, an intellectual convenience at the most? Or are they realities, as the Realists maintained, having an existence quite independent of and apart from the particular individuals in which they may be for the moment objectified? A mere matter of logical terminology, you may say, of no importance in the actual world. Yet much depends upon the application. Apply the nominalistic doctrine to God, and the indivisible Trinity dissolves into three persons. Apply it to the Church, and the Church ceases to be a divine institution with a life of its own and becomes merely a convenient designation for the whole body of individual Christians. Apply to it the State, and where does political authority reside, in a sovereign whole or in the individual citizens? In this form, at least, the problem is still with us. Practical thinking cannot entirely shake itself free from logic, and, conversely, logic has sometimes practical consequences not at first realized.

The debate respecting universals has its roots in Boethius and Porphyry, but it comes into the foreground with Roscellinus, an extreme Nominalist, condemned in 1092 for tritheism at the instance of Anselm. Against the extreme realism represented in various forms by William of Champeaux, Abaelard maintained a more moderate view, a doctrine which he worked out with his usual brilliancy and which we have just begun to understand with the publication, now proceeding, of his *Glosses on Porphyry*. As here explained, this resembles closely the doctrine of later orthodoxy. In an age, however, when theology was a prime object of attention, the logicians were always under the temptation of applying their dialectic to fundamental problems concerning the nature of God, and it is not surprising to find that Abaelard, like Roscellinus before him, ran into difficulties on the subject of the Trinity, being condemned for heresy at Soissons in 1121 and at Sens in 1141. Such conflicts were inevitable with one of Abaelard's radical temper, who courted opposition and combat. . . .

In another way Abaelard contributed to the formation of scholasticism, namely, in his *Sic et non,* or *Yes* and *No.* True, the method of collecting and arranging passages from the Fathers on specific topics had been used before, as in the *Sentences* of Anselm of Laon, but Abaelard gave it a pungency and a wide popularity which associate it permanently with his name. Like everything he did, it was well advertised. His method was to take significant topics of theology and ethics and to collect from the Fathers their opinions pro and con, sharpening perhaps the contrast and being careful not to solve the real or seeming contradiction. Inerrancy he grants only to the Scriptures, apparent contradictions in which must be explained as due to scribal mistakes or defective understanding; subsequent authorities may err for other reasons, and when they disagree he claims the right of going into the reasonableness of the doctrine itself, of proving all things in order to hold fast that which is good. He has accordingly collected divergent sayings of the Fathers as they have come to mind, for the purpose of stimulating tender readers to the utmost effort in seeking out truth and of making them more acute as the result of such inquiry. "By doubting we come to inquiry, and by inquiry we perceive truth." The propositions cover a wide range of topics and of reading; some are dismissed briefly, while others bring forth long citations. . . . Some . . . , one can almost imagine briefed on either side in modern manuals for the training of debaters. Some such purpose, the stimulating of discussion among his pupils, seems to have been Abaelard's primary object, but the emphasis upon contradiction rather than upon agreement and the failure to furnish any solutions, real or superficial, tended powerfully to expose the weaknesses in the orthodox position and to undermine authority generally.

The Substance of Abelard
DAVID KNOWLES

To Haskins belongs the well-deserved credit, if not for "discovering"
Abelard, at least for giving him a setting in which he can be seen with some
clarity. More recent scholarship, however, has moved beyond the
conception of Abelard as an example of the medieval Renaissance man—
no matter how brilliant, fascinating, and attractive—to the larger question
of his importance as a substantive figure in medieval intellectual history.
Much of this new scholarship is summarized, and some of it anticipated,
by the distinguished British medievalist and ecclesiastical historian
Dom David Knowles in his The Evolution of Medieval Thought.
     We turn now to that summary.

UNTIL VERY RECENT years all discussions of Abelard centred upon his
alleged heretical and rationalistic teaching. At the present day, as a result
both of research among unpublished manuscripts and of critical methods
applied to his works, he can be seen as a figure of positive import, as a
logician of supreme ability and as the originator of ideas as well as of
methods that were to have a long life. Not only is it now possible to grasp
more fully than before what Abelard taught and thought, but it has been
shown conclusively that throughout his life he was constantly rewriting and
reconsidering his works, and that his opinions grew more orthodox and
more carefully expressed with the passage of the years.
     Was Abelard a rationalist? The question has been variously answered.
Eighty years ago, the rationalists of the nineteenth century, Renan among
them, saw in Abelard a herald of their enlightenment, and some of the
historians of the day agreed with them; such was the opinion of Charles
de Rémusat and Victor Cousin, and to their names, with some reserves,
may be added the more recent opinion of Maurice de Wulf: "Exaggerat-
ing the rights of dialectic in theological matters, Peter Abelard established
the relations of theology and philosophy on rationalistic principles."
Others, even, have not hesitated to reverse Anselm's motto for Abelard;
he would have said: "I understand in order that I may believe." Nevertheless, even at the beginning of this century some of the most distinguished names were found among Abelard's advocates, among them those
of Harnack and Portalié, the latter of whom remarks: "In theory at least,
Abelard never desired to give a philosophical demonstration of a mystery

of the faith; still less did he profess himself a rationalist." This, expressed
in various forms, is the almost unanimous verdict of recent scholars—
Geyer, Chenu, Grabmann, de Ghellinck, Gilson—and we may agree with
the judgment of the last-named of these, that the legend of Abelard the
free-thinker has now become an exhibit of the historical curiosity-shop.
Of a truth, Abelard was never a rebel against the authority of the
Church, and never a rationalist in the modern sense. He never persisted
in teaching what had been censured, even though until censured he may
have protested vehemently that he had been misrepresented. Similarly, he
never intended that his dialectic should attack or contradict or replace the
doctrines of the Church as formulated by tradition. In this, full weight
must be given to his words in his *Introduction to Theology:* "Now therefore it remains for us, after having laid down the foundation of authority,
to place upon it the buttresses of reasoning." This is unquestionably a
genuine expression of his programme, as are also the celebrated and moving words of his letter to Héloise after the condemnation of 1141: "I will
never be a philosopher, if this is to speak against St Paul; I would not be
an Aristotle, if this were to separate me from Christ. . . . I have set my
building on the corner-stone on which Christ has built his Church . . .
if the tempest rises, I am not shaken; if the winds rave, I am not fearful. . . . I rest upon the rock that cannot be moved." These are not the
words of a deliberate heretic or of a professed rationalist.

There are, in fact, two quite distinct questions. Did Abelard intend to
formulate the doctrines of the faith in terms of dialectic, and to establish
or invalidate them by this means? And, did Abelard in fact, in his writing
and teaching, err from the orthodox teaching of the Church?

As we have seen, the answer to the first question, if it were needful to
give it in a single word, would be negative. Such a simple answer, however, does not meet the complexity of the matter. . . . Abelard knew
Anselm's work, and though he does not mention his motto, *credo ut in-
telligam,*[4] would certainly have echoed it, though perhaps on a slightly
more superficial level and with more emphasis on the last word. But
Abelard, besides having his full share of the contemporary trust in dialectic as the mistress of all truth, had a far greater acquaintance with, and
trust in, the current *sprachlogik,* the conviction that just as words and
terms and methods could be found to express truth with absolute fidelity,
so all speculation, and indeed the nature and modes of acting of things in
themselves, must follow and in a sense be modified by, the words and
terms used by the skilled dialectician. *A fortiori,* the theological expression
of religious truths must conform to dialectical practice; only so could any
discussion or explanation of the mysteries of the faith be practicable. This
postulate was probably at the root of Berengar's controversy with Lan-
franc. It was certainly a prime cause of misunderstanding between Bernard

4 "I believe in order that I might understand."—ED.

and Gilbert de la Porrée. So it was with Abelard. By genius, choice and practice he was a dialectician, and a dialectician he almost always remained. The dogmas of the faith are not for him wells of infinite depth, the reflection in words of luminous supernatural truth. Rather, they are so many propositions or facts thrown, so to say, to the Christian philosopher, upon which he may exercise his ingenuity and to which he can apply no laws but those of logic and grammar. . . .

As to the second question, Abelard was unquestionably technically unorthodox in many of his expressions. Though his opponents, and in particular St Bernard, may have erred in the severity of their attacks and in the universality of their suspicions, and though recent scholarship has shown that some, at least, of his expressions can, in their context, bear an orthodox interpretation, and that Abelard became more, and not less, respectful of tradition as the years passed, yet many of his pronouncements on the Trinity, the Incarnation, and Grace were certainly incorrect by traditional standards and, if carried to their logical issue, would have dangerously weakened the expression of Christian truth. The catalogue of erroneous, or at least of erratic, propositions in his writings drawn up by Portalié sixty years ago cannot be wholly cancelled by explanations of a verbal or logical nature. Error, however, is not always heretical. In the theological controversies of every age there have always been two families among those accused of heresy. There are those who, whatever their professions, are in fact attacking traditional doctrine, and those who, despite many of their expressions have, as we may say, the root of the matter in them . . . and there can be no doubt to which of the families Abelard belongs.

Abelard's genius was versatile, and left a mark on everything he touched. We have already considered his important contribution to logic, and in particular his solution of the problem of universals. In methodology he marked an epoch with his *Sic et non*. This short treatise, composed perhaps in its earliest form *c.* 1122, is perhaps the most celebrated (though not necessarily the most important) of Abelard's contributions to the development of medieval thought; it has in recent years been the occasion of a number of controversies. It consists of a relatively short prologue explaining its purpose and giving rules for the discussion of what follows; then comes a series of texts from Scripture and the Fathers on 150 theological points. The texts are given in groups, and in each case are apparently mutually contradictory. The essence of the work is the exposition of methodical doubt. As Abelard has it, "careful and frequent questioning is the basic key to wisdom," or, as he writes in the same prologue: "By doubting we come to questioning, and by questioning we perceive the truth."

Opinions have been divided as to how far the *Sic et non* is original, how far it is an instrument of scepticism, and what was its influence on the development of scholastic method. It was for long the common opinion

that it was completely original, an innovation with resounding consequences as great in its own field as the invention of the spinning-jenny or
the mechanical reaper in the world of economics. This view, usually held
in conjunction with that which saw in Abelard the first great apostle of
free thought, was convincingly refuted by the researches of Fournier
and Grabmann, who showed that the juxtaposition of seemingly contradictory authorities was already a method in common use in Abelard's day
by compilers of canonical collections, who had not only amassed texts
but given rules for criticism and harmonization. Bernold of Constance and
Ivo of Chartres in particular had employed this technique, and the *Decre-
tum* and *Panormia* of the latter were shown to have furnished Abelard
with some of his quotations from the Fathers.

As regards the primary aim of the *Sic et non,* there have been two views.
Many in the past, Harnack among them, have seen in it an attempt to
undermine tradition by showing its essentially self-contradictory character,
in order to make way for a more rational approach. Others, and among
them the greatest names among historians of medieval thought, have
strenuously opposed this view, seeing in the *Sic et non* simply an exercise
for explaining and harmonizing discrepancies and difficulties in the authorities. This opinion gains additional support from the fact that the work
was never used by his opponents as a stick with which to beat Abelard.
Such a view might well allow that *Sic et non* was a reaction against the
purely traditionalist teaching of the day, and that it was intended to open
a wide new field to dialectic, for which only a few samples were given.

As for the influence of the work upon the schools, the verdict of the
early historians was summary, and Abelard was hailed as the creator of
the scholastic method, and even Denifle in his early days regarded it as
the basis of the method of question and disputation. As we have seen,
all now admit that the borrowing was on Abelard's side. . . .

In theology, the main achievement of Abelard was to discuss and explain, where others merely asserted or proved, and to provide an outline
of the whole field of doctrines. It would seem, indeed, that he was the
first to use the Latin word *theologia* in the sense that is now current in all
European languages; the word had previously borne the connotation familiar in the Greek Fathers and the pseudo-Denis, of the mystical or at
least the expert knowledge of God and His attributes. By giving, in versions of increasing length and scope, an "introduction" or survey of
Christian teaching, Abelard's writings are an important link in the development of the *summa,* the typical medieval survey of theology.

When thus "introducing" his disciples to theology, Abelard met, as he
himself tells us, a genuine demand for an explanation of the mysteries of
the faith, and he gave this explanation with opinions that were often original, and which aimed at being reasonable. Abelard was in many ways a
humanist; he stressed the exemplary purpose of the Incarnation and
Crucifixion at the expense of the redemptive, and minimized the concep-

tion of original sin, regarding it as a penalty rather than a stain and regarding grace as an assistance rather than as an enablement. He reacted against all legalistic interpretations, such as the opinion that the death or blood of Christ was a discharge of the rights claimed over mankind by the devil. In his Trinitarian theology, which was the head and front of his offending at Soissons and remained a charge at Sens, the principal accusation was that in reaction from the "tritheism" of Roscelin he founded the distinctions within the Godhead upon the traditional "appropriations" ("power" of the Father, "wisdom" of the Word, and "love" of the Holy Spirit) thereby either reducing them to aspects of the one Godhead (Sabellianism) or, by an exclusive appropriation, limiting the equality of the persons. He was further accused of obscuring the personal union of the divine and human natures in Christ by treating the humanity as something assumed, as it were, as a garment by the divine Son. This, and other questionable propositions, make up an impressive total of erroneous opinions, and although some were due to faulty terminology and others were tacitly dropped from later versions of the same work—for Abelard, resembling other lecturers before and since, was always rewriting and adding precision to his treatises—too much smoke remains to allow the cry of fire to be ignored. Above and through all else was the charge that Abelard left no place in his system for faith. . . .

In yet one more important field, that of ethics, Abelard was destined to leave a durable mark. In his discussion of moral problems in *Scito te ipsum* [5] he showed his originality in such a way as to be one of the founders of scholastic moral theology. Reacting against the view then current which placed moral goodness solely in the conformity of an act to the declared law of God, and which tended to see sin as the factual transgression of the law, even if unknown or misunderstood (e.g. the obligation of certain degrees of fasting on certain days), Abelard placed goodness wholly in the intention and will of the agent, and saw sin not as the actual transgression of the law, but as a contempt of God the lawgiver. . . . Abelard, in commenting upon the text, "Father, forgive them, for they know not what they do," tended to excuse wholly from sin the agents of the Crucifixion, stressing "they know not what they do" rather than the implicit sin that needed forgiveness. This shocked current susceptibilities, and was one of the charges against him. In another direction his opinions minimized the conception of the law of God and of the absolute ethical goodness of particular actions. Abelard, anticipating with strange exactness the opinions of some fourteenth century "voluntarists," suggested that with God as with man the good depended upon the free choice, and that God might have established canons of morality other than, and even contrary to, those of the Hebrew and Christian revelation.

Look at him how we will, and when full weight has been given to the

[5] "Know thyself."—ED.

impression of restlessness, vanity and lack of spiritual depth given by his
career and some of his writings, Abelard remains, both as a teacher and as
a thinker, one of the half-dozen most influential names in the history of
medieval thought. . . . As a theologian, he was the first to see his subject as a whole, and to conceive the possibility of a survey or synthesis
for his pupils, thus taking an important part in fixing the method of teaching. Finally, and perhaps most significantly, he approached theological and
ethical problems as questions that could be illuminated, explained and
in part comprehended by a carefully reasoned approach, and still more
by a humane, practical attitude which took account of difficulties and of
natural, human feelings, and he endeavoured to solve problems of belief
and conscience not by the blow of an abstract principle, but by a consideration of circumstances as they are in common experience. Abelard
failed to become a much-cited authority by reason of his double condemnation and the attacks of celebrated adversaries, but his ideas lingered
in the minds of his disciples, and many of them came to the surface, un-
acknowledged, in the golden age of scholasticism.

Suggestions for Further Reading

ABELARD'S AUTOBIOGRAPHY, which is excerpted in this chapter and which
took the form of a letter to a friend, is available in another translation
along with seven additional letters exchanged between Abelard and Eloise,
The Letters of Abelard and Eloise, tr. C. K. Scott-Moncrieff (New York:
Knopf, 1926). There are a number of biographical treatments of Abelard.
One of the best is a small and elegant book by Etienne Gilson, *Héloïse
and Abelard*, tr. L. K. Shook (Ann Arbor: University of Michigan Press,
1963 [1951]), in which the great French medievalist retells the familiar
story with scholarship and insight. He also includes an appendix in which
he argues for the authenticity of the letters. R. W. Southern, the distinguished British medievalist, also deals with the letters and some related
topics in a collection of his articles, *Medieval Humanism and Other
Studies* (Oxford, England: Blackwell, 1970). There is a first-rate historical novel by Helen J. Waddell, *Peter Abelard, A Novel* (New York:
Barnes and Noble, 1971 [1933]). J. G. Sikes, *Peter Abelard* (New York:

Russell and Russell, 1965 [1932]), is largely about Abelard's thought rather than about his life and is complex and difficult, as is the more recent detailed documentary study of Abelard's influence, D. E. Luscombe, *The School of Peter Abelard, The Influence of Abelard's Thought in the Early Scholastic Period* (Cambridge, England: Cambridge University Press, 1969), but the latter is an important revisionist work, showing Abelard as less the founder of a distinctive school and more a journeyman critic.

It was, of course, largely Abelard's thought that got him in trouble with the church and with St. Bernard of Clairvaux. Their differences are dealt with in Denis Meadows, *A Saint and a Half: A New Interpretation of Abelard and St. Bernard of Clairvaux* (New York: Devin-Adair, 1963); it is less a new interpretation than an attempt to soften the disagreements between them. A sharper treatment of their differences is to be found in A. Victor Murray, *Abelard and St. Bernard, A Study in Twelfth Century "Modernism"* (New York: Barnes and Noble, 1967). For the church itself in Abelard's time, the best brief general survey of the papacy is G. Barraclough, *The Medieval Papacy* (New York: Harcourt, Brace, 1968). Equally authoritative and readable but more comprehensive for this period is H. Daniel-Rops, *Cathedral and Crusade, Studies of the Medieval Church 1050–1350,* tr. John Warrington (New York: Dutton, 1957). As for the more specific environment of Abelard, the medieval schools, the best and most readable works are still the old classics, Helen Waddell, *The Wandering Scholars* (New York: Holt, 1934 [1927]), Charles Homer Haskins, *The Rise of Universities* (New York: P. Smith, 1940 [1923]), and his *Studies in Medieval Culture* (New York: Ungar, 1958 [1929]). Haskins' notions about the Renaissance of the twelfth century are still being debated: see the review of the literature in C. Warren Hollister (ed.), *The Twelfth-Century Renaissance* (New York: Wiley, 1969); Christopher Brooke, *The Twelfth-Century Renaissance* (New York: Harcourt, Brace, 1969), not so much a revision of Haskins' classic work as an updating and extension; and the graceful and learned work of Sidney R. Packard, *12th Century Europe, An Interpretive Essay* (Amherst: University of Massachusetts Press, 1973).

For the relationship of Abelard to medieval learning and scholasticism, further reading in Dom David Knowles, *The Evolution of Medieval Thought* (New York: Vintage, 1962), is recommended, along with Gordon Leff, *Medieval Thought* (Harmondsworth, England: Penguin, 1958). Two more straightforward surveys are Meyrick H. Carré, *Realists and Nominalists* (London: Oxford University Press, 1946), and F. C. Copleston, *A History of Medieval Philosophy* (New York: Harper & Row, 1972 [1952]).

Finally, students must remember that the towns and schools of the twelfth century were the products of the economic revolution that was sweeping Europe. The best and most comprehensive treatment of the new medieval economic history is *The Cambridge Economic History of Europe*, 2nd ed., vols. 1–3 (Cambridge, England: Cambridge University Press, 1952–1966). Three additional works may also be recommended, one by the American economic historian Robert S. Lopez, *The Commercial Revolution of the Middle Ages, 950–1350* (Englewood Cliffs, N.J.: Prentice-Hall, 1971), and two by French authorities, R. H. Bautier, *The Economic Development of Medieval Europe*, tr. H. Karolyi (New York: Harcourt, Brace, 1971), and Georges Duby, *The Early Growth of the European Economy*, tr. H. B. Clarke (Ithaca, N.Y.: Cornell University Press, 1974).

Eleanor of Aquitaine
and the
Wrath of God

Eleanor of Aquitaine was one of the most remarkable and important figures in medieval history. In her own right, she was duchess of the vast domain of Aquitaine and countess of Poitou, the wife first of Louis VII of France and then of Henry II of England, the mother of "good King Richard" and "bad King John," patroness of poets and minstrels. Tradition remembers her as beautiful and passionate, headstrong and willful. But beyond that intriguing traditional reputation, she is a figure only imperfectly seen and, ironically enough, seen at all largely through the accounts of her enemies.

The sources of medieval history are scanty at best and tend, moreover, to record men's doings in a preponderantly man's world. Even the greatest of medieval women appear in the records of their time as conveyors of properties and channels for noble blood lines, and we know of them only that they were "good and faithful wives"—or that they were not. So it is with Eleanor. We do not even have a contemporary description of her. Troubadour poets sang rapturously of her "crystal cheeks," her "locks like threads of gold," her eyes "like Orient pearls." One even proclaims,

> Were the world all mine,
> From the sea to the Rhine,
> I'd give it all
> If so be the Queen of England
> Lay in my arms.

In sober fact, we do not know what color her eyes were, nor her hair, whether it was indeed "like threads of gold" or raven black. Even the few pictorial representations we have of her—including her tomb effigy at the Abbey of Fontevrault—are purely conventional.

But Eleanor's part in the great events of her time was real enough. It began with her marriage, at the age of fifteen, to Louis the young king, son of Louis VI (Louis the Fat) of France. Her father, the turbulent Duke William X of Aquitaine, had died suddenly and unexpectedly on pilgrimage to Spain, leaving Eleanor his heiress. And, in feudal law, the disposition of both Eleanor and her fiefs was a matter to be decided by her father's overlord, Louis VI of France. Duke William had been Louis' most intractable vassal, and his death was a priceless opportunity not only to put an end to the contumaciousness of Aquitaine but to tie that large and wealthy duchy to the French realm. Louis decided that the interests of his house were best served by the marriage of Eleanor to his son. And so, it was done. There is no record of how either the young bride or the young groom responded, only an account of the brilliant assemblage that gathered to witness the ceremony in Bordeaux and to accompany the happy couple back by weary stages to Paris. In the course of this journey, the aged King Louis died. His son was now Louis VII, the Duchess Eleanor now queen of France. The year was 1137.

We must not imagine that Eleanor was a very happy bride in those first years of her marriage. Paris was a cold and gloomy northern city, very different from sunny Provence, and the Capetian castles in which she lived were dark and uncomfortable. The king her husband had an inexhaustible thirst for devotion and piety and surrounded himself with ecclesiastical advisors, confessors, theologians, and barren, quibbling scholars, so unlike the more robust and charming practitioners of the *gai savoir* (merry learning) with whom Eleanor had grown up at her father's court. Nor was Louis very happy, for his young wife gave him two daughters and no son, no member of "the better sex" to be groomed for the Capetian throne.

Then word reached Paris of the fall of Edessa in the distant Latin Kingdom of Jerusalem, one of those fortress principalities to secure the Holy Land dating from the first crusade almost half a century before. The resurgence of Moslem power was clearly seen to threaten the Holy Land, and the call for a second crusade went out. The pious King Louis took the cross—to the consternation of his more realistic advisors. And Eleanor insisted upon accompanying him. Whatever Louis and his fellow crusaders may have thought about this matter, Eleanor's position as a great vassal who could summon a substantial host of warriors from her own lands made her support crucial: and her support was contingent upon her going in person. There is a persistent legend that the queen and her ladies decked themselves out as Amazons in anticipation of their role in the coming military adventure.

But the military adventure itself turned into a military disaster. The second crusade was a dismal failure. The French forces of Louis VII were seriously defeated by the Turks, and the German contingent led by the Emperor Conrad III was almost wiped out. Both the French and the Germans accused the Byzantine Greeks of treachery. There were disagreements among the Western knights, and many of them simply abandoned the crusade and returned home. There were divided counsels among those who remained and mistrust between them and the Christian lords of the Eastern principalities. And there were continued military blunders and defeats. Tempers were short, old quarrels flared, new ones commenced.

In this atmosphere, what had apparently been a growing estrangement between King Louis and Queen Eleanor became an open break. Their troubles were aggravated by the boldness and outspokenness of the queen and in particular by her attentions to her handsome uncle, only eight years older than she, Raymond of Poitiers, Prince of Antioch. It may have been no more than an innocent flirtation. But Louis thought otherwise. He brooded not only on his queen's conduct but on her failure to produce a son for him, and his mind turned to divorce, the grounds for which were to be found in consanguinity, a marriage within the prohibited degree of blood relationship, which was the usual legal pretext for the dissolution of feudal marriages no longer bearable or profitable.

Eleanor and the Chroniclers
WILLIAM OF TYRE AND JOHN OF SALISBURY

Eleanor's role in the second crusade is scarcely mentioned by the chroniclers who recorded the deeds of its other leading figures. Odo of Deuil, a monk of the French royal monastery of St. Denis and the chaplain of Louis VII, wrote the most detailed account of Louis' part in the crusade—De profectione Ludovici VII in orientem—but he makes only four passing references to the queen in the entire narrative. Odo clearly had reason to favor the cause of the king his master. And, for one reason or another, so did the few other chroniclers who give any account at all of the estrangement between Louis and Eleanor. The most detailed is that of William Archbishop of Tyre. William is generally regarded as the best of all the chroniclers of the crusades, but he was not present at the time of this crisis and we do not know what source he used. In any event, he regarded the behavior of the queen and the resulting breach with her husband as part of a cynical attempt by Raymond of Antioch to turn the crusade to his own advantage. Here is the account of William of Tyre.

FOR MANY DAYS Raymond, prince of Antioch, had eagerly awaited the arrival of the king of the Franks. When he learned that the king had landed in his domains, he summoned all the nobles of the land and the chief leaders of the people and went out to meet him with a chosen escort. He greeted the king with much reverence and conducted him with great pomp into the city of Antioch, where he was met by the clergy and the people. Long before this time—in fact, as soon as he heard that Louis was coming—Raymond had conceived the idea that by his aid he might be able to enlarge the principality of Antioch. With this in mind, therefore, even before the king started on the pilgrimage, the prince had sent to him in France a large store of noble gifts and treasures of great price in the hope of winning his favor. He also counted greatly on the interest of the queen with the lord king, for she had been his inseparable companion on his pilgrimage. She was Raymond's niece, the eldest daughter of Count William of Poitou, his brother.

As we have said, therefore, Raymond showed the king every attention on his arrival. He likewise displayed a similar care for the nobles and chief men in the royal retinue and gave them many proofs of his great liberality. In short, he outdid all in showing honor to each one according to his rank and handled everything with the greatest magnificence. He felt a lively hope that with the assistance of the king and his troops he would be able to subjugate the neighboring cities, namely, Aleppo, Shayzar, and several others. Nor would this hope have been futile, could he have induced the king and his chief men to undertake the work. For the arrival of King Louis had brought such fear to our enemies that now they not only distrusted their own strength but even despaired of life itself.

Raymond had already more than once approached the king privately in regard to the plans which he had in mind. Now he came before the members of the king's suite and his own nobles and explained with due formality how his request could be accomplished without difficulty and at the same time be of advantage and renown to themselves. The king, however, ardently desired to go to Jerusalem to fulfil his vows, and his determination was irrevocable. When Raymond found that he could not induce the king to join him, his attitude changed. Frustrated in his ambitious designs, he began to hate the king's ways; he openly plotted against him and took means to do him injury. He resolved also to deprive him of his wife, either by force or by secret intrigue. The queen readily assented to this design, for she was a foolish woman. Her conduct before and after this time showed her to be, as we have said, far from circumspect. Contrary to her royal dignity, she disregarded her marriage vows and was unfaithful to her husband.

As soon as the king discovered these plots, he took means to provide for his life and safety by anticipating the designs of the prince. By the advice of his chief nobles, he hastened his departure and secretly left Antioch with his people. Thus the splendid aspect of his affairs was completely changed, and the end was quite unlike the beginning. His coming had been attended with pomp and glory; but fortune is fickle, and his departure was ignominious.

The only other substantial account of the events leading to the divorce of Louis and Eleanor is that of the great twelfth-century ecclesiastic and intellectual, John of Salisbury, in his Historia Pontificalis. *In one respect, John was even further removed from the events than William of Tyre. He had no direct knowledge of the East at all and was, at this time, in Rome on a mission from the see of Canterbury and attached to the papal court. We do not know what source he used for the events in Antioch. It is likely that he is simply repeating the story as he heard it from members of Louis' retinue, for the hostility against Eleanor that already animated Louis' close supporters is clearly present in John's account. It is also possible that the hostility of the account and its strong pro-French bias is related to the later time at which John's work was actually written, about 1163. At this time, John was involved in the growing bitterness between Thomas Becket, whom he supported, and Henry II of England, who had just sent John into exile for his support of Becket. John found refuge in France.*

But in any event, the account in the Historia Pontificalis *is strongly favorable to Louis, even to the extent of ascribing to Eleanor the initiative in the proposal for the divorce.*

IN THE YEAR of grace 1149 the most Christian king of the Franks reached Antioch, after the destruction of his armies in the east, and was nobly entertained there by Prince Raymond, brother of the late William, count of Poitiers. He was as it happened the queen's uncle, and owed the king loyalty, affection and respect for many reasons. But whilst they remained there to console, heal and revive the survivors from the wreck of the army, the attentions paid by the prince to the queen, and his constant, indeed almost continuous, conversation with her, aroused the king's suspicions. These were greatly strengthened when the queen wished to remain behind, although the king was preparing to leave, and the prince made every effort to keep her, if the king would give his consent. And when the king made haste to tear her away, she mentioned their kinship, saying it was not lawful for them to remain together as man and wife, since they were related in the fourth and fifth degrees. Even before their departure a rumour to that effect had been heard in France, where the late Bartholomew bishop of Laon had calculated the degrees of kinship; but it was not certain whether the reckoning was true or false. At this the king was deeply moved; and although he loved the queen almost beyond reason he consented to divorce her if his counsellors and the French nobility would allow it. There was one knight amongst the king's secretaries, called Terricus Gualerancius, a eunuch whom the queen had always hated and mocked, but who was faithful and had the king's ear like his father's before him. He boldly persuaded the king not to suffer her to dally longer at Antioch, both because "guilt under kinship's guise could lie concealed," and because it would be a lasting shame to the kingdom of the Franks if in addition to all the other disasters it was reported that the king had been deserted by his wife, or robbed of her. So he argued, either because he hated the queen or because he really believed it, moved perchance by widespread rumour. In consequence, she was torn away and forced to leave for Jerusalem with the king; and, their mutual anger growing greater, the wound remained, hide it as best they might.

In the next passage, John is on more familiar ground since he was in Rome, a familiar of the curia and of Pope Eugenius III, and perhaps even a witness to some of the events he describes.

In the year of grace eleven hundred and fifty the king of the Franks returned home. But the galleys of the Emperor of Constantinople lay in wait for him on his return, capturing the queen and all who were journeying in her ship. The king was appealed to to return to his Byzantine brother and friend, and force was being brought to bear on him when the galleys of the king of Sicily came to the rescue. Freeing the queen and releasing the king, they escorted them back to Sicily rejoicing, with honour and triumph. This was done by order of the king of Sicily, who feared the wiles of the Greeks and desired an opportunity of showing his devotion to the king and queen of the Franks. Now therefore he hastened to meet him with an ample retinue, and escorted him most honourably to Palermo, heaping gifts both on him and on all his followers; thereafter he travelled with him right across his territory to Ceprano, supplying all his needs on the way. This is the last point on the frontier between the principality of Capua and Campania, which is papal territory.

At Ceprano the cardinals and officials of the church met the king and, providing him with all that he desired, escorted him to Tusculum to the lord pope, who received him with such tenderness and reverence that one would have said he was welcoming an angel of the Lord rather than a mortal man. He reconciled the king and queen, after hearing severally the accounts each gave of the estrangement begun at Antioch, and forbade any future mention of their consanguinity: confirming their marriage, both orally and in writing, he commanded under pain of anathema that no word should be spoken against it and that it should not be dissolved under any pretext whatever. This ruling plainly delighted the king, for he loved the queen passionately, in an almost childish way. The pope made them sleep in the same bed, which he had had decked with priceless hangings of his own; and daily during their brief visit he strove by friendly converse to restore love between them. He heaped gifts upon them; and when the moment for departure came, though he was a stern man, he could not hold back his tears, but sent them on their way blessing them and the kingdom of the Franks, which was higher in his esteem than all the kingdoms of the world.

Eleanor the Queen of Hearts
AMY KELLY

In spite of "the lord pope's" good offices, his tears and his blessing, even his threat of anathema, the estrangement between Louis and Eleanor continued. Louis was adamant, and finally, in the spring of 1152 at a solemn synod in Beaugency on the Loire, Louis' spokesmen argued the case of the consanguinity of their lord and his queen, and the Archbishop of Sens proclaimed their marriage invalid. The Archbishop of Bordeaux, the queen's surrogate, sought only the assurance that her lands be restored. But this had already been arranged, as had all the other details of this elaborate royal charade. Eleanor was not even present. She had already returned to Poitou.

But Eleanor was not destined to reign as a dowager duchess in her own domains. Within two months, she had married Henry, Duke of Normandy. He was not only the Norman duke but also the heir to the fiefs of his father, Geoffrey Plantagenet, Count of Maine and Anjou. These already substantial lands, when joined to those of his new bride, made Henry lord of a nearly solid block of territories that stretched from the English Channel to the Mediterranean and from Bordeaux to the Vexin, hardly a day's ride from Paris. At one stroke, Henry of Anjou had become the greatest feudatory of France, with lands and resources many times the size of those held by his nominal overlord, King Louis VII. Two years later, another piece of Henry's inheritance came into his hands. His mother, Matilda, was the daughter of the English King Henry I and had never ceased to press the claim of her son to the English throne. The reign of King Stephen was coming to an end, and he had no surviving heirs. At his death in 1154, Henry of Anjou claimed his crown, and there was none to deny him. Eleanor was a queen once more.

But this time, she had a very different king. Henry II was as godless as Louis had been pious, as flamboyant as Louis had been humble. Where Louis was stubborn and persistent, Henry was furiously energetic and decisive. The setting was at hand for one of the classic confrontations of medieval history that was to stretch into the following generation of the kings of both France and England.

As for Eleanor, the sources are once more silent. We know that she produced for Henry the family of sons she had denied to Louis. The eldest, William, born before the succession to England, died in childhood. But in 1155 came Henry, in 1157, Richard—to be called the Lion-Hearted—and in 1158, Geoffrey, in 1166 came John, the last of her sons, and there were by this time two daughters as well. We know that through the early years of her marriage to Henry, Eleanor was often with him at court and sometimes presided in his absence, a fact attested by writs and seals. But her marriage was by no means serene. There were long periods of separation during which the king was known to be unfaithful. The incidents of his infidelity had grown more flagrant with the passing years. At about the time of prince John's birth in 1166, Henry was involved with a paramour of spectacular beauty, Rosamond Clifford. Their affair was the object of such celebration by poets, balladeers, and wags alike that Eleanor may have decided that her bed and her dignity could no longer endure such an affront. But there may have been other matters at issue. The queen may have become alarmed at her husband's efforts to substitute his rule for hers in her dower lands.

In any case, about 1170 she returned to Poitou with her favorite among her sons, Richard, whom she installed as her heir for the lands of Poitou and Aquitaine. For the next three or four years she lived in her old capital of Poitiers, separated from her husband. In these years of self-imposed exile, Eleanor not only reasserted her rights to her own lands, but created a center in Poitiers for the practice of the troubadour culture and l'amour courtois that had long been associated with her family.

The following passage, from Amy Kelly's Eleanor of Aquitaine and the Four Kings—*the book that has come to be regarded as the standard work on Eleanor—is a brilliant reconstruction of this period of Eleanor's life.*

WHEN THE COUNTESS of Poitou settled down to rule her own heritage, she took her residence in Poitiers, which offered a wide eye-sweep on the world of still operative kings. In the recent Plantagenet building program her ancestral city, the seat and necropolis of her forebears, had been magnificently enlarged and rebuilt, and it stood at her coming thoroughly renewed, a gleaming exemplar of urban elegance. The site rose superbly amidst encircling rivers. Its narrow Merovingian area had lately been extended to include with new and ampler walls parishes that had previously straggled over its outer slopes; ancient quarters had been cleared of immemorial decay; new churches and collegials had sprung up; the cathedral of Saint Pierre was enriched; markets and shops of tradesmen and artisans bore witness to renewed life among the *bourgeoisie*; bridges fanned out to suburbs and monastic establishments lying beyond the streams that moated the city. Brimming with sunshine, the valleys ebbed far away below—hamlet and croft, mill and vineyard—to a haze as blue as the vintage. . . .

When Eleanor came in about 1170 to take full possession of her newly restored city of Poitiers and to install her favorite son there as ruling count and duke in her own patrimony, she was no mere game piece as were most feudal women, to be moved like a queen in chess. She had learned her role as *domina* in Paris, Byzantium, Antioch, London, and Rouen, and knew her value in the feudal world. She was prepared of her own unguided wisdom to reject the imperfect destinies to which she had been, as it were, assigned. In this, her third important role in history, she was the pawn of neither prince nor prelate, the victim of no dynastic scheme. She came as her own mistress, the most sophisticated of women, equipped with plans to establish her own assize, to inaugurate a regime dedicated neither to Mars nor to the Pope, nor to any king, but to Minerva, Venus, and the Virgin. She was resolved to escape from secondary roles, to assert her independent sovereignty in her own citadel, to dispense her own justice, her own patronage, and when at leisure, to survey, like the Empress of Byzantium, a vast decorum in her precincts. . . .

The heirs of Poitou and Aquitaine who came to the queen's high place for their vassals' homage, their squires' training, and their courtiers' service, were truculent youths, boisterous young men from the baronial strongholds of the south without the Norman or Frankish sense of nationality, bred on feuds and violence, some of them with rich fiefs and proud lineage, but with little solidarity and no business but local warfare and daredevil escapade. The custom of lateral rather than vertical inheritance of fiefs in vogue in some parts of Poitou and Aquitaine—the system by which lands passed through a whole generation before descending to the next generation—produced a vast number of landless but expectant younger men, foot-loose, unemployed, ambitious, yet dependent upon the reluctant bounty of uncles and brothers, or their own violent exploits.

These wild young men were a deep anxiety not only to the heads of their houses, but to the Kings of France and England and to the Pope in Rome. They were the stuff of which rebellion and schism are made. For two generations the church had done what it could with the problem of their unemployment, marching hordes out of Europe on crusade and rounding other hordes into the cloister.

It was with this spirited world of princes and princesses, of apprentice knights and chatelaines, at once the school and the court of young Richard, that the duchess, busy as she was with the multifarious business of a feudal suzerain, had to deal in her palace in Poitiers. . . .

Eleanor found a willing and helpful deputy to assist her in the person of her daughter by Louis of France, now entrusted to her tutelage, a young woman already well grown, well educated, and apparently well disposed to her mother and to her mother's plans—Marie, Countess of Champagne.

. . . The character of the milieu which Marie appears to have set up in Poitiers suggests a genuine sympathy between the queen and her daughter who had so long been sundered by the bleak fortuities of life. Old relationships were knit up. Something native blossomed in the countess, who shone with a special luster in her mother's court. The young Count of Poitou learned to love particularly his half sister Marie and forever to regard the Poitiers of her dispensation as the world's citadel of valor, the seat of courtesy, and the fountainhead of poetic inspiration. Long after, in his darkest hours, it was to her good graces he appealed. The countess, having carte blanche to proceed with the very necessary business of getting control of her academy, must have striven first for order. Since the miscellaneous and high-spirited young persons in her charge had not learned order from the liturgy nor yet from hagiography, the countess bethought her, like many an astute pedagogue, to deduce her principles from something more germane to their interests. She did not precisely invent her regime; rather she appropriated it from the abundant resources at her hand.

The liberal court of Eleanor had again drawn a company of those gifted persons who thrive by talent or by art. Poets, *conteurs* purveying romance, ecclesiastics with Latin literature at their tongues' end and mere clerks with smatterings of Ovid learned from quotation books, chroniclers engaged upon the sober epic of the Plantagenets, came to their haven in Poitiers. The queen and the countess, with their native poetic tradition, were the natural patrons of the troubadours. It will be seen that the Countess Marie's resources were rich and abundant, but not so formalized as to afford the disciplines for a royal academy nor give substance to a social ritual. The great hall was ready for her grand assize; the expectant court already thronged to gape at its suggestive splendors. . . .

At least one other important source Marie employed. She levied upon the social traditions of her Poitevin forebears. Nostredame relates that in Provence chatelaines were accustomed to entertain their seasonal assemblies with so-called "courts of love," in which, just as feudal vassals brought their grievances to the assizes of their overlords for regulation, litigants in love's thrall brought their problems for the judgment of the ladies. André in his famous work [1] makes reference to antecedent decisions in questions of an amatory nature by "les dames de Gascogne," and the poetry of the troubadours presupposes a milieu in which their doctrines of homage and deference could be exploited. Thus we have in André's *Tractatus* the framework of Ovid with the central emphasis reversed, the Arthurian code of manners, the southern ritual of the "courts of love," all burnished with a golden wash of troubadour poetry learned by the queen's forebears and their vassals in the deep Midi, probably beyond the barrier of the Pyrenees. Marie made these familiar materials the vehicle for her woman's doctrine of civility, and in so doing, she transformed the gross and cynical pagan doctrines of Ovid into something more ideal, the woman's canon, the chivalric code of manners. Manners, she plainly saw, were after all the fine residuum of philosophies, the very flower of ethics. . . .

With this anatomy of the whole corpus of love in hand, Marie organized the rabble of soldiers, fighting cocks, jousters, springers, riding masters, troubadours, Poitevin nobles and debutantes, young chatelaines, adolescent princes, and infant princesses in the great hall of Poitiers. Of this pandemonium the countess fashioned a seemly and elegant society, the fame of which spread to the world. Here was a woman's assize to draw men from the excitements of the tilt and the hunt, from dice and games to feminine society, an assize to outlaw boorishness and compel the tribute of adulation to female majesty. . . .

While the ladies, well-accoutered, sit above upon the dais, the sterner portion of society purged, according to the code, from the odors of the kennels and the highway and free for a time from spurs and falcons, range themselves about the stone benches that line the walls, stirring the fragrant rushes with neatly pointed shoe. There are doubtless preludes of music luring the last reluctant knight from the gaming table, *tensons* or *pastourelles*, the plucking of rotes, the "voicing of a fair song and sweet," perhaps even some of the more complicated musical harmonies so ill-received by the clerical critics in London; a Breton *lai* adding an episode to Arthurian romance, or a chapter in the tale of "sad-man" Tristram, bringing

---

[1] André, simply known as the Chaplain, a scholar of this court whose work *Tractatus de Amore* is referred to here, one of the basic works on medieval chivalry and the courts of love.—ED.

a gush of tears from the tender audience clustered about the queen and the Countess of Champagne.

After the romance of the evening in the queen's court, the jury comes to attention upon petition of a young knight in the hall. He bespeaks the judgment of the queen and her ladies upon a point of conduct, through an advocate, of course, so he may remain anonymous. A certain knight, the advocate deposes, has sworn to his lady, as the hard condition of obtaining her love, that he will upon no provocation boast of her merits in company. But one day he overhears detractors heaping his mistress with calumnies. Forgetting his vow in the heat of his passion, he warms to eloquence in defense of his lady. This coming to her ears, she repudiates her champion. Does the lover, who admits he has broken his pledge to his mistress, deserve in this instance to be driven from her presence?

The Countess of Champagne, subduing suggestions from the floor and the buzz of conference upon the dais, renders the judgment of the areopagus. The lady in the case, anonymous of course, is at fault, declares the Countess Marie. She has laid upon her lover a vow too impossibly difficult. The lover has been remiss, no doubt, in breaking his vow to his mistress, no matter what cruel hardship it involves; but he deserves leniency for the merit of his ardor and his constancy. The jury recommends that the stern lady reinstate the plaintiff. The court takes down the judgment. It constitutes a precedent. Does anyone guess the identity of the young pair whose estrangement is thus delicately knit up by the countess? As a bit of suspense it is delicious. As a theme for talk, how loosening to the tongue!

A disappointed petitioner brings forward a case, through an advocate, involving the question whether love survives marriage. The countess, applying her mind to the code, which says that marriage is no proper obstacle to lovers (*Causa coniugii ab amore non est excusatio recta*), and after grave deliberation with her ladies, creates a sensation in the court by expressing doubt whether love in the ideal sense can exist between spouses. This is so arresting a proposition that the observations of the countess are referred to the queen for corroboration, and all wait upon the opinion of this deeply experienced judge. The queen with dignity affirms that she cannot gainsay the Countess of Champagne, though she finds it admirable that a wife should find love and marriage consonant. Eleanor, Queen of France and then of England, had learned at fifty-two that, as another medieval lady put it, "Mortal love is but the licking of honey from thorns."

Eleanor the Regent
MARION MEADE

*During the years of Eleanor's dalliance at Poitiers, her husband's larger
world had been turned upside down by his quarrel with Thomas Becket.
It had not ended even with the martyrdom of that troublesome prelate at
the altar of Canterbury in 1170. The question of whether Henry ordered
Becket's murder or not—and he probably did not—is quite immaterial.
For he bore its consequences. And its principal consequence was to
give to the French king a priceless justification to move against Henry
and his fiefs. What is more, Henry's own sons were as often as not in
league with the French king. With some of this devil's brood of offspring
Henry had been too hard, with others too soft. And when he favored one,
the others feared and plotted against the favorite of the moment. Even
Henry's proposed disposition of his estates and titles served only to
further their quarrels with each other and with him. These quarrels
reached their first climax in the great rebellion of 1173, in which Henry
the young king, Richard, and Geoffrey were in open alliance with Louis of
France against their father. To the alliance flocked rebellious barons
from Scotland to Aquitaine. Henry charged Eleanor with sedition and
with embittering his sons against him. As the rebellion faltered and then
was quelled, Henry was reconciled, however fitfully, with his sons but not
their mother. With Eleanor, Henry was unyielding. She was imprisoned,
first at Salisbury Castle, later at Winchester and other places, for the next
sixteen years. One must imagine that the captivity was genteel, but it was
nonetheless real. From time to time, she was released for a holiday visit
to court or to participate in some stormy family council.*

*In the last years of her imprisonment two of her sons, Henry and
Geoffrey, had died, but the surviving sons, Richard and John, could still
intrigue against their father. They did so in league with a new and more
dangerous Capetian enemy, Philip II Augustus, the able and energetic
son of Louis VII, who had followed him to the throne in 1180. Henry II's
final years were filled with his sons' rebellion, and he died in 1189
shamed by defeat at their hands. It was only after Henry's death and the
succession of Richard that Eleanor was released from her captivity.*

*With none of her ardor dimmed, the queen, now almost seventy, set
about to serve her favored son, now king at last. While Richard was still on
the Continent, Eleanor assumed the regency and on her own authority
convoked a court at Westminster to demand the oaths of loyalty from the
English feudality to their new king. She then traveled to other centers to
take similar obeisances and to set the affairs of the kingdom in order.*

Her son arrived for an undisputed coronation in the summer of 1189.
But Richard's thoughts in that triumphal summer season were not
upon the affairs of England or any of his other lands. He had already
taken the cross almost two years before, and the third crusade was about
to begin. The Lion-Hearted was to be its greatest hero.
The third crusade, despite Richard's heroics, was as unsuccessful as the
second. And, after three years, during which most of his fellow crusaders
had declared their vows discharged and returned to their own lands—
including his Capetian rival, Philip Augustus—Richard started for home.
We pick up the story of his return—with its delays and betrayals—
and of Eleanor's role in it from her most recent biography, by Marian
Meade, Eleanor of Aquitaine, A Biography. Meade's book is broadly
revisionist, and the basis of her revisionism is her feminist sympathy. She
observes that "the historical record, written to accommodate men" has
judged Eleanor ". . . a bitch, harlot, adultress, and monster" and that
this is not surprising "for she was one of those rare women who altogether
refused to be bound by the rules of proper behavior for her sex; she did
as she pleased, although not without agonizing personal struggle"
(p. ix). In Meade's account, as in any other account of Eleanor, there is
much latitude for interpretation, given the pervasive silence of
contemporary chronicles. Meade further argues that even these are
"riddled with lies since monks and historians—in the twelfth century one
and the same—have always abhorred emancipated women" (p. xi).
Meade intends to redress the balance. And she does so, in no part of her
account more forcefully than in the following passage.

IN ENGLAND, Eleanor was expecting her son home for Christmas. All
through November and early December companies of Crusaders had
begun arriving in the kingdom; in the ports and marketplaces there were
firsthand reports of the king's deeds in Palestine and plans for celebrations
once he arrived. But the days passed without news, and newly arrived
contingents of soldiers expressed astonishment that they had beaten the
king home although they had left Acre after Richard. Along the coast,
lookouts peered into the foggy Channel in hope of sighting the royal ves-
sel, and messengers waited to race over the frozen roads toward London
with the news of the king's landing. Eleanor learned that Berengaria and
Joanna [2] had safely reached Rome, but of her son, weeks overdue, there
was an alarming lack of information. She held a cheerless Christmas court
at Westminster, her apprehension mounting with each day, her silent fears
being expressed openly in the ale houses along the Thames: The king had

[2] Berengaria was Richard's wife—a Spanish princess he had married, at Eleanor's
urging, on his way to the crusade. Joanna was Richard's sister, the widowed Queen
of Sicily, whom he had taken under his protection to Palestine.—ED.

encountered some calamity, a storm along the Adriatic coast no doubt, and now he would never return.

Three days after Christmas, the whereabouts of the tardy Richard Plantagenet became known, not at Westminster but at the Cité Palace in Paris. On December 28, Philip Augustus received an astounding letter from his good friend Henry Hohenstaufen, the Holy Roman emperor: [3]

> We have thought it proper to inform your nobleness that while the enemy of our empire and the disturber of your kingdom, Richard, King of England, was crossing the sea to his dominions, it chanced that the winds caused him to be shipwrecked in the region of Istria, at a place which lies between Aquila and Venice. . . . The roads being duly watched and the entire area well-guarded, our dearly beloved cousin Leopold, Duke of Austria, captured the king in a humble house in a village near Vienna. Inasmuch as he is now in our power, and has always done his utmost for your annoyance and disturbance, we have thought it proper to relay this information to your nobleness.

Shortly after the first of the new year, 1193, the archbishop of Rouen was able to send Eleanor a copy of the letter, accompanied by a covering note in which he cited whatever comforting quotations he could recall from Scripture to cover an outrage of this magnitude.

Eleanor's most imperative problem—finding the location where Richard was being held prisoner—she tackled with her usual energy and resourcefulness. From all points, emissaries were dispatched to find the king: Eleanor herself sent the abbots of Boxley and Pontrobert to roam the villages of Bavaria and Swabia, following every lead and rumor; Hubert Walter, bishop of Salisbury, stopping in Italy on his way home from the Crusade, changed course and hastened to Germany; even William Longchamp, the exiled chancellor, set out at once from Paris to trace his master. It was not until March, however, that Richard's chaplain, Anselm, who had shared many of the king's misadventures, arrived in England, and Eleanor was able to obtain authentic details [including the fact that Richard was being held in a remote castle of Durrenstein in Austria].

Treachery was rife not only in Germany but in Paris and Rouen; it even percolated rapidly in the queen's own family. Before Eleanor could take steps to secure Coeur de Lion's release, she was faced with more immediate catastrophes in the form of Philip Augustus and his newest ally, her son John. These two proceeded on the assumption that Richard, king of England, was dead. Or as good as dead. But before Eleanor could take her youngest son in hand, he fled to Normandy, where he declared him-

---

[3] The Plantagenet kings were related by marriage to the great German feudal family, the Welfs, who were the most dangerous rivals to the imperial house of Hohenstaufen. The Angevins, including Richard, had frequently supported the Welfs, hence the emperor's hostility.—ED.

self the king's heir, an announcement the Norman barons greeted with disdain. John did not wait to convince them, proceeding instead to Paris, where he did homage to Philip for the Plantagenet Continental domains and furthermore agreeing to confirm Philip's right to the Vexin.[4] . . . In the meantime, Eleanor, "who then ruled England," had taken the precaution of closing the Channel ports and ordering the defense of the eastern coast against a possible invasion, her hastily mustered home guard being instructed to wield any weapon that came to hand, including their plowing tools.

At this point, Eleanor's dilemma in regard to her sons would have taxed the most patient of mothers. John, returning to England, swaggered about the countryside proclaiming himself the next king of England —perhaps he sincerely believed that Richard would never be released alive—and, never known for his sensitivity, constantly regaled Eleanor with the latest rumors concerning the fate of her favorite son. Her actions during this period indicate clearly that she failed to take John seriously. Although he was twenty-seven, she thought of him as the baby of the family, always a child showing off and trying to attract attention. Her attitude was probably close to that of Richard's when, a few months later, he was informed of John's machinations: "My brother John is not the man to subjugate a country if there is a person able to make the slightest resistance to his attempts." With one hand, Eleanor deftly managed to anticipate John's plots and render him harmless; with the other, she worked for Richard's release. After Easter, the king had been removed from Durrenstein Castle and the hands of Duke Leopold and, after some haggling, had been taken into custody by Leopold's suzerain, the Holy Roman emperor. As the emperor's prisoner, Richard found himself the object of high-level decisions. His death, it was decided, would achieve no useful purpose; rather the arrogant Plantagenets, or what remained of them, should be made to redeem their kin, but at a price that would bring their provinces to their knees: 100,000 silver marks with two hundred hostages as surety for payment. The hostages, it was specified, were to be chosen from among the leading barons of England and Normandy or from their children.

Relieved as Eleanor must have felt to learn that her son could be purchased, she could only have been appalled at the size of the ransom. The prospect of collecting such an enormous sum, thirty-five tons of pure silver, seemed impossible after Henry's Saladin tithe [5] and Richard's great sale before the Crusade.[6] Where was the money to be found? Where were two hundred noble hostages to be located? At a council convened at Saint

---

[4] The Vexin was an area at the juncture of Normandy, Anjou, and the Ile de France, long disputed by the English and French kings.—ED.

[5] A tax that Henry had levied for a crusade, hence called after the great Moslem leader Saladin.—ED.

[6] A sale not only of movable property of the crown but that of such protected folk as foreign and Jewish merchants, and what could be extracted from the nobility.—ED.

Albans on June 1, 1193, she appointed five officers to assist with the dreaded task. During the summer and fall, England became a marketplace to raise the greatest tax in its history. The kingdom was stripped of its wealth: "No subject, lay or clerk, rich or poor, was overlooked. No one could say, 'Behold I am only So-and-So or Such-and-Such, pray let me be excused.'" Barons were taxed one-quarter of a year's income. Churches and abbeys were relieved of their movable wealth, including the crosses on their altars. The Cistercians, who possessed no riches, sheared their flocks and donated a year's crop of wool. Before long, the bars of silver and gold began slowly to pile up in the crypt of Saint Paul's Cathedral under Eleanor's watchful eyes. But not quickly enough to comfort her. Even more painful was the job of recruiting hostages from the great families, their lamentations and pleadings rising like a sulphurous mist all over the kingdom and providing constant agony for the queen.

From Haguenau, where Richard was incarcerated, came a flood of letters to his subjects and most especially to his "much loved mother." He had been received with honor by the emperor and his court, he is well, he hopes to be home soon. He realizes that the ransom will be difficult to raise but he feels sure that his subjects will not shirk their duty; all sums collected should be entrusted to the queen. . . .

It is said that in her anguish she addressed three letters to Pope Celestine III imploring his assistance in securing Richard's release and in her salutation addressed the pontiff as "Eleanor, by the wrath of God, Queen of England." . . . Why, she demands, does the sword of Saint Peter slumber in its scabbard when her son a "most delicate youth," the anointed of the Lord, lies in chains? Why does the pope, a "negligent," "cruel" prevaricator and sluggard, do nothing?

These letters, supposedly written for her by Peter of Blois, are so improbable that it is surprising that many modern historians have accepted them as authentic. While preserved among the letters of Peter of Blois, who is undoubtedly their author—they are characteristic of his style and use his favorite expressions—there is no evidence that they were written for Eleanor or that they were ever sent. Most likely they were rhetorical exercises. No contemporary of Eleanor's mentioned that she wrote to the pope, and not until the seventeenth century were the letters attributed to her. From a diplomatic point of view, they are too fanciful to be genuine; Eleanor, clearheaded and statesmanlike, was never a querulous old woman complaining of age, infirmities, and weariness of life. On the contrary, her contemporaries unanimously credit her with the utmost courage, industry, and political skill. A second point to notice is that the details of the letters misrepresent the facts of Richard's imprisonment. He was never "detained in bonds," and as both she and the pope knew, Celestine had instantly, upon receiving news of Richard's capture, excommunicated Duke Leopold for laying violent hands on a brother Crusader; he had threatened Philip Augustus with an interdict if he trespassed upon Plantagenet territories; and he had menaced the English with interdict should they fail to collect the ransom. Under the circumstances, Celestine had done all he could. In the last analysis, the letters must be viewed as Peter of Blois's perception of Eleanor's feelings, a view that may or may not be accurate.

In December 1193, Eleanor set sail with an imposing retinue of clerks, chaplains, earls, bishops, hostages, and chests containing the ransom. By January 17, 1194, the day scheduled for Richard's release, she had presented herself and the money at Speyer, but no sooner had they arrived than, to her amazement, Henry Hohenstaufen announced a further delay. He had received letters that placed an entirely new light on the matter of the king's liberation. As the gist of the problem emerged, it seemed Philip Augustus and John Plantagenet had offered the emperor an equivalent amount of silver if he could hold Coeur de Lion in custody another nine months, or deliver him up to them. These disclosures, and Henry's serious consideration of the counteroffer, provoked horror from the emperor's own vassals, and after two days of argument, Henry relented. He would liberate Richard as promised if the king of England would do homage to him for all his possessions, including the kingdom of England. This request, a calculated humiliation, would have made Richard a vassal of the Holy Roman emperor, a degradation that the Plantagenets were hard put to accept. Quick to realize the meaninglessness, as well as the illegality, of the required act, Eleanor made an on-the-spot decision. According to Roger of Hovedon, Richard, "by advice of his mother Eleanor, abdicated the throne of the kingdom of England and delivered it to the emperor as the lord of all." On February 4, the king was released "into the hands of his mother" after a captivity of one year six weeks and three days.

Seven weeks later, on March 12, the king's party landed at Sandwich and proceeded directly to Canterbury, where they gave thanks at the tomb of Saint Thomas. By the time they reached London, the city had been decorated, the bells were clanging furiously, and the Londoners ready to give a rapturous welcome to their hero and champion. Her eldest son "hailed with joy upon the Strand," Eleanor looked in vain for the remaining male member of her family, but the youngest Plantagenet was nowhere to be found. Once Richard's release had been confirmed, he had fled to Paris upon Philip Augustus's warning that "beware, the devil is loose." . . .

According to the chronicles, "the king and John became reconciled through the mediation of Queen Eleanor, their mother." In the circumstances, it seemed the safest course as well as the wisest. There was no doubt in Eleanor's mind that the boy, now twenty-eight, could not be held responsible for his actions, that he was, as Richard of Devizes termed him, "light-minded." But at that moment, he was the last of the Plantagenets. With luck, Richard might reign another twenty-five years or more. Who was to say that he would not produce an heir of his own? Thus the queen must have reasoned in the spring of 1194 when her son, after so many adversities, had come home to her.

Suggestions for Further Reading

SEVERAL OF THE general works listed for the last chapter will also be useful for this one since Abelard and Eleanor of Aquitaine were both figures of the twelfth century. But, as we have seen, despite her importance and inherent interest there are virtually no contemporary source materials for Eleanor. Thus, whether hostile or sympathetic, the treatments of Eleanor have had to be not so much biographies as life-and-times books. This is true even of the best modern works. Two of them, Amy Kelly, *Eleanor of Aquitaine and the Four Kings* (Cambridge, Mass.: Harvard University Press, 1950), and Marion Meade, *Eleanor of Aquitaine, A Biography* (New York: Hawthorn, 1977), are excerpted in this chapter, and students are encouraged to read further in them. Two additional works are also recommended: Curtis H. Walker, *Eleanor of Aquitaine* (Chapel Hill: University of North Carolina Press, 1950), and Regine Pernoud, *Eleanor of Aquitaine*, tr. P. Wiles (New York: Coward-McCann, 1967), both well written, lively, and fast moving. *Eleanor of Aquitaine, Patron and Politician*, ed. Wm. W. Kibler (Austin: University of Texas Press, 1976), is a series of specialized papers on aspects of Eleanor's life and reign.

Of Eleanor's contemporaries, the best, most comprehensive, and up-to-date work on Henry II is W. L. Warren, *Henry II* (London: Eyre Methuen, 1973). Somewhat less intimidating are the smaller but entirely competent Richard Barber, *Henry Plantagenet* (Totowa, N.J.: Rowman and Littlefield, 1964), and John Schlight, *Henry II Plantagenet*, "Rulers and Statesmen of the World" (New York: Twayne, 1973). Probably the best biography of Richard I is Philip Henderson, *Richard Coeur de Lion, A Biography* (New York: Norton, 1959), but students are also encouraged to read James A. Brundage, *Richard Lion Heart* (New York: Scribners, 1974), largely a study of Richard as soldier and crusader and a tough, realistic work. The standard work on John is Sidney Painter, *The Reign of King John* (Baltimore: Johns Hopkins University Press, 1949). W. J. Warren, *King John* (New York: Norton, 1961), is a somewhat revisionist treatment of John showing him as a hard-working monarch and more the victim than the causer of his troubles—but he still is a far from attractive figure. For Eleanor's French royal contemporaries see R. Fawtier, *The Capetian Kings of France*, tr. Lionel Butler and R. J. Adam (London: Macmillan, 1960). There are a handful of studies of important nonroyal figures whose lives intertwined with Eleanor's: Sidney Painter, *William Marshall, Knight Errant, Baron, and Regent of England* (Baltimore: Johns Hopkins University Press, 1933); Charles

R. Young, *Hubert Walter, Lord of Canterbury and Lord of England* (Durham, N.C.: Duke University Press, 1968); and a number of books on the durable subject of Henry and Becket—the best are Richard Winston, *Thomas Becket* (New York: Knopf, 1967), a tough, skeptical, but solidly source-based work; Dom David Knowles, *Thomas Becket* (London: A. and C. Black, 1970), a scrupulously objective account by a great ecclesiastical historian, but, naturally, most occupied with the arguments of Thomas and the church; and finally, Alfred L. Duggan, *My Life for My Sheep* (New York: Coward-McCann, 1955), a lively novelized account by an experienced historical novelist.

Two special topics relate to Eleanor throughout her life—chivalry and courtly love and the crusades. Both have been much studied and written about. On chivalry and courtly love, see two excellent and well-written background works—John C. Moore, *Love in Twelfth-Century France* (Philadelphia: University of Pennsylvania Press, 1972), and Jack Lindsay, *The Troubadours and Their World of the Twelfth and Thirteenth Centuries* (London: Frederick Muller, 1976), and two equally interesting ones dealing with the actual operation of knightly chivalry as well as its romanticized literary aspects—Sidney Painter, *French Chivalry, Chivalric Ideas and Practices in Medieval France* (Baltimore: Johns Hopkins University Press, 1940), and the more comprehensive Richard Barber, *The Knight and Chivalry* (New York: Scribners, 1970). The standard work on the crusades is now *The History of the Crusades* (Philadelphia: University of Pennsylvania Press, 1955–1962), a great multiauthored work under the general editorship of Kenneth M. Setton: vol. 1, *The First Hundred Years*, ed. M. W. Baldwin, and vol. 2, *The Later Crusades, 1189–1311*, ed. R. L. Wolff. Steven Runciman, *A History of the Crusades*, 3 vols. (Cambridge, England: Cambridge University Press, 1951–1954), may, however, still be the best account. Students may prefer Zoé Oldenbourg, *The Crusaders,* tr. Anne Carter (New York: Pantheon, 1966), somewhat less successful than her famous historical novels but still excellent and exciting.

The Meaning
of Dante

The ambitious title of this chapter does not announce a new breakthrough in Dante scholarship. It refers instead to the sampling of views presented here from the incredible volume of writing that has been done in an attempt to determine what Dante means—as historical figure, as historical symbol, or as a symbol of eternal truths. The need to "interpret" Dante in order to discover his meaning arises in part from the great complexity and range of his work and its seeming obscurity to many modern readers and in part from the contradictory rather than conforming nature of Dante himself.

In his youth Dante fought for the Guelf cause and was a functionary of Guelf Florence. As a mature exile he reviled his city—"ingrato popolo maligno"—revived classical Ghibellinism, made an unlikely hero of the Emperor Henry VII, and lodged Pope Boniface VIII in hell! Although he remained a layman, Dante was as learned in theology as any clerical theologian of his time. He wrote a book defending the use of the vernacular, but he wrote it in Latin, *De Vulgari Eloquentia,* and then chose to write his greatest work, *The Divine Comedy,* in the vernacular Italian.

The problem of interpreting Dante is further complicated by the nature of our information about him. Dante was reticent and prickly, stiff, aloof, and secretive about himself, and, as a result, few of the routine facts of his life were recorded. We have, of course, the great corpus of his work, which even contains, in the *Vita Nuova,* what one scholar has called "one of the great spiritual autobiographies of all time." But Dante himself leaves many important questions unanswered, and his contemporaries are not much more helpful. In spite of the fact that Dante was the most famous poet of his time, with an international reputation and following, he had no contemporary biographer. The earliest life of Dante appeared some half century after his death, written by his fellow Florentine, Giovanni Boccaccio.

The Life of Dante
BOCCACCIO

*Boccaccio (1313–1375), like Dante earlier, was one of the most celebrated
literary figures of his own generation. Yet his* Vita di Dante *is, in many
respects, an unsatisfactory biography. The humanist Leonardo Bruni,
who wrote a short sketch of Dante still another generation later, found
it so. He took Boccaccio to task for his failure to collect the physical
evidence about Dante's life and the recollections of contemporaries
while they were still available. He criticized him for dwelling on the poet
rather than the man. But Boccaccio, a poet himself, was much more
interested in this aspect of his subject. We owe to Boccaccio the first body
of serious, systematic Dante criticism, as well as the earliest biography.
Indeed, Boccaccio was drawn to Dante in many ways and for many
reasons, not the least of which was that Boccaccio was a master of the
Italian language second only to Dante among its early literary users.*

*But the generation gap between Dante and Boccaccio was also an
important factor. For, unlike Dante, Boccaccio clearly lived across
whatever line we may use to separate the Middle Ages from the
Renaissance. Moreover, he was not only "in" but "of" the early
Renaissance. He was a friend and disciple of Petrarch, "the Father of
Humanism," and, while he did not share his master's snobbish disdain
for the vernacular, he adopted a great many of his other notions and
prejudices. One of these was a propensity to see the age in which he
lived as a new age—"novus ordo saeculorum"—rather sharply set off from
the barbaric period of the recent past, which later humanists would
contemptuously dub "the Middle Ages," "the Dark Ages," or "the Gothic
Age." And in his enthusiasm for Dante, Boccaccio tended to carry him
across into his own new age, to view him as the first "modern" poet who
had rescued literary art from the darkness, obscurity, and ignorance in
which it had languished since antiquity.*

We turn now to Boccaccio's account from The Life of Dante.

. . . I AM GOING to record the banishment of that most illustrious man,
Dante Alighieri, an ancient citizen and born of no mean parents, who
merited as much through his virtue, learning, and good services as is
adequately shown and will be shown by the deeds he wrought. If such
deeds had been done in a just republic, we believe they would have earned
for him the highest rewards.

O iniquitous design! O shameless deed! O wretched example, clear proof of ruin to come! Instead of these rewards there was meted to him an unjust and bitter condemnation, perpetual banishment with alienation of his paternal goods, and, could it have been effected, the profanation of his glorious renown by false charges. The recent traces of his flight, his bones buried in an alien land, and his children scattered in the houses of others, still in part bear witness to these things. If all the other iniquities of Florence could be hidden from the all-seeing eyes of God, should not this one suffice to provoke his wrath upon her? Yea, in truth. . . .

But inasmuch as we should not only flee evil deeds, albeit they seem to go unpunished, but also by right action should strive to amend them, I, although not fitted for so great a task, will try to do according to my little talent what the city should have done with magnificence, but has not. For I recognize that I am a part, though a small one, of that same city whereof Dante Alighieri, if his merits, his nobleness, and his virtue be considered, was a very great part, and that for this reason I, like every other citizen, am personally responsible for the honors due him. Not with a statue shall I honor him, nor with splendid obsequies—which customs no longer hold among us, nor would my powers suffice therefor—but with words I shall honor him, feeble though they be for so great an undertaking. Of these I have, and of these will I give, that other nations may not say that his native land, both as a whole and in part, has been equally ungrateful to so great a poet. . . .

This special glory of Italy was born in our city in the year of the saving incarnation of the King of the universe 1265, when the Roman Empire was without a ruler owing to the death of the [Emperor] Frederick, and Pope Urban the Fourth was sitting in the chair of Saint Peter. The family into which he was born was of a smiling fortune—smiling, I mean, if we consider the condition of the world that then obtained. I will omit all consideration of his infancy—whatever it may have been—wherein appeared many signs of the coming glory of his genius. But I will note that from his earliest boyhood, having already learned the rudiments of letters, he gave himself and all his time, not to youthful lust and indolence, after the fashion of the nobles of to-day, lolling at ease in the lap of his mother, but to continued study, in his native city, of the liberal arts, so that he became exceedingly expert therein. And as his mind and genius ripened with his years, he devoted himself, not to lucrative pursuits, whereto every one in general now hastens, but, with a laudable desire for perpetual fame, scorning transitory riches, he freely dedicated himself to the acquisition of a complete knowledge of poetic creations and of their exposition by rules of art. In this exercise he became closely intimate with Virgil, Horace, Ovid, Statius, and with every other famous poet. And not only did he delight to know them, but he strove to imitate them in lofty song, even as his works demonstrate, whereof we shall speak at the proper time. . . .

. . . . And to the end that no region of philosophy should remain unvisited by him, he penetrated with acute genius into the profoundest depths of theology. Nor was the result far distant from the aim. Unmindful of heat and cold, vigils and fasts, and every other physical hardship, by assiduous study he grew to such knowledge of the Divine Essence and of the other Separate Intelligences as can be compassed here by the human intellect. And as by application various sciences were learned by him at various periods, so he mastered them in various studies under various teachers. . . .

Studies in general, and speculative studies in particular—to which, as has been shown, our Dante wholly applied himself—usually demand solitude, remoteness from care, and tranquility of mind. Instead of this retirement and quiet, Dante had, almost from the beginning of his life down to the day of his death, a violent and insufferable passion of love, a wife, domestic and public cares, exile, and poverty, not to mention those more particular cares which these necessarily involve. The former I deem it fitting to explain in detail, in order that their burden may appear the greater.

In that season wherein the sweetness of heaven reclothes the earth with all its adornments, and makes her all smiling with varied flowers scattered among green leaves, the custom obtained in our city that men and women should keep festival in different gatherings, each person in his neighborhood. And so it chanced that among others Folco Portinari, a man held in great esteem among his fellow-citizens, on the first day of May gathered his neighbors in his house for a feast. Now among these came the aforementioned Alighieri, followed by Dante, who was still in his ninth year; for little children are wont to follow their fathers, especially to places of festival. And mingling here in the house of the feast-giver with others of his own age, of whom there were many, both boys and girls, when the first tables had been served he boyishly entered with the others into the games, so far as his tender age permitted.

Now amid the throng of children was a little daughter of the aforesaid Folco, whose name was Bice, though he always called her by her full name, Beatrice. She was, it may be, eight years old, very graceful for her age, full gentle and pleasing in her actions, and much more serious and modest in her words and ways than her few years required. Her features were most delicate and perfectly proportioned, and, in addition to their beauty, full of such pure loveliness that many thought her almost a little angel. She, then, such as I picture her, or it may be far more beautiful, appeared at this feast to the eyes of our Dante; not, I suppose, for the first time, but for the first time with power to inspire him with love. And he, though still a child, received the lovely image of her into his heart with so great affection that it never left him from that day forward so long as he lived.

Now just what this affection was no one knows, but certainly it is true that Dante at an early age became a most ardent servitor of love. . . .

Forsaking, therefore, all other matters, with the utmost solicitude he went wherever he thought he might see her, as if he were to attain from her face and her eyes all his happiness and complete consolation.

O insensate judgment of lovers! who but they would think to check the flames by adding to the fuel? Dante himself in his *Vita Nuova* in part makes known how many and of what nature were the thoughts, the sighs, the tears, and the other grievous passions that he later suffered by reason of this love, wherefore I do not care to rehearse them more in detail. This much alone I do not wish to pass over without mention, namely, that according as he himself writes, and as others to whom his passion was known bear witness, this love was most virtuous, nor did there ever appear by look or word or sign any sensual appetite either in the lover or in the thing beloved; no little marvel to the present world, from which all innocent pleasure has so fled, and which is so accustomed to have the thing that pleases it conform to its lust before it has concluded to love it, that he who loves otherwise has become a miracle, even as a thing most rare.

If such love for so long season could interrupt his eating, his sleep, and every quietness, how great an enemy must we think it to have been to his sacred studies and to his genius? Certainly no mean one, although many maintain that it urged his genius on, and argue for proof from his graceful rimed compositions in the Florentine idiom, written in praise of his beloved and for the expression of his ardors and amorous conceits. But truly I should not agree with this, unless I first admitted that ornate writing is the most essential part of every science—which is not true.

As every one may plainly perceive, there is nothing stable in this world, and, if anything is subject to change, it is our life. A trifle too much cold or heat within us, not to mention countless other accidents and possibilities, easily leads us from existence to non-existence. Nor is gentle birth privileged against this, nor riches, nor youth, nor any other worldly dignity. Dante must needs experience the force of this general law by another's death before he did by his own. The most beautiful Beatrice was near the end of her twenty-fourth year when, as it pleased Him who governs all things, she left the sufferings of this world, and passed to the glory that her virtues had prepared for her.

. . . By her departure Dante was thrown into such sorrow, such grief and tears, that many of those nearest him, both relatives and friends, believed that death alone would end them. They expected that this would shortly come to pass, seeing that he gave no ear to the comfort and consolation offered him. The days were like the nights, and the nights like the days. Not an hour of them passed without groans, and sighs, and an abundant quantity of tears. His eyes seemed two copious springs of welling water, so that most men wondered whence he received moisture enough for his weeping. . . .

In Dante's time the citizens of Florence were perversely divided into two factions, and by the operations of astute and prudent leaders each party was very powerful, so that sometimes one ruled and sometimes the other, to the displeasure of its defeated rival. . . .

Dante decided, then, to pursue the fleeting honor and false glory of public office. Perceiving that he could not support by himself a third party, which, in itself just, should overthrow the injustice of the two others and reduce them to unity, he allied himself with that faction which seemed to him to possess most of justice and reason—working always for that which he recognized as salutary to his country and her citizens. But human counsels are commonly defeated by the powers of heaven. Hatred and enmities arose, though without just cause, and waxed greater day by day; so that many times the citizens rushed to arms, to their utmost confusion. They purposed to end the struggle by fire and sword, and were so blinded by wrath that they did not see that they themselves would perish miserably thereby.

After each of the factions had given many proofs of their strength to their mutual loss, the time came when the secret counsels of threatening Fortune were to be disclosed. Rumor, who reports both the true and the false, announced that the foes of Dante's faction were strengthened by wise and wonderful designs and by an immense multitude of armed men, and by this means so terrified the leaders of his party that she banished from their minds all consideration, all forethought, all reason, save how to flee in safety. Together with them Dante, instantly precipitated from the chief rule of his city, beheld himself not only brought low to the earth, but banished from his country. Not many days after this expulsion, when the populace had already rushed to the houses of the exiles, and had furiously pillaged and gutted them, the victors reorganized the city after their pleasure, condemning all the leaders of their adversaries to perpetual exile as capital enemies of the republic, and with them Dante, not as one of the lesser leaders, but as it were the chief one. Their real property was meanwhile confiscated or alienated to the victors.

This reward Dante gained for the tender love which he had borne his country! . . .

In such wise, then, Dante left that city whereof not only he was a citizen, but of which his ancestors had been the rebuilders. . . .

Boccaccio recounts Dante's exile and his wandering from court to court, city to city, and his hopes for a restoration of order in Italy dashed by the death of the Emperor Henry VII.

Since all hope, though not the desire, of ever returning to Florence was gone, Dante continued in Ravenna several years, under the protection of its gracious lord. And here he taught and trained many scholars in poetry, and especially in the vernacular, which he first, in my opinion, exalted and made esteemed among us Italians, even as Homer did his tongue among the Greeks, and Virgil his among the Latins. Although the vulgar tongue is supposed to have originated some time before him, none thought or dared to make the language an instrument of any artistic matter, save in the numbering of syllables, and in the consonance of its endings. They employed it, rather, in the light things of love. Dante showed in effect that every lofty subject could be treated of in this medium, and made our vulgar tongue above all others glorious.

But even as the appointed hour comes for every man, so Dante also, at or near the middle of his fifty-sixth year, fell ill. And having humbly and devoutly received the sacraments of the Church according to the Christian religion, and having reconciled himself to God in contrition for all that he, as a mortal, had committed against His pleasure, in the month of September in the year of Christ 1321, on the day whereon the Exaltation of the Holy Cross is celebrated by the Church, not without great sorrow on the part of the aforesaid Guido and in general of all the other citizens of Ravenna, he rendered to his Creator his weary spirit. . . .

Our poet was of moderate height, and, after reaching maturity, was accustomed to walk somewhat bowed, with a slow and gentle pace, clad always in such sober dress as befitted his ripe years. His face was long, his nose aquiline, and his eyes rather large than small. His jaws were large, and the lower lip protruded beyond the upper. His complexion was dark, his hair and beard thick, black, and curled, and his expression ever melancholy and thoughtful.

Our poet, in addition . . . was of a lofty and disdainful spirit. On one occasion a friend, moved by entreaties, labored that Dante might return to Florence—which thing the poet desired above all else—but he found no way thereto with those who then held the government in their hands save that Dante should remain in prison for a certain time, and after that be presented as a subject for mercy at some public solemnity in our principal church, whereby he should be free and exempt from all sentences previously passed upon him. But this seemed to Dante a fitting procedure for abject, if not infamous, men and for no others. Therefore, notwithstanding his great desire, he chose to remain in exile rather than return home by such a road. O laudable and magnanimous scorn, how manfully hast thou acted in repressing the ardent desire to return, when it was only possible by a way unworthy of a man nourished in the bosom of philosophy! . . .

This glorious poet composed many works during his lifetime, an orderly arrangement of which would, I think, be fitting, in order that his works may not be attributed to some one else, and that the works of another may not be ascribed to him.

In the first place, while his tears still flowed for the death of Beatrice, in his twenty-sixth year or thereabouts, he brought together in a little volume, entitled *Vita Nuova*, certain marvelously beautiful pieces in rime, like sonnets and canzoni, which he had previously written at various times.

Before each one he wrote in order the causes that had led him to compose it, and after each one he placed its divisions. Although in his maturer years he was greatly ashamed of this little book, nevertheless, if his age be considered, it is very beautiful and pleasing, especially to the common people.

. . . Having long premeditated what was to be done, in his thirty-fifth year he began to put into effect what he had before deliberated upon, namely, to censure and reward the lives of men according to the diversity of their merits. And inasmuch as he saw that life was of three sorts—the vicious life, the life of departing from vice and advancing toward virtue, and the virtuous life—he admirably divided his work, which he entitled *Commedia*, into three books, in the first of which he censured the wicked and in the last rewarded the good. The three books he again divided into cantos, and the cantos into rhythms (*ritmi*), as may be plainly seen. He composed it in rime and in the vernacular with such art, and in so wonderful and beautiful an order, that there has yet been none who could justly find any fault therewith.

The Historical Dante
HENRY OSBORN TAYLOR

Although at the present time Dante is usually considered to be at least a transitional figure between the Middle Ages and the Renaissance, historians have traditionally viewed him as the summation of all the trends and tendencies of the Middle Ages. No one exemplifies this interpretive approach better than the American medievalist Henry Osborn Taylor (d. 1941). Taylor's most important book was his massive, brilliant, and original The Mediaeval Mind, *still one of the standard works in medieval intellectual history. The following selection is from the chapter on Dante, subtitled "The Mediaeval Synthesis," in which Dante is seen as bringing together all the strands of medieval thought and temperament.*

. . . [DANTE] IS NOT merely mediaeval; he is the end of the mediaeval development and the proper issue of the mediaeval genius.

Yes, there is unity throughout the diversity of mediaeval life; and Dante is the proof. For the elements of mediaeval growth combine in him, demonstrating their congruity by working together in the stature of the fullgrown mediaeval man. When the contents of patristic Christianity and the surviving antique culture had been conceived anew, and had been felt as well, and novel forms of sentiment evolved, at last comes Dante to possess the whole, to think it, feel it, visualize its sum, and make of it a poem. He had mastered the field of mediaeval knowledge, diligently cultivating parts of it, like the Graeco-Arabian astronomy; he thought and reasoned in the terms and assumptions of scholastic (chiefly Thomist-Aristotelian) philosophy; his intellectual interests were mediaeval; he felt the mediaeval reverence for the past, being impassioned with the ancient greatness of Rome and the lineage of virtue and authority moving from it to him and thirteenth-century Italy and the already shattered Holy Roman Empire. He took earnest joy in the Latin Classics, approaching them from mediaeval points of view, accepting their contents uncritically. He was affected with the preciosity of courtly or chivalric love, which Italy had made her own along with the songs of the Troubadours and the poetry of northern France. His emotions flowed in channels of current convention, save that they overfilled them; this was true as to his early love, and true as to his final range of religious and poetic feeling. His was the emotion and the cruelty of mediaeval religious conviction; while in his mind (so worked the genius of symbolism) every fact's apparent meaning was clothed with the significance of other modes of truth.

Dante was also an Italian of the period in which he lived; and he was a marvellous poet. One may note in him what was mediaeval, what was specifically Italian, and what, apparently, was personal. This scholar could not but draw his education, his views of life and death, his dominant inclinations and the large currents of his purpose, from the antecedent mediaeval period and the still greater past which had worked upon it so mightily. His Italian nature and environment gave point and piquancy and very concrete life to these mediaeval elements; and his personal genius produced from it all a supreme poetic creation.

The Italian part of Dante comes between the mediaeval and the personal, as species comes between the genus and the individual. The tremendous feeling which he discloses for the Roman past seems, in him, specifically Italian: child of Italy, he holds himself a Latin and a direct heir of the Republic. Yet often his attitude toward the antique will be that of mediaeval men in general, as in his disposition to accept ancient myth for fact; while his own genius appears in his beautifully apt appropriation of the Virgilian incident or image; wherein he excels his "Mantuan" master, whose borrowings from Homer were not always felicitous. Frequently the specifically Italian in Dante, his yearning hate of Florence, for example, may scarcely be distinguished from his personal temper; but its civic bitterness is different from the feudal animosities or promiscuous rages which were more generically mediaeval. . . .

Again, Dante's arguments in the *De monarchia* seem to be those of an Italian Ghibelline. Yet beyond his intense realization of Italy's direct succession to the Roman past, his reasoning is scholastic and mediaeval, or springs occasionally from his own reflections. The Italian contribution to the book tends to coalesce either with the general or the personal elements. . . .

The *De vulgari eloquentia* illustrates the difference between Dante accepting and reproducing mediaeval views, and Dante thinking for himself. . . . And in the *De Vulgari Eloquentia,* as in the *Convivio,* Dante is deeply conscious of the worth of the Romance vernacular. . . .

Certainly the *Convivio* gives evidence touching the writer's mental processes and the interests of his mind. Except for its lofty advocacy of the *volgare* and its personal apologetic references, it contains little that is not blankly mediaeval. . . . [A] significant phrase may be drawn from it: "Philosophy is a loving use of wisdom (*uno amoroso uso di sapienza*) which chiefly is in God, since in Him is utmost wisdom, utmost love, and utmost actuality." A loving use of wisdom—with Dante the pursuit of knowledge was no mere intellectual search, but a pilgrimage of the whole nature, loving heart as well as knowing mind, and the working virtues too. This pilgrimage is set forth in the *Commedia,* perhaps the supreme creation of the Middle Ages, and a work that by reason of the beautiful affinity of its speech with Latin, exquisitely expressed the matters which in Latin had been coming to formulation through the mediaeval centuries.

The *Commedia* (*Inferno, Purgatorio, Paradiso*) is a *Summa,* a *Summa salvationis,* a sum of saving knowledge. It is such just as surely as the final work of Aquinas is a *Summa theologiae.* But Aquinas was the supreme mediaeval theologian-philosopher, while Dante was the supreme theologian-poet; and with both Aquinas and Dante, theology includes the knowledge of all things, but chiefly of man in relation to God. Such was the matter of the *divina scientia* of Thomas, and such was the subject of the *Commedia,* which was soon recognized as the *Divina Commedia* in the very sense in which Theology was the divine science. The *Summa* of Thomas was *scientia* not only in substance, but in form; the *Commedia* was *scientia,* or *sapientia,* in substance, while in form it was a poem, the epic of man the pilgrim of salvation. . . . The *Commedia* rested upon the entire evolution of the Middle Ages. Therein had lain its spiritual preparation. To be sure it had its casual forerunners (*precursori*): narratives, real or feigned, of men faring to the regions of the dead. But these signified little; for everywhere thoughts of the other life pressed upon men's mind: fear of it blanched their hearts; its heavenly or hellish messengers had been seen, and not a few men dreamed that they had walked within those gates and witnessed clanging horrors or purgatorial pain. Heaven had been more rarely visited.

Dante gave little attention to any so-called "forerunners," save only two, Paul and Virgil. The former was a warrant for the poet's reticence as to the manner of his ascent to Heaven; the latter supplied much of his scheme of Hell. . . .

One observes mediaeval characteristics in the *Commedia* raised to a higher power. The mediaeval period was marked by contrasts of quality and of conduct such as cannot be found in the antique or the modern age. And what other poem can vie with the *Commedia* in contrasts of the beautiful and the loathsome, the heavenly and the hellish, exquisite refinement of expression and lapses into the reverse, love and hate, pity and cruelty, reverence and disdain? These contrasts not only are presented by the story; they evince themselves in the character of the author. Many scenes of the *Inferno* are loathsome: Dante's own words and conduct there may be cruel and hateful or show tender pity; and every reader knows the poetic beauty which glorifies the *Paradiso,* renders lovely the *Purgatorio,* and ever and anon breaks through the gloom of Hell.

Another mediaeval quality, sublimated in Dante's poem, is that of elaborate plan, intended symmetry of composition, the balance of one incident or subject against another. And finally one observes the mediaeval inclusiveness which belongs to the scope and purpose of the *Commedia* as a *Summa* of salvation. Dante brings in everything that can illuminate and fill out his theme. Even as the *Summa* of St. Thomas, so the *Commedia* must present a whole doctrinal scheme of salvation, and leave no loopholes, loose ends, broken links of argument or explanation.

The substance of the *Commedia,* practically its whole content of thought, opinion, sentiment, had source in the mediaeval store of antique culture and the partly affiliated, if not partly derivative, Latin Christianity. The mediaeval appreciation of the Classics, and of the contents of ancient philosophy, is not to be so very sharply distinguished from the attitude of the fifteenth or sixteenth, nay, if one will, the eighteenth, century, when the *Federalist* in the young inchoately united States, and many an orator in the revolutionary assemblies of France, quoted Cicero and Plutarch as arbiters of civic expediency. Nevertheless, if we choose to recognize deference to ancient opinion, acceptance of antique myth and poetry as fact, unbounded admiration for a shadowy and much distorted ancient world, as characterizing the mediaeval attitude toward whatever once belonged to Rome and Greece, then we must say that such also is Dante's attitude, scholar as he was; and that in his use of the Classics he differed from other mediaeval men only in so far as above them all he was a poet. . . .

Yet however universally Dante's mind was solicited by the antique matter and his poet's nature charmed, he was profoundly and mediaevally Christian. The *Commedia* is a mediaeval Christian poem. Its fabric, springing from the life of earth, enfolds the threefold quasi-other world of damned, of purging, and of finally purified, spirits. It is dramatic and doctrinal. Its drama of action and suffering, like the narratives of Scripture, offers literal fact, moral teaching, and allegorical or spiritual significance. The doctrinal contents are held partly within the poem's dramatic action and partly in expositions which are not fused in the drama. Thus, whatever else it is, the poem is a *Summa* of saving doctrine, which is driven home by illustrations of the sovereign good and abysmal ill coming to man under the providence of God. One may perhaps discern a twofold purpose in it, since the poet works out his own salvation and gives precepts and examples to aid others and help truth and righteousness on earth. The subject is man as rewarded or punished eternally by God—says Dante in the letter to Can Grande.[1] This subject could hardly be conceived as veritable, and still less could it be executed, by a poet who had no care for the effect of his poem upon men. Dante had such care. But whether he, who was first and always a poet, wrote the *Commedia* in order to lift others out of error to salvation, or even in order to work out his own salvation,—let him say who knows the mind of Dante. No divination, however, is required to trace the course of the saving teaching, which, whether dramatically exemplified or expounded in doctrinal statement, is embodied in the great poem; nor is it hard to note how Dante drew its substance from the mediaeval past.

Dante's Relevance Today
PHILIP MC NAIR

In our truncated search for "the meaning of Dante" we have examined that meaning as seen by the fourteenth-century Florentine poet and littérateur Boccaccio and the early twentieth-century American historian Henry Osborn Taylor. Boccaccio expressed the view that Dante was (or should be) the great preceptor of his ungrateful mother city, Taylor that he is the exemplification of the medieval mind. We turn now to a third view, in an essay by the Cambridge Italian scholar Philip McNair —"Dante's Relevance Today," one of the many works on Dante published in 1965 to commemorate the seven hundredth anniversary of the poet's birth. McNair finds the relevance of Dante today (and every day) in the fact that Dante, more than any other poet or most philosophers, deals "with the things which affect us most—and these things do not alter from one millennium to another"—things such as God, grace, sin, love, justice, and human nature.

"*Poeta nascitur non fit*"[2] is a well-worn tag, and a true one; and that is why the birth of a supreme poet is supremely worth celebrating. Last

---

[1] Can Grande della Scala, the Lord of Verona, to whom Dante dedicated part of the *Commedia*. Dante wrote a letter to Can Grande explaining the meaning of the poem.—ED.
[2] "Poets are born, not made."—ED.

year it was Shakespeare; this year it is Dante: and the conjunction of these two great names could hardly be happier, for in the words of the late T. S. Eliot: "Dante and Shakespeare divide the modern world between them; there is no third" (Weimar's objection overruled).[3]

"The modern world"—Eliot said—and at first blush "modern" may seem quite the wrong word to use when talking about Dante. Shakespeare, after all, stands closer to us by three centuries and half-a-dozen revolutions in taste and outlook, such as the Renaissance and the Reformation. But a cursory glance at *The Divine Comedy* discovers a medieval world reflected in a medieval mind. We are back in a pre-Copernican cosmology with God at the circumference and Satan at the centre, exploring a three-storeyed universe crammed with scholastic bric-à-brac and Christian myths. . . .

But dip deeper into Dante and we find how curiously relevant he is today—far more so than Virgil, for instance, or Homer, or practically any other poet who wrote before Shakespeare. Perhaps "perennial" is a better word than "modern," for, like the *philosophia perennis* [4] which it reflects, his poem just goes on applying to the human situation year after year and from age to age. Dante is 700 years old this summer, yet he is still the most topical poet for a cosmonaut floating in space to read; and seven centuries from now, when the science-fiction of his *Comedy* has come true, the men who contemplate this world from the stars will not have outsoared the shadow of his genius or exhausted the meaning of his poem.

Dante's relevance today stems from the fact that he is one of the most engaged writers of all time, as well as one of the most engaging. In commemorating him it is all too easy to slip into superlatives, and say that he is the poet "with the mostest" (most understanding, most insight, most vision, and so on); but surely we may make the modest claim that in the *Comedy*, despite its medieval structure, Dante is dealing with the things which affect us most—and these things do not alter from one millennium to another. God, grace, sin, love, justice, and human nature have not changed since Moses knew them. Dante's total involvement in them is best explained in terms of his purpose in writing the poem at all.

Apart from the basic urge which every poet feels to express himself, Dante's particular poetic reason for projecting the *Comedy* seems to have been his desire to measure up to an exacting challenge, to stretch his technique to breaking-point in doing what no other poet had ever done before—to pioneer in the vernacular, indeed in language itself. . . .

But Dante is more than a poet and his *Comedy* more than a poem. His prime purpose in writing is missionary and prophetic, and concerns the state of the world, the redemption of mankind. You do not have to

[3] A reference to the claim for similar stature for the German author Goethe.—ED.
[4] Eternal philosophy.—ED.

read very far to know that he is not out simply to entertain—"A funny thing happened to me in the dark wood"—although reading him *is* tremendous fun. His aim, says that problematic letter to Cangrande della Scala, "is to rescue those living in this life from a state of misery and bring them to a state of bliss." It is, of course, the same end proposed by the Christian Gospel, and springs from the same realism about sin and damnation: in fact this led one nineteenth-century Pope to dub the *Divine Comedy* the "Fifth Gospel." But Dante is less an evangelist than a prophet.

If poets are born and not made, prophets are called by God and fitted by experience. Dante is robustly conscious of his call, but that is his own private affair and inscrutable. What falls under our survey is his experience as a man among men, and the most important thing that happened to him —apart from being born a poet in 1265—was banishment from his native Florence in January 1302, unjustly charged with injustice in the form of political corruption. Important, because it made him brood on justice: not only in his own life, but also in the history of the world. His exile from Florence is due to Man's injustice, but Man's exile from paradise is due to the justice of God. What then is this Divine Justice? How does it operate? And how does it square with God's love?

Here we have one of the *Comedy's* central themes which must be seen against the dark background of human injustice. God's in His heaven, but all is *not* right with the world. Fallen Man is unjust because sin in him has disturbed the balance between reason and desire and warped his will. When we reach the poem's end we find Dante's *disio* and his *velle*[5] harmonized by the Divine Love which keeps the solar system in equilibrium. But the first note he strikes is the reality of sin. He begins with his own predicament—astray in a dark wood, having left the right road—and little by little reveals that this is the predicament of Man, of human nature, of every human institution. Florence is astray, Italy is astray, the papacy is astray, and so is the empire; the entire world is astray through sin, and therefore Dante is called to write *"in pro del mondo che mal vive."*[6] Karl Vossler described the *Comedy* as the whole course of a religious conversion, but it is more than that: it is the whole programme of the world's redemption to God from sin. Dante sees himself not only as a sinner being saved, but in some sense as an agent of the salvation of others. This accounts for the fact that at times his tone is positively Messianic, for we have no evidence that he underrated his mission.

For Dante, as for all prophets, *hora novissima, tempora pessima sunt.*[7] The end of the world is at hand, the number of the Elect is almost complete, nearly all the seats in heaven are already taken. But his prophetic

[5] "Desire" and "ambition."—ED.
[6] "On behalf of the world that lives in evil."—ED.
[7] The most recent times are the worst.—ED.

burden is not Bunyanesque; he does not suggest fleeing from the wrath to come, or abandoning the world to its doom. He does not even "look for new heavens and a new earth, wherein dwelleth righteousness"; he looks rather for a regeneration of this earth, for the coming of the Kingdom of God. The point of his allegory of hell, purgatory, and heaven is not so much pie-in-the-sky as the reorganization of this world in love and justice. . . .

It seems to me that Dante might have pictured hell in one of two ways: either like a concentration camp, with Satan as its commandant, in which sinners are at the mercy of a power more evil than themselves; or like a penitentiary, in which a just government exacts retributive punishment for sin. Following Christ and the Church, he has chosen the second way in his *Inferno*, where Divine Justice is seen as Vengeance. This is never stressed more starkly than in the Third Ring of the Seventh Circle, where the violent against God suffer the inexorable rain which falls in broad flakes of fire upon them in a slow downward drift "as Alpine snows in windless weather fall."

But God's justice is not only punitive. In purgatory, the "Mount where Justice probes us," it sets the desire of the repentant toward their purging pains as once that desire was set on sin. In heaven it rewards the blessed with the vision of God. But it is also active in the history of the world for Man's good and salvation. Here Dante's most distinctive idea is that Divine Justice master-minded the rise and rule of the Roman Empire, *"che 'l buon mondo feo."* [8] In fact, this is one of his key concepts, discussed in detail in the *Monarchia*, and informing the *Comedy* from beginning to end. . . .

Of course Dante, like all political thinkers, starts out from the existing situation in his own day, dominated by the two great institutions of the empire and the papacy, yet menaced by the rising power of French nationalism and the emergence of city-states like Florence. But with a prophet's mind he argues back to God's purpose behind Rome's two suns —her *due soli*—and with a prophet's eye he sees their destiny in God's salvation, when Man has attained his *duo ultima*—his two supreme ends of temporal and eternal happiness. For God's plan of salvation is one and indivisible, and Dante's study of history has taught him how dovetailed that immense operation of love and justice is: David contemporary with Aeneas; Christ, the Son of David, contemporary with Augustus, the son of Aeneas; the Roman Pope, Christ's Vicar, the complement of the Roman Emperor, Augustus Caesar's successor. And not only is there a developed parallelism in Dante's mind, which condemns Judas to the same fate as Brutus and Cassius, but also an ingenious interaction which provides the legal basis of his soteriology.[9]

[8] "that the good world might come about."—ED.
[9] Doctrine of salvation.—ED.

For the Roman Emperor is the fount of Roman law, and is declared
de jure the governing power in the world by God Himself in two great
acts of Divine Vengeance. God willed that His Son should be born under
the *Pax-Romana* and suffer under Pontius Pilate, Caesar's Procurator.
Thereby He willed that the Roman Emperor should perform a crucial
function in the Atonement; for it was by the authority of Tiberius Caesar
that God avenged the sin of Adam in the crucifixion of Christ, in whom
the whole human race was vicariously punished to satisfy Divine Justice.
But having avenged Man's sin in Christ's death under Tiberius, Justice
avenged Christ's death upon the Jews by the destruction of Jerusalem
under Titus. This devious doctrine is propounded to Dante in the Heaven
of Mercury by no less an authority than the Emperor Justinian, who,
inspired by *il primo amore* and *la viva giustizia,*[10] traces the course of
Rome's rise to world dominion in a panoramic unfolding of history from
the divine standpoint. But the sweep and scope of his review is capped
by Beatrice, who takes his cryptic words on divine vengeance and explains them to Dante in one of the most impressive expositions of the
Atonement to be found in non-canonical literature.

Echoing the Anselmian [11] doctrine of satisfaction, Beatrice proves how
the justice and the love of God meet in the cross, where divine vengeance
is exhausted and divine compassion expressed. Ruined by his fall, Adam's
helpless race lay sick for many a century until it pleased the Word of God
to descend and unite Man's estranged nature to Himself "with the sole act
of His eternal love." The love that is the life of the Trinity, that binds the
leaves of the volume of the universe together, the love that moves the sun
and the other stars, that moved Beatrice to seek out Virgil on Dante's
behalf—it is this primal eternal love that was kindled in the Virgin's
womb and bore our nature to judicial execution on the cross.

In that Man was punished, the penalty was just; in that God suffered,
it was outrageously *unjust.* Why God should take this way to redeem His
creature "is buried from the eyes of all whose wit is not matured within
Love's flame." But—Beatrice explains—if Man were to be saved at all,
one of two fords must be passed: either God of His sole courtesy must
remit the debt, or Man of himself must make satisfaction for his sin. . . .

What the love and justice of God mean to the sinner saved by grace
is witnessed throughout the *Purgatorio* and *Paradiso* as Dante's mind and
heart are conformed to the pleasure of God. To take one instance, it is
seen in Manfred,[12] whom we meet at the mountain's foot. He repented at
the point of death, but died excommunicate. His dead body was cast out
of the kingdom of Naples, but his undying soul was received into the
Kingdom of God. Why? Because weeping he gave himself up to Him

10 "The first love" and "the living justice."—ED.
11 St. Anselm of Canterbury, medieval theologian (d. 1109).—ED.
12 The son and successor of Emperor Frederick II.—ED.

Who willingly pardons. Horrible though he confessed his sins to be, "Infinite Goodness has such wide arms that she accepts all who turn to her." The bishop and the pope who banned his corpse had read only the one face of God, His inexorable justice; but Manfred saw the face of everlasting love. God receives him because Christ has borne the penalty of his sins; but the laws of the kingdom still operate even though Manfred is forgiven, and Justice excludes him from purgatory until thirty times the period of his presumption is fulfilled.

Although Dante can write movingly about the wide arms of Infinite Goodness and the two faces of God, His justice and His love, it is disappointing to find that to the end of the *Comedy* his God remains strangely impersonal. Consummate poet though he is, Dante's greatest omission is his failure to portray Christ, the very personification of the justice and the love of God. Only three times do we glimpse Him in heaven, but although He is the Incarnate Word on no occasion does He speak. . . .

In the *Divine Comedy* we see the unveiled mystery and the radiant hosts, the uncreated light and the vision of God; but we do not see the Lamb, without Whose sacrifice we could not see heaven at all.

Suggestions for Further Reading

DANTE IS, first and foremost, a poet—one of the two or three greatest of all time—and students ought to sample his poetry, no matter how difficult, abstruse, or philosophical it may seem. Dante's greatest work, *The Divine Comedy*, is available in many translations, but students will probably be most pleased with the contemporary verse translation by the popular poet-critic John Ciardi, *The Inferno* (New Brunswick, N.J.: Rutgers University Press, 1954), *The Purgatorio* (New York: New American Library, 1961), and *The Paradiso* (New York: New American Library, 1970). It is not entirely faithful to the letter (more so to the spirit) of the original but it is a lively, often earthy, and always entertaining effort. Somewhat less successful is Dorothy L. Sayers' translation, *The Comedy of Dante Alighieri, the Florentine*, 3 vols. (Harmondsworth, England: Penguin, 1955–1973), which attempts the almost impossible task of duplicating

Dante's interlocking three-line rhyme scheme. The translation suffers from it in places, but it is generally readable; the long introduction and critical notes are, however, first class and an enormous help. For a sampling of Dante's other writings, the most convenient work is *The Portable Dante*, ed. Paolo Milano (New York: Viking, 1968), with the complete text of the *Divine Comedy* and *Vita Nuova* and excerpts from his other verse and Latin prose works. Two conventional guides to the *Divine Comedy* are *Companion to the Divine Comedy*, ed. C. S. Singleton (Cambridge, Mass.: Harvard University Press, 1975), and *A Concordance to the Divine Comedy of Dante Alighieri*, ed. Ernest Hatch Wilkins and Thomas G. Bergin (Cambridge, Mass.: Harvard University Press, 1965).

There is an enormous literature of Dante criticism, much of it as difficult and obscure as the poet himself. A handful of works, however, can be recommended for beginning students. The most readable and among the most sensible are two collections of essays by Dorothy L. Sayers, *Introductory Papers on Dante* (New York: Barnes and Noble, 1969 [1954]), and *Further Papers on Dante* (New York: Harper, 1957). Thomas G. Bergin is one of the world's great authorities on Dante, and three of his books are so clear and readable that they can be recommended even to those with little or no prior exposure to Dante—*Dante* (Boston: Houghton Mifflin, 1965); *Perspectives on the Divine Comedy* (New Brunswick, N.J.: Rutgers University Press, 1967); and *A Diversity of Dante* (New Brunswick, N.J.: Rutgers University Press, 1969). Two older famous books of Dante criticism are also recommended: Erich Auerbach, *Dante, Poet of the Secular World*, tr. Ralph Manheim (Chicago: University of Chicago Press, 1961 [1929]), and Etienne Gilson, *Dante and Philosophy*, tr. David Moore (New York: Harper, 1963 [1949]).

Most of the foregoing books deal not only with Dante the poet but also with his life and times. The following works deal more explicitly with the man and his age. The most authoritative modern biography of Dante is by the great Italian Dante scholar Michele Barbi, *Life of Dante*, tr. and ed. Paul G. Ruggiers (Berkeley and Los Angeles: University of California Press, 1954 [1933]). The more bulky and comprehensive Karl Vossler, *Mediaeval Culture: An Introduction to Dante and His Times*, tr. Wm. C. Lawton (New York: Harcourt, Brace, 1929), is also a standard work. Highly recommended is Domenico Vittorini, *The Age of Dante* (Westport, Conn.: Greenwood Press, 1975 [1957]), which can serve as a corrective to the views of Vossler and Henry Osborn Taylor (excerpted in this chapter), in that Vittorini ties Dante into the new scholarly views on the early Renaissance.

Leonardo da Vinci: Universal Man of the Renaissance

While scholars may still argue whether Dante belongs in the Renaissance or the Middle Ages, there is no question where Leonardo da Vinci belongs. More than any other figure, he is commonly regarded as the exemplar of that uniquely Renaissance ideal *uomo universale,* the universal man.

Leonardo, the spoiled, loved, and pampered illegitimate son of a well-to-do Florentine notary, was born in 1452 at the very midpoint of Florence's magnificent Renaissance century, the Quattrocento. The boy grew up at his father's country home in the village of Vinci. His precocious genius and his talent for drawing led his father to apprentice Leonardo to the artist Verrocchio in Florence. While Verrocchio is best remembered as a sculptor, it should be noted that he was, like most Florentine artists of his time, a versatile master of other artistic crafts, and that his *bottega*—like Ghiberti's earlier or Michelangelo's later— was not only a lively school of craftsmanship and technique but a place where people gathered to gossip and talk over on a wide range of subjects. Here the young Leonardo's multiple talents bloomed.

At the age of twenty Leonardo was admitted to the painters' guild and soon after set up his own shop and household. He was well enough received and commissions came his way. But, for reasons that are not entirely clear, he seems not to have been marked for the lavish patronage of the Medici family—as were so many of his fellow artists—or of any other great Florentine houses. The fashion of the moment preferred those artists like Alberti and Botticelli who mingled learned humanism with their art and could converse in Latin with the humanists, poets, and philosophers who dominated the intellectual scene in Florence. But Leonardo knew no Latin. His education consisted only of apprenticeship training and beyond that a hodge-podge of self-instruction directed to his own wide-ranging interests, in some areas profound and original, in others hopelessly limited and naive. It is also possible that Leonardo may simply have set himself apart from the circle of his fellow artists and their patrons. There are hints of alienation and jealousy and even a vaguely worded reference to a homosexual charge against him that was brought before a magistrate and then dropped. But it is most likely that Leonardo's own restless curiosity was already carrying him beyond the practice of his art.

In 1482 Leonardo left Florence for Milan and the court of its lord, Ludovico Sforza, one of the most powerful princes of Italy. In the letter Leonardo wrote commending himself to Ludovico, which has been preserved, he described himself as a military architect, siege and hydraulic engineer, ordnance and demolition expert, architect, sculptor, and painter; he ended the letter, "And if any one of the above-named things seems to anyone to be impossible or not feasible, I am most ready to make the experiment in your park, or in whatever place may please your Excellency, to whom I commend myself with the utmost humility." [1] Humility indeed! The universal man had declared himself.

Leonardo spent the next seventeen years—the most vigorous and productive of his life—at the court of Milan. He painted *The Last Supper* for the Dominican Convent of Santa Maria delle Grazie. He conceived and created the model for what might well have been the world's greatest equestrian statue; but the statue, memorializing Ludovico Sforza's father, the old soldier-duke Francesco, was never cast, and the model was destroyed. In addition, Leonardo created gimcrackery for court balls and fetes—costumes, jewelry, scenery, engines, floats, spectacles. But increasingly he was occupied with studies of a bewildering variety of subjects. The notebooks he kept reveal drawings and notes on the flight of birds and the possibility of human flight; military engineering, tanks, submarines, exploding shells, rapid-firing artillery pieces, and fortifications; bold schemes for city planning and hydraulic engineering; plans for machinery of every sort, pulleys, gears, self-propelled vehicles, a mechanical clock, and a file cutter; detailed studies of plant, animal, and human anatomy that go well beyond the needs of an artist; a complete treatise on painting and another on the comparison of the arts. Despite the fact that much of this

[1] Quoted in E. G. Holt (ed.), *A Documentary History of Art* (New York: Doubleday, 1957), vol. I, pp. 273–275.

body of work—including a treatise on perspective that was reputed to be far in advance of other such works—was scattered and lost, some seven thousand pages have survived, all written in a code-like, left-handed, mirror script.

Leonardo's handwriting is of particular interest, for it is indicative of a special side of his nature—almost obsessively secretive, aloof, touchy and suspicious of others. These qualities are part of the traditional image of Leonardo that has been passed down to us, beginning with his earliest biography, by his younger contemporary Vasari.

In Praise of Leonardo
GIORGIO VASARI

Giorgio Vasari (1511–1574) was himself something of a universal man. He was an artist of more than middling ability who worked all over Italy. He was also a respected man of affairs, the familiar of popes, princes, and dignitaries, as well as artists and scholars. But his most important achievement was his book Lives of the Most Eminent Painters, Sculptors & Architects from Cimabue until our own Time, *the first edition published in Florence in 1550. Wallace K. Ferguson has called it "a masterpiece of art history."* [2] *In fact, the book is more than a masterpiece of art history, for it virtually created the concept of art history itself.*

Vasari introduces "our present age" with his treatment of Leonardo. But this biography, despite its extravagant praise of Leonardo's genius, is seriously limited. Vasari had access to many of Leonardo's notes, even some that we no longer have. But he was most familiar with the art and artists of Tuscany. It is clear that he had not actually seen several of Leonardo's most important works, in Milan and elsewhere. And much of the information he provided on Leonardo's life was nothing more than current rumor or gossip about him. Vasari, furthermore, was himself a pupil and lifelong admirer of Leonardo's great contemporary Michelangelo (1475–1564), and it was Vasari's thesis that the whole tradition of Italian art reached its fulfillment in Michelangelo. It

[2] In *The Renaissance in Historical Thought: Five Centuries of Interpretation* (Boston: Houghton Mifflin, 1948), 60.

might be recalled also that Michelangelo despised Leonardo; they had at least one nasty quarrel. And Michelangelo was fond of saying that Leonardo was a technically incompetent craftsman, who could not complete the projects he began. Whether by design or not, this charge became the main line of criticism in Vasari's biography of Leonardo, and it has persisted alongside Leonardo's reputation as an enigmatic genius.
We look now at Vasari's account from Lives of the Most Eminent Painters, Sculptors & Architects.

THE GREATEST GIFTS are often seen, in the course of nature, rained by celestial influences on human creatures; and sometimes, in supernatural fashion, beauty, grace, and talent are united beyond measure in one single person, in a manner that to whatever such an one turns his attention, his every action is so divine, that, surpassing all other men, it makes itself clearly known as a thing bestowed by God (as it is), and not acquired by human art. This was seen by all mankind in Leonardo da Vinci, in whom, besides a beauty of body never sufficiently extolled, there was an infinite grace in all his actions; and so great was his genius, and such its growth, that to whatever difficulties he turned his mind, he solved them with ease. In him was great bodily strength, joined to dexterity, with a spirit and courage ever royal and magnanimous; and the fame of his name so increased, that not only in his lifetime was he held in esteem, but his reputation became even greater among posterity after his death.

Truly marvellous and celestial was Leonardo, the son of Ser Piero da Vinci; and in learning and in the rudiments of letters he would have made great proficience, if he had not been so variable and unstable, for he set himself to learn many things, and then, after having begun them, abandoned them. Thus, in arithmetic, during the few months that he studied it, he made so much progress, that, by continually suggesting doubts and difficulties to the master who was teaching him, he would very often bewilder him. He gave some little attention to music, and quickly resolved to learn to play the lyre, as one who had by nature a spirit most lofty and full of refinement; wherefore he sang divinely to that instrument, improvising upon it. Nevertheless, although he occupied himself with such a variety of things, he never ceased drawing and working in relief, pursuits which suited his fancy more than any other. Ser Piero, having observed this, and having considered the loftiness of his intellect, one day took some of his drawings and carried them to Andrea del Verrocchio, who was much his friend, and besought him straitly to tell him whether Leonardo, by devoting himself to drawing, would make any proficience. Andrea was astonished to see the extraordinary beginnings of Leonardo, and urged Ser Piero that he should make him study it; wherefore he arranged with Leonardo that he should enter the workshop of Andrea, which Leonardo did with the greatest willingness in the world. And he practised not one branch of art only, but all those in which drawing played a part; and having an intellect so divine and marvellous that he was also an excellent geometrician, he not only worked in sculpture, making in his youth, in clay, some heads of women that are smiling, of which plaster casts are still taken, and likewise some heads of boys which appeared to have issued from the hand of a master; but in architecture, also, he made many drawings both of ground-plans and of other designs of buildings; and he was the first, although but a youth, who suggested the plan of reducing the river Arno to a navigable canal from Pisa to Florence. He made designs of flour-mills, fulling-mills, and engines, which might be driven by the force of water: and since he wished that his profession should be painting, he studied much in drawing after nature. . . . He was continually making models and designs to show men how to remove mountains with ease, and how to bore them in order to pass from one level to another; and by means of levers, windlasses, and screws, he showed the way to raise and draw great weights, together with methods for emptying harbours, and pumps for removing water from low places, things which his brain never ceased from devising; and of these ideas and labours many drawings may be seen, scattered abroad among our craftsmen; and I myself have seen not a few. . . .

He was so pleasing in conversation, that he attracted to himself the hearts of men. And although he possessed, one might say, nothing, and worked little, he always kept servants and horses, in which latter he took much delight, and particularly in all other animals, which he managed with the greatest love and patience; and this he showed when often passing by the places where birds were sold, for, taking them with his own hand out of their cages, and having paid to those who sold them the price that was asked, he let them fly away into the air, restoring to them their lost liberty. For which reason nature was pleased so to favour him, that, wherever he turned his thought, brain, and mind, he displayed such divine power in his works, that, in giving them their perfection, no one was ever his peer in readiness, vivacity, excellence, beauty, and grace.

It is clear that Leonardo, through his comprehension of art, began many things and never finished one of them, since it seemed to him that the hand was not able to attain to the perfection of art in carrying out the things which he imagined; for the reason that he conceived in idea difficulties so subtle and so marvellous, that they could never be expressed by the hands, be they ever so excellent. And so many were his caprices, that, philosophizing of natural things, he set himself to seek out the properties of herbs, going on even to observe the motions of the heavens, the path of the moon, and the courses of the sun. . . .

He began a panel-picture of the Adoration of the Magi, containing many beautiful things, particularly the heads, which was in the house of Amerigo Benci, opposite the Loggia de' Peruzzi; and this, also, remained unfinished, like his other works.

It came to pass that Giovan Galeazzo, Duke of Milan, being dead, and

Lodovico Sforza raised to the same rank, in the year 1494,[3] Leonardo was summoned to Milan in great repute to the Duke, who took much delight in the sound of the lyre, to the end that he might play it: and Leonardo took with him that instrument which he had made with his own hands, in great part of silver, in the form of a horse's skull—a thing bizarre and new—in order that the harmony might be of greater volume and more sonorous in tone; with which he surpassed all the musicians who had come together there to play. Besides this, he was the best improviser in verse of his day. The Duke, hearing the marvellous discourse of Leonardo, became so enamoured of his genius, that it was something incredible: and he prevailed upon him by entreaties to paint an altar-panel containing a Nativity, which was sent by the Duke to the Emperor.

He also painted in Milan, for the Friars of S. Dominic, at S. Maria delle Grazie, a Last Supper, a most beautiful and marvellous thing; and to the heads of the Apostles he gave such majesty and beauty, that he left the head of Christ unfinished, not believing that he was able to give it that divine air which is essential to the image of Christ.[4] This work, remaining thus all but finished, has ever been held by the Milanese in the greatest veneration, and also by strangers as well; for Leonardo imagined and succeeded in expressing that anxiety which had seized the Apostles in wishing to know who should betray their Master. . . .

While he was engaged on this work, he proposed to the Duke to make a horse in bronze, of a marvellous greatness, in order to place upon it, as a memorial, the image of the Duke.[5] And on so vast a scale did he begin it and continue it, that it could never be completed. And there are those who have been of the opinion (so various and so often malign out of envy are the judgments of men) that he began it with no intention of finishing it, because, being of so great a size, an incredible difficulty was encountered in seeking to cast it in one piece; and it might also be believed that, from the result, many may have formed such a judgment, since many of his works have remained unfinished. But, in truth, one can believe that his vast and most excellent mind was hampered through being too full of desire, and that his wish ever to seek out excellence upon excellence, and perfection upon perfection, was the reason of it. "Tal che l' opera fosse ritardata dal desio," [6] as our Petrarca has said. And, indeed, those who saw the great model that Leonardo made in clay vow that they have never seen a more beautiful thing, or a more superb; and it was preserved until the French came to Milan with King Louis of France, and broke it all to pieces.[7] Lost, also, is a little model of it in wax, which was

---

[3] The date was actually 1482.—ED.

[4] The head of Christ was finished, along with the rest of the painting. Vasari was repeating gossip and had not seen the work.—ED.

[5] Rather of the Duke's father, Francesco, the founder of the Sforza dynasty.—ED.

[6] "So that the work was retarded by the very desire of it."—ED.

[7] Louis XII of France. The incident of the model's destruction took place during the French occupation of Milan in 1499.—ED.

held to be perfect, together with a book on the anatomy of the horse made
by him by way of study.

He then applied himself, but with greater care, to the anatomy of man,
assisted by and in turn assisting, in this research, Messer Marc' Antonio
della Torre, an excellent philosopher, who was then lecturing at Pavia,
and who wrote of this matter; and he was one of the first (as I have heard
tell) that began to illustrate the problems of medicine with the doctrine of
Galen, and to throw true light on anatomy, which up to that time had
been wrapped in the thick and gross darkness of ignorance. And in this
he found marvellous aid in the brain, work, and hand of Leonardo, who
made a book drawn in red chalk, and annotated with the pen, of the
bodies that he dissected with his own hand, and drew with the greatest
diligence; wherein he showed all the frame of the bones; and then added
to them, in order, all the nerves, and covered them with muscles; the first
attached to the bone, the second that hold the body firm, and the third
that move it; and beside them, part by part, he wrote in letters of an
ill-shaped character, which he made with the left hand, backwards; and
whoever is not practised in reading them cannot understand them, since
they are not to be read save with a mirror. . . .

*With the fall of Ludovico Sforza and the French occupation of Milan
in 1499, the artist returned to Florence.*

Leonardo undertook to execute, for Francesco del Giocondo, the portrait
of Monna Lisa, his wife; and after toiling over it for four years, he left it
unfinished; and the work is now in the collection of King Francis of
France, at Fontainebleau. In this head, whoever wished to see how closely
art could imitate nature, was able to comprehend it with ease; for in it
were counterfeited all the minutenesses that with subtlety are able to be
painted. . . .

By reason, then, of the excellence of the works of this divine craftsman,
his fame had so increased that all persons who took delight in art—nay,
the whole city of Florence—desired that he should leave them some
memorial, and it was being proposed everywhere that he should be com-
missioned to execute some great and notable work, whereby the commonwealth might be honoured and adorned by the great genius, grace and
judgment that were seen in the works of Leonardo. And it was decided
between the Gonfalonier [8] and the chief citizens, the Great Council Chamber
having been newly built . . . and having been finished in great haste, it
was ordained by public decree that Leonardo should be given some
beautiful work to paint; and so the said hall was allotted to him by Piero
Soderini, then Gonfalonier of Justice. Whereupon Leonardo, determining
to execute this work, began a cartoon in the Sala del Papa, an apartment

---

[8] The title of the chief magistrate of Florence.—Ed.

in S. Maria Novella, representing the story of Niccolò Piccinino,[9] Captain of Duke Filippo of Milan; wherein he designed a group of horsemen who were fighting for a standard, a work that was held to be very excellent and of great mastery, by reason of the marvellous ideas that he had in composing that battle. . . . It is said that, in order to draw that cartoon, he made a most ingenious stage, which was raised by contracting it and lowered by expanding. And conceiving the wish to colour on the wall in oils, he made a composition of so gross an admixture, to act as a binder on the wall, that, going on to paint in the said hall, it began to peel off in such a manner that in a short time he abandoned it, seeing it spoiling.[10] . . .

He went to Rome with Duke Giuliano de' Medici, at the election of Pope Leo,[11] who spent much of his time on philosophical studies, and particularly on alchemy; where, forming a paste of a certain kind of wax, as he walked he shaped animals very thin and full of wind, and, by blowing into them, made them fly through the air, but when the wind ceased they fell to the ground. . . .

He made an infinite number of such follies, and gave his attention to mirrors; and he tried the strangest methods in seeking out oils for painting, and varnish for preserving works when painted. . . . It is related that, a work having been allotted to him by the Pope, he straightway began to distil oils and herbs, in order to make the varnish; at which Pope Leo said: "Alas! this man will never do anything, for he begins by thinking of the end of the work, before the beginning."

There was very great disdain between Michelagnolo Buonarroti and him, on account of which Michelagnolo departed from Florence, with the excuse of Duke Giuliano, having been summoned by the Pope to the competition for the façade of S. Lorenzo. Leonardo, understanding this, departed and went into France, where the King, having had works by his hand, bore him great affection; and he desired that he should colour the cartoon of S. Anne, but Leonardo, according to his custom, put him off for a long time with words.

Finally, having grown old, he remained ill many months, and, feeling himself near to death, asked to have himself diligently informed of the teaching of the Catholic faith. . . . [He] expired in the arms of the King, in the seventy-fifth year of his age.[12]

---

[9] A mercenary commander who had worked for Florence.—ED.

[10] Michelangelo was assigned a companion panel and also abandoned his work on it before it was completed.—ED.

[11] Pope Leo X, the former Giovanni Cardinal dei Medici.—ED.

[12] Vasari is inaccurate. In the year Leonardo died, 1519, he actually was sixty-seven.—ED.

Leonardo the Scientist
JOHN HERMAN RANDALL, JR.

From Vasari's time to the present, there has clung to the image of Leonardo da Vinci a kind of Faustian quality, linking him to the origins of modern science. Throughout his life, and increasingly from middle age on, Leonardo was preoccupied with technical studies and scientific experiments, often to the detriment of his art. But the judgments of modern scholars on "Leonardo the scientist" are much more varied and more circumspect than those upon "Leonardo the artist."

We turn first to the views of a distinguished philosopher and historian of science, especially medieval and Renaissance science, the long-time Columbia University Professor of Philosophy, John Herman Randall, Jr. This selection is from his article "The Place of Leonardo da Vinci in the Emergence of Modern Science."

LEONARDO WAS NOT himself a scientist. "Science" is not the hundred-odd aphorisms or "pensieri" that have been pulled out of his Codici and collected, by Richter, Solmi, and others. "Science" is not oracular utterances, however well phrased; it is not bright ideas jotted down in a notebook. "Science" is systematic and methodical thought. . . .

"Science" is not just the appeal to experience, though it involves such an appeal, as Leonardo stated in answering those critics who had censured him as a mere empiric: "If I could not indeed like them cite authors and books, it is a much greater and worthier thing to profess to cite experience, the mistress of their masters." "Science" is not the mere rejection of authority, the case for which is well put by Leonardo: "He who argues by citing an authority is not employing intelligence but rather memory." . . .

It is true that during Leonardo's youth—the second half of the Quattrocento—the intellectual influence of the non-scientific humanists had been making for a kind of St. Martin's summer of the "authority" of the ancients, and that his life coincides with this rebirth of an authoritarian attitude toward the past. Leonardo's protests were magnificent, and doubtless pertinent. But they are not enough to constitute "science." "Science" is not merely fresh, first-hand observation, however detailed and accurate.

Above all, "science" is not the intuitions of a single genius, solitary and alone, however suggestive. It is cooperative inquiry, such as had prevailed in the Italian schools from the time of Pietro d'Abano († 1315; his

Conciliator appeared earlier)—and such as was to continue till the time of Galileo—the cumulative cooperative inquiry which actually played so large a part in the emergence of modern science. . . .

In practice, Leonardo always becomes fascinated by some particular problem—he has no interest in working out any systematic body of knowledge. His artist's interest in the particular and the concrete, which inspires his careful, precise and accurate observation, is carried further by his inordinate curiosity into a detailed analytic study of the factors involved. His thought seems always to be moving from the particularity of the painter's experience to the universality of intellect and science, without ever quite getting there. . . .

No evidence has ever been offered that anybody in the sixteenth century capable of appreciating scientific ideas ever saw the Codici of Leonardo. . . . But since the scientific ideas expressed therein were all well-known in the universities of Leonardo's day, and were accessible in much more elaborated form in the books the scientists were reading, there seems to be no "problem" of tracing any presumed "influence" of Leonardo on the development of sixteenth-century scientific thought in Italy.

The *Trattato de la Pittura,* or *Paragone,* was not printed until 1651, but its existence in manuscript form suggests that it had been read much earlier by the Urbino circle. It was put together from various manuscripts of Leonardo by an editor whose identity is not known, but who seems to have been responsible for its systematic organization—an organization which later editors have uniformly tried to improve upon.

With Leonardo's anatomical studies, the story is somewhat different. There is no evidence that Vesalius [13] ever actually saw his drawings; but in view of the marked similarities between them and his own much more systematically planned and organized series of drawings, it is difficult to think that he did not. . . .

Turning now from the things that Leonardo, despite all the adulations of his genius, was clearly not, let us try to state what seems to have been his real genius in scientific matters. During the Renaissance, as a result of the surprising dissolution of the rigid boundaries which had previously kept different intellectual traditions, as it were, in watertight compartments, the many different currents of thought which had long been preparing and strengthening themselves during the Middle Ages managed to come together, and to strike fire. The explanation of this phenomenon can ultimately be only sociological—the breaking down of the fairly rigid boundaries that had hitherto shut off one discipline and one intellectual tradition from another. Whatever its cause, the confluence of many different intellectual traditions in the fertile, all-too-fertile mind of Leonardo renders

---

[13] The Flemish anatomist at the University of Padua who in 1543 published the first modern, scientific descriptive treatise on human anatomy.—ED.

his views an unusually happy illustration of the way in which very diverse intellectual traditions managed during the Renaissance to unite together to create what we now call "modern science."

There is first the "scientific tradition," the careful, intelligent, cooperative and cumulative criticism of Aristotelian physics, which began with William of Ockham.[14] . . . In his reading Leonardo was in touch with this scientific tradition, as Duhem has shown.

There is secondly Leonardo's enthusiasm for mathematics, which goes far beyond its obvious instrumental use. It is very hard to assay the precise sense in which Leonardo thought of mathematics as the alphabet of nature: in this area much work remains to be done. There seems to be in Leonardo no trace of the popular contemporary Pythagoreanism or Platonism. If we examine Leonardo's conception of mathematics as depicted in his drawings, not as inadequately stated in his prose, we find that it differs markedly from the static and very geometrical notion of Dürer.[15] It is movement, not geometrical relations, that Leonardo is trying to capture. There is much in his drawings that suggests a world envisaged in terms of the calculus—like the world of Leibniz [16]—rather than in terms of the purely geometrical vision of the Greek tradition. In his mathematical vision of the world, Leonardo seems to belong to the realm of "dynamic" and "Faustian" attitudes, rather than to the static geometrical perfection of Greek thought.

There is thirdly the tradition of what Edgar Zilsel has called the "superior craftsman"—the man who is not afraid to take an idea and try it out, to experiment with it. . . . As a pupil of Verrocchio [Leonardo] had no fastidious objections to sullying his hands with "experiment." This habit of Leonardo's of descending from the academic cathedra and actually trying out the ideas of which he read had broad repercussions: it is one of the activities of Leonardo that seems to have become generally known, and to have awakened emulation. The consequences of Leonardo's willingness to experiment are to be found in the "practical geometry" of Tartaglia, the greatest of the sixteenth-century Italian mathematicians. Galileo, of course, was in this tradition of the "practical geometers"; he too was an indefatigable inventor. Indeed, Leonardo can fairly claim to belong not to the line of scientists but to the noble tradition of the inventors. . . .

Many of Leonardo's aphorisms treat the matter of the proper intellectual method. He has much to say on the relation between "reason" and "experience," and what he says used to lead commentators to impute to him the anticipation of Francis Bacon's "inductive method"—God save the mark, as though that had anything to do with the method employed by the pioneering scientists of the seventeenth century!

Neither experience alone nor reason alone will suffice. "Those who are enamored of practice without science are like the pilot who boards his ship

[14] The important nominalist philosopher of the early fourteenth century.—ED.

[15] The great German artist, a contemporary of Leonardo.—ED.

[16] The great German philosopher and mathematician of the seventeenth century who shares with Newton the discovery of the calculus.—ED.

without helm or compass, and who is never certain where he is going."
On the other hand, pure reasoning is without avail: "Should you say that
the sciences which begin and end in the mind have achieved truth, that
I will not concede, but rather deny for many reasons; and first, because
in such mental discourse there occurs no experience, without which there is
no certainty to be found."

But Leonardo does not bother to give any precise definition of what
he means by his key terms, "experience," "reason," "certainty," or "truth."
Certainty depends on "experience," but "there is no certainty where one
of the mathematical sciences cannot apply, or where the subject is not
united with mathematics." And—maxim for all inventors!—"Mechanics
is the paradise of the mathematical sciences, because in it they come to
bear their mathematical fruits." . . .

These aphorisms as to the relation between reason and experience are
no doubt rhetorically effective. But we have only to compare such vague
utterances with the very detailed analyses of precisely the same methodological relation which were being carried out at this very time in the
Aristotelian schools of the Italian universities to realize the difference between an artist's insights and the scientist's analysis.

Leonardo was above all else the anatomist of nature. He could see, and
with his draughtsmanship depict clearly, the bony skeleton of the world—
the geological strata and their indicated past. He could also see everywhere
nature's simple machines in operation—in man and in the non-human world
alike. . . .

As a genuine contributor, then, to the descriptive sciences, Leonardo
reported with his pencil fundamental aspects of nature the great machine—
in anatomy, geology, and hydrostatics. As a writer rather than as a graphic
reporter, Leonardo shows himself an extremely intelligent reader. But he
was clearly never so much the scientist as when he had his pencil in hand,
and was penetrating to the mechanical structure of what he was observing.

Leonardo the Technologist
LADISLAO RETI

A substantial group of modern scholars agrees with Randall. Some, however, do not. In the following selection, we will sample the views of one of them, Ladislao Reti, an historian of science and medicine and an authority on Leonardo's scientific and technical manuscripts. Reti not only attaches more importance to Leonardo's scientific work than does Randall; he vigorously denies Randall's charges that Leonardo failed to exhibit a sustained, systematic body of scientific thought; that he stood alone outside the tradition of science; that he failed to develop a methodological terminology; and that he failed to influence the evolution of science beyond his own time. But most of all, Reti disputes Randall's view that science is abstract conception. Rather, he takes the position that science must be the accumulation of particular observations and applications. Reti views "Leonardo the scientist" as "Leonardo the technologist," and he insists that a technologist of such brilliance and inventiveness as Leonardo cannot be so readily dismissed. "The greatest engineer of all times" surely deserves a place in the history of science.

VARIED AS LEONARDO'S interests were, statistical analysis of his writings points to technology as the main subject. As was acutely pointed out by Bertrand Gille in a recent book, judging by the surviving original documents, Leonardo's métier was rather an engineer's than an artist's.

However we may feel about this opinion, it is disturbing to take an inventory of Leonardo's paintings, of which no more than half a dozen are unanimously authenticated by the world's leading experts.

Contrast this evident disinclination to paint with the incredible toil and patience Leonardo lavished on scientific and technical studies, particularly in the fields of geometry, mechanics, and engineering. Here his very indulgence elicited curious reactions from his contemporaries and in the minds of his late biographers. They regretted that a man endowed with such divine artistic genius should waste the precious hours of his life in such vain pursuits. And, of course, as the well-known episodes of his artistic career testify, this exposed him not only to criticism but also to serious inconveniences.

But were Leonardo's nonartistic activities truly marginal?

Documentary evidence proves that every official appointment refers to him not only as an artist but as an engineer as well.

At the court of Ludovico il Moro he was *Ingeniarius et pinctor*.[17] Cesare Borgia called him his most beloved *Architecto et Engengero Generale*.[18] When he returned to Florence he was immediately consulted as military engineer. . . . Louis XII called him *nostre chier et bien amé Léonard da Vincy, nostre paintre et ingenieur ordinaire*.[19] Even in Rome, despite the pope's famous remark on hearing of Leonardo's experiments with varnishes preparatory to beginning an artistic commission, Leonardo's duties clearly included technical work, as is documented by three rough copies of a letter to his patron Giuliano de' Medici. Nor was his position different when he went to France at the invitation of Francis I. The official burial document calls him *Lionard de Vincy, noble millanois, premier peinctre et ingenieur et architecte du Roy, mescanichien d'Estat, et anchien directeur du peincture du Duc de Milan*.[20]

We can thus see that Leonardo had a lively interest in the mechanical arts and engineering from his earliest youth, as evidenced by the oldest drawing in the Codex Atlanticus, to the end of his industrious life. Thousands of his drawings witness to it, from fleeting sketches (though always executed with the most uncanny bravura) to presentation projects finished in chiaroscuro wash. Often these sketches and drawings are accompanied by a descriptive text, comments, and discussion.

The drawings and writings of Leonardo on technical matters, though scattered throughout the notebooks and especially in the Codex Atlanticus (a true order probably never existed nor did the author attempt to make one), represent an important and unique source for the history of technology. . . .

It is far from my intention and beyond my possibilities to discuss Leonardo's technology as a whole on this occasion. Enough is said when we remember that there is hardly a field of applied mechanics where Leonardo's searching mind has left no trace in the pages of his notebooks. To illustrate Leonardo's methods I shall limit myself to discussing some little-known aspects of how he dealt with the main problem of technology, the harnessing of energy to perform useful work.

At the time of Leonardo the waterwheel had been improved and in some favored places wind was used to grind corn or pump water. But the main burden of human industry still rested on the muscle power of man or animal. Little thought was given to how this should be used. Animals were

---

[17] Engineer and painter.—ED.

[18] Architect and Engineer-General.—ED.

[19] Our dear and well-loved Leonardo da Vinci, our painter and engineer ordinary.—ED.

[20] Leonardo da Vinci, Milanese nobleman, first painter and engineer and architect of the King, state technician, and former director of painting of the Duke of Milan.—ED.

attached to carts or traction devices; fortunately collar harness was already in use, multiplying by five the pulling strength of the horse. Men worked tools by hand, turned cranks, or operated treadmills. Of course, power could be gained, sacrificing time, with the help of levers, screws, gears, and pulleys. Little attention was given to the problems of friction, strength of materials, and to the rational development of power transmission. At least this is the picture suggested by studying the few manuscripts that precede Leonardo, devoted to technological matters.

Leonardo's approach was fundamentally different. He firmly believed that technological problems must be dealt with not by blindly following traditional solutions but according to scientific rules deduced from observation and experiment.

When Leonardo searched for the most efficient ways of using the human motor, the force of every limb, of every muscle, was analyzed and measured. Leonardo was the first engineer who tried to find a quantitative equivalent for the forms of energy available.

In MS H (written *ca.* 1494) on folios 43*v* and 44*r* (figs. 1 and 2) there are two beautiful sketches showing the estimation of human muscular effort with the help of a dynamometer. The force is measured in pounds which represent the lifting capacity of the group of muscles under scrutiny. In figure 1 no less than six different cases covering the whole body are examined, while in figure 2 Leonardo tries to compare the force of the arm in different positions and points of attachment. Between the last two draw-

Figure 1
MS H, fol. 43*v*.

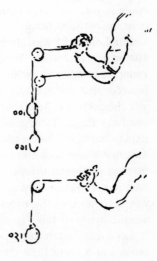

Figure 2
MS H, fol. 44*r*.

ings a diagram shows the arm as a compound lever. In many other instances Leonardo compares the human body with a mechanical system, anticipating Borelli. We shall see one of them on folio 164r, a of the Codex Atlanticus. . . .

The interest of Leonardo in the maximum efficiency of muscle power is understandable. It was the only motor he could have used in a flying machine; a project that aroused his ambition as early as the year 1488 and in which he remained interested till the end of his life.

The efficiency of the human motor depends not only on its intrinsic strength but also on the ways the force is applied. Indeed, what is the greatest strength a man can generate, without the help of mechanical devices like levers, gears, or pulleys? In a very interesting passage of MS A, folio 30v (fig. 3), Leonardo answers the question:

A man pulling a weight balanced against himself (as in lifting a weight with the help of a single block) cannot pull more than his own weight. And if he has to raise it, he will raise as much more than his weight, as his strength may be more than that of another man. The greatest force a man can apply, with equal velocity and impetus, will be when he sets his feet on one end of the balance and then leans his shoulders against some stable support. This will raise, at the other end of the balance, a weight equal to his own, and added to that, as much weight as he can carry on his shoulders.

Masterly executed marginal sketches illustrate the three different cases. The problem has been already touched on folio 90v of MS B, where the following suggestion is made beside a similar sketch: "See at the mill how much is your weight, stepping on the balance and pressing with your shoulders against something."

But Leonardo was always anxious to integrate theory with application. His own advice was: "When you put together the science of the motions of water, remember to include under each proposition its application and use, in order that this science may not be useless" (MS F, fol. 2v).

I should like to select, among many, a few cases in which Leonardo demonstrates the usefulness of his rules. One of them is pile driving for foundation work or the regulation of river banks. The simplest pile-driving machine consists of a movable frame, provided with a drop hammer raised by men pulling at a rope provided with hand lines. After being raised, the hammer is released by a trigger. The operation is repeated until the pile has been sunk to the necessary depth. In Belidor's classic treatise we may see the figure of this age-old device (fig. 4).

Leonardo, often engaged in architectural and hydraulic projects, obviously had a more than theoretical interest in the operation. . . .

As for the practical improvements, I should like to present a group of notes on this subject, from the Leicester Codex, folio 28v, which so far

Figure 3
MS A, fol. 30*v*.

Figure 4
Belidor, *Architecture Hydraulique,*
pt. 2, p. 128, pl. 8.

as I know have never been reproduced, commented upon, or translated. Marginal drawings (figs. 5 and 6) illustrate the text.

The very best way to drive piles (*ficcare i pali a castello*) is when the man lifts so much of the weight of the hammer as is his own weight. And this shall be done in as much time as the man, without burden, is able to climb a ladder quickly. Now, this man shall put his foot immediately in the stirrup and he will descend with so much weight as his weight exceeds that of the hammer. If you want to check it thoroughly, you can have him carry a stone weighing a pound. He will lift so much weight as is his own on descending from the top of the ladder and the hammer will raise and remain on top, locked by itself, until the man dismounts the stirrup and again climbs the ladder. When you unlock the hammer with a string, it will descend furiously on top of the pile you want to drive in. And with the same speed the stirrup will rise again

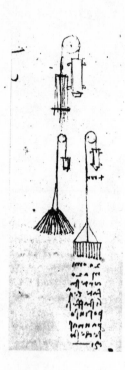

Figure 5
MS Leicester, fol. 28v.

Figure 6
MS Leicester, fol. 28v.

to the feet of the man. And this shall be done again and again. And if you want to have more men, take several ropes that end in one rope and several ladders to allow the men to reach the top of the ladders at the same time. Now, at a signal from the foreman, they shall put their feet in the stirrups and climb the ladder again. They will rest while descending and there is not much fatigue in climbing the ladders because it is done with feet and hands, and all the weight of the man that is charged on the hands will not burden the feet. But one man shall always give the signal.

Pile driving by raising the hammer by hand is not very useful, because a man cannot raise his own weight if he does not sustain it with his arms. This cannot be done unless the rope he is using is perpendicular to the center of his gravity. And this happens only to one of the men in a crowd who is pulling on the hammer.

We can further observe in the sketches of the Leicester Codex that Belidor's first two improvements had already been considered by Leonardo:

the substitution of a large wheel for the block and use of a capstan or a winch. . . .

A last word on the pile driver of Leonardo. He spoke of a hammer that is locked and unlocked by itself. In the pile driver drawn on folio 289*r*, *e* of the Codex Atlanticus (fig. 7) we can observe the kind of mechanism Leonardo was hinting at. It is amazing to verify the identity of this device with that of the mentioned, improved pile driver of Belidor (fig. 8). According to the French author, the machine had been invented by Vauloue, a London watchmaker, and used at the construction of the famous Westminster bridge, that is, in 1738–1750. The story is recorded also by Desaguliers. Devices of this type are still used.

Many notes and sketches of Leonardo refer to the construction of canals, a subject that often turns up in the manuscripts. . . .

He began by analyzing the best ways of disposing men to work if this had to be done by hand. For those calculations Leonardo even constructed a kind of chronometer on the nature of which Augusto Marinoni tells us more. He filled many sheets, extremely interesting in themselves, with calculations and sketches (e.g., C.A., fol. 210*r*, *a*), arriving at the conclusion that the only reasonable solution was to mechanize the whole operation.

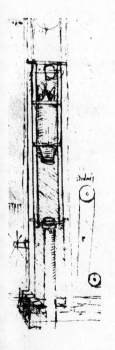

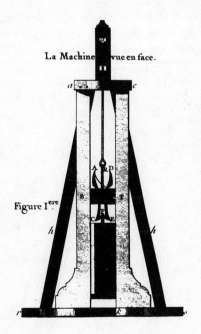

Figure 7
Codex Atlanticus, fol. 289*r*, *e*.

Figure 8
Belidor, *Architecture Hydraulique*.

It was not only a matter of digging. The excavated material had to be cleared and transported a long way. For this purpose wheeled vehicles were considered next and rejected.

Leonardo did not underestimate wheeled vehicles. He notes that "the cart has the first place among all human inventions, particularly when it has the right proportions, although I have never seen such a one." But a cart is useful only on level ground; on steep runs the weight nullifies the effort of the animal. Besides, "to fill the carts requires more time than needed for the transport itself" (C.A., fol. 164r, a). . . .

The well-known folio 211r, a of the Codex Atlanticus shows the theoretical justification of this statement; less noticed are the beautiful sketches above the main drawing, where the influence of the relative thickness of the axle on the movement is measured by an amazingly modern-looking dynamometer. On folio 340v, d, of the same codex, a similar arrangement is suggested for the measurement of the force required in pulling a four-wheeled vehicle. Leonardo was to use the same type of apparatus to gauge the force of a waterfall (C. Fors. III, fol. 47r) and to determine the power requirement of a grain mill (ibid., fol. 46v), anticipating the classic experiments of Smeaton.

After rejecting wheeled vehicles as unsuitable for excavation work and recognizing that a large and deep canal could not economically be dug by hand, Leonardo examined the possibility of substituting progressive hand shoveling from level to level by excavation machines combined with a system of cranes. Power was again his main concern.

To activate a crane, in addition to a horse-driven capstan, the only transportable motor available at the time would have been a treadmill, a machine that converts muscle power into rotary motion. . . .

Leonardo did not invent the external treadmill; there are older examples as far back as Vitruvius. But he was the first to use the principle rationally and in accordance with sound engineering principles. . . .

However, the increasing size of the complex machines created by the imagination of Leonardo required more power than that which could be supplied by the weight of a few men walking on a treadmill, even admitting the most rational mechanical arrangements. Leonardo was well aware of the situation, and wrote: "There you see the best of all motors, made by the ancient architects, that I cleaned from every fault and reduced to the ultimate perfection, with improvements that were not and could not be in its simple state. But I am still not satisfied and I intend to show a way of quicker motion of more usefulness and brevity" (C.A., fol. 370v, c). . . .

Still, the ultimate perfection had not yet been achieved. There was too much human work in filling and emptying the buckets and, particularly, in the excavation itself, the breaking up and the shoveling of the soil. Let us see how Leonardo the engineer tackled these problems.

Amazingly modern systems for the emptying of the buckets are described and shown on other pages of the Codex Atlanticus. The box is discharged

Leonardo da Vinci 235

Figure 9
Codex Atlanticus, fol. 363r, a.

by hitting the ground as in folio 363r, a (fig. 9), or by releasing the bottom with a string (C.A., fol. 344r, a), or it is ingeniously overturned with the least possible effort as in folio 294r, a. As for the mechanization of the excavation itself, Leonardo offered several solutions that command the admiration of the modern engineer. He devised wheeled scrapers that with the aid of a horse could dig and remove the earth. Their design contains all the main features of modern tools (C.A., fols. 294r, a; 389r, b; 389v, c).

Leonardo's aim, however, was total mechanization. He declared emphatically that in the making of canals "the most useful method would be one by which the soil, removed, would jump by itself quickly on the instrument that will transport it" (C.A., fol. 164r, a; C. Ar., fol. 127r–v). . . .

A number of reasonable questions advanced by several authors will be echoed at this point. Those marvelously modern-looking projects of Leonardo, do they have reality or are they to be considered as the unfulfilled dreams of an inventor? Are they original or do they come from a long tradition of engineering experience?

These questions can be answered both ways. Leonardo did find ample inspiration in the deeds and writings of his predecessors in the technical arts, and some of his projects were so advanced that they could not have been carried out, for lack of adequate technical support. Others, even if brilliantly conceived, were based on faulty theories and would not work (e.g., the use of syphons more than 30 feet tall).

There can be no doubt, however, that most of Leonardo's technical ideas were grounded in firm and actual experience, even if the corresponding historical records are meager. His canal-building activity in the Romagnas, while in the service of Cesare Borgia, must have been successful in view of his immediate appointment by the Signoria of Florence in a similar capacity after the downfall of his frightful patron. Leonardo's innovations and inventions in the field of mechanical engineering can be traced in the writings of a number of sixteenth- and seventeenth-century authors, especially Cardan, Besson, Ramelli, Zonca, Castelli, Verantius, De Caus, etc. It is useless to speculate about the fact that Leonardo's manuscripts were hardly accessible to those writers: his technological ideas, like those related to the arts, were already incorporated in the common knowledge of the epoch.

But arts and techniques can be easily lost when genius is not understood and assimilated. The technology of the sixteenth and seventeenth centuries was much inferior to the standards set by Leonardo; only at the end of the seventeenth century was there a renewal that led to the beginning of modern engineering. A thorough study of Leonardo's technical activities and ideas, even if presented in the disorderly state of the mutilated and plundered heritage, points to him, as Feldhaus has correctly remarked, as the greatest engineer of all times.

Suggestions for Further Reading

THERE ARE TWO standard editions of Leonardo's notebooks, Leonardo da Vinci, *Notebooks*, tr. and ed. Edward McCurdy, 2 vols. (London: Cape,

1956), and *The Notebooks of Leonardo da Vinci*, ed. Jean Paul Richter, 2 vols. (New York: Dover, 1970), as well as a small collection of excerpts, Leonardo da Vinci, *Philosophical Diary*, tr. and ed. Wade Baskin (New York: Philosophical Library, 1959). Of the many collections of his artistic works, one of the best is *Leonardo da Vinci* (New York: Reynal, 1956), the catalogue of the comprehensive Milan Leonardo Exposition of 1938.

Two general works on Leonardo can be recommended—*Leonardo da Vinci, Aspects of the Renaissance Genius,* ed. Morris Philipson (New York: Braziller, 1966), a well-selected set of articles and special studies, and Cecil H. M. Gould, *Leonardo: the Artist and the Non-artist* (Boston: New York Graphic Society, 1975). Both these books recognize the two aspects of Leonardo's life and work that are generally dealt with, the scientific and the artistic. Of the works on Leonardo the artist, the best is Kenneth M. Clark, *Leonardo da Vinci, An Account of His Development as an Artist,* rev. ed. (Baltimore: Penguin, 1958); it may well be the best work on him of any sort. For Leonardo's mechanical engineering interests, the pioneer study is Ivor B. Hart, *The Mechanical Investigations of Leonardo da Vinci,* 2nd ed. (Berkeley: University of California Press, 1963 [1925]), and a later work by Hart updating the research, *The World of Leonardo, Man of Science, Engineer, and Dreamer of Flight* (New York: Viking, 1961). For Leonardo's anatomical studies see Elmer Belt, *Leonardo the Anatomist* (New York: Greenwood, 1955).

A special interest in Leonardo was stirred by two works of Sigmund Freud, *Leonardo da Vinci: A Study in Psychosexuality,* tr. A. A. Brill (New York: Random House, 1947), and *Leonardo da Vinci and a Memory of His Childhood,* tr. Alan Tyson (New York: Norton, 1964), in which Freud treated Leonardo as the subject of his most extensive attempt at psychohistory. The works are full of errors and not solidly based on research, but they thrust into the forefront of controversy about Leonardo the questions of his homosexuality and the paralyzing duality of his interests in science and art. There are two later important books in this controversy: Kurt R. Sissler, *Leonardo da Vinci: Psychoanalytic Notes on an Enigma* (New York: International Universities Press, 1961), and Raymond S. Stites, *The Sublimation of Leonardo da Vinci, with a Translation of the Codex Trivulzianus* (Washington: Smithsonian, 1970), the latter a large, detailed, and difficult book but an important revisionist study on Freud's tentative conclusions.

Although its assertions and research are now dated, students may still enjoy a famous historical novel, Dmitrii Merezhkovskii, *The Romance of Leonardo da Vinci,* tr. B. G. Guerney (New York: Heritage, 1938).

For the background to Leonardo's biography and the Renaissance, see Wallace K. Ferguson, *Europe in Transition, 1300–1520* (Boston: Houghton Mifflin, 1962), and Ernst Breisach, *Renaissance Europe, 1300–1517* (New York: Macmillan, 1973).

Martin Luther: Protestant Saint or "Devil in the Habit of a Monk"?

On a summer day in the year 1505, a young German law student was
returning to the University of Erfurt after a visit home. He was overtaken
by a sudden, violent thunderstorm and struck to the ground by a bolt
of lightning. Terrified, he cried out, "St. Anne, help me! I will become a
monk." Such vows were usually quickly forgotten, but not this one,
for the student was Martin Luther, the man who was to bring about
the most profound revolution in the history of the Christian faith.
Within a matter of weeks, he disposed of his worldly goods, including
his law books, and joined the order of the Augustinian Eremites in
Erfurt. His father was furious; his friends were dismayed. And historians
and theologians since the sixteenth century have speculated about the
motives that compelled him. But this is only one of the questions
about Martin Luther that have fascinated scholars and made him the
subject of more writing than any other figure in European history.

There was seemingly nothing in his youth or adolescence to account
for his decision to become a monk. But once that decision was made,
Luther was swept by such a tidal wave of religious intensity that it
troubled even his monastic superiors. He prayed for hours on end;
he subjected himself to such ascetic rigors that he almost ruined his
health; and he confessed his sins over and over again. He was assaulted
by what one modern scholar has aptly called "the terror of the holy."
God was for him a terrible judge, so perfect and so righteous that

sinful man could not even begin to deserve anything at His hands but
eternal damnation. Martin Luther was beginning his search for
"justification," the sense that somehow, against all odds, he might earn
God's grace and escape damnation.

The terror of the holy remained, and the monastic life gave Luther
no assurance that God's grace was close at hand. But the very religious
disquiet that tormented the young monk also caused his superiors
to single him out, for this was the stuff that the great figures of religion
were made of—St. Francis, St. Bernard, St. Benedict. Moreover, Brother
Martin, for all his inner turmoil, was a bright and capable young man
and already well educated, a Master of Arts. Soon he was ordained
priest. He was sent on a matter of chapter business to Rome. And his
education was continued, but now in theology rather than law.

Then the Elector of Saxony, Frederick the Wise, approached the
Erfurt Augustinians in search of faculty members for the newly founded
university in his capital town of Wittenberg. Brother Martin was
sent. In Wittenberg he taught the arts course, worked at his own studies,
and assumed more than a fair share of the parish duties. By 1513 he
earned his doctor's degree and began to teach theology. As he
prepared a series of lectures on the Psalms, he began to gain new
understanding of his texts. And then, while he was working out his
lectures on the Epistles of St. Paul, he found meaning in the familiar
passage from Romans 1:17 that he had never before perceived. "For
therein is the righteousness of God revealed from faith to faith: as
it is written, the just shall live by faith." Later Luther said, "This
passage of Paul became to me a gate to heaven." Here was the
"justification" he had sought so long in vain. Man is justified by faith, by
the simple act of belief in Christ, in a way that no amount of works,
however pious and well intended, no amount of prayers or anguish or
penance can insure. Justification by faith was to become the cardinal
doctrine of a new religious sect.

But Luther's inward revelation might never have led to a separate
sect, much less a Reformation, except for a chain of events external
to him. It began with a particularly scandalous sale of indulgences
in the neighboring lands of the Archbishop of Mainz. The doctrine of
indulgences was the basis of the church's profitable traffic in "pardons,"
as they were sometimes called, remissions of the temporal penalties
for sin. Although the doctrine was an outgrowth of the sacrament of
penance, many churchmen were troubled by it. To Luther, the
indulgences that had been bought across the border by some of his
parishioners and the outrageous claims for their effectiveness that were
being made by the indulgence preacher, the Dominican Johann Tetzel,
seemed a surpassingly bad example of the concept of "works,"
especially in light of his own increasing conviction that works cannot
work salvation in man—only faith "sola fides." In response to this

scandalous situation, Luther was led to propose his ninety-five theses against indulgences. The document was dated October 31, 1517, the most famous date in Protestantism. The theses were written in Latin, intended for academic disputation, but somehow they were translated into German and found their way into print. Despite their dry, scholarly prose and formal organization they became a popular, even an inflammatory manifesto. Ecclesiastical authorities, including the offended Archbishop of Mainz, complained to Luther's superiors and eventually to Rome. Luther was pressed to recant, but he refused. Instead, he clung stubbornly not only to his basic position on indulgences but to the ever more revolutionary implications of his belief in justification by faith. Within three years, he had come to reject much of the sacramental theory of the church, nearly all its traditions, and the authority of the pope. In 1520 he defied Pope Leo X's bull of condemnation; in the following year he defied the Emperor Charles V in the famous confrontation at the Diet of Worms. The Lord's good servant had become, in Charles' phrase, "that devil in the habit of a monk." The Catholic Luther had become the Protestant Luther.

The Protestant Luther
MARTIN LUTHER

The image of Luther the Protestant results most directly, of course, from Luther's deeds—his successful act of defiance against established church and established state, his uncanny ability not only to survive but to build around him a new political-religious community vital enough to maintain itself. Luther's Protestant image is also based upon the incredible quantity of his writings—tracts and treatises, sermons, commentaries, translations, disputations, hymns, and letters—nearly a hundred heavy volumes in the standard modern edition. But his image also rests upon an elaborate Protestant tradition that can be traced to Luther himself.

Luther was a voluble and expansive man. Even his formal treatises are rich in anecdotes from his own experience and filled with autobiographical detail. These qualities carried over into his talk, and Luther loved to talk. As the Reformation settled into a political and social reality and Luther married—for he rejected clerical celibacy along with the other doctrines of the old church—his kitchen table became the center of the Protestant world. In addition to his own large family, there were always people visiting—friends and associates, wandering scholars and churchmen, professors and students, and religious refugees. After dinner, when the dishes were cleared and the beer steins passed around, they would talk, Luther usually taking the lead. He had opinions on practically everything—politics, people, theology, education, child raising—and he would reminisce about his own life as well.

Some of the guests took notes on these conversations, and a great many of them have been preserved—six volumes in the German Weimar edition—appropriately called the Tabletalk. *The following selections are from the* Tabletalk. *They are fragments of Luther's own recollections of his experience of monasticism, his inward struggle to gain a sense of justification, and his defiance of the old church.*

HE [MARTIN LUTHER] became a monk against the will of his father. When he celebrated his first mass and asked his father why he was angry about the step he took, the father replied reproachfully, "Don't you know that

it's written, Honor your father and your mother" [Exod. 20:12]? When
he excused himself by saying that he was so frightened by a storm that
he was compelled to become a monk, his father answered, "Just so it
wasn't a phantom you saw!" . . .

[Luther recalled] "later when I stood there during the mass and began
the canon, I was so frightened that I would have fled if I hadn't been
admonished by the prior. For when I read the words, 'Thee, therefore,
most merciful Father,' etc., and thought I had to speak to God without a Mediator, I felt like fleeing from the world like Judas. Who
can bear the majesty of God without Christ as Mediator? In short, as
a monk I experienced such horrors; I had to experience them before I
could fight them.". . . "I almost fasted myself to death, for again and
again I went for three days without taking a drop of water or a morsel
of food. I was very serious about it. I really crucified the Lord Christ. I
wasn't simply an observer but helped to carry him and pierce [his hands
and feet]. God forgive me for it, for I have confessed it openly! This is
the truth: the most pious monk is the worst scoundrel. He denies that
Christ is the mediator and highpriest and turns him into a judge."

"I chose twenty-one saints and prayed to three every day when I celebrated mass; thus I completed the number every week. I prayed especially
to the Blessed Virgin, who with her womanly heart would compassionately
appease her Son. . . ."

"When I was a monk I was unwilling to omit any of the prayers, but
when I was busy with public lecturing and writing I often accumulated
my appointed prayers for a whole week, or even two or three weeks. Then
I would take a Saturday off, or shut myself in for as long as three days
without food and drink, until I had said the prescribed prayers. This
made my head split, and as a consequence I couldn't close my eyes for five
nights, lay sick unto death, and went out of my senses. Even after I had
quickly recovered and I tried again to read, my head went 'round and
'round. Thus our Lord God drew me, as if by force, from that torment
of prayers. To such an extent had I been captive [to human tradi-
tions]. . . ."

"I wouldn't take one thousand florins for not having seen Rome because
I wouldn't have been able to believe such things if I had been told by
somebody without having seen them for myself. We were simply laughed
at because we were such pious monks. A Christian was taken to be
nothing but a fool. I know priests who said six or seven masses while I
said only one. They took money for them and I didn't. In short, there's no
disgrace in Italy except to be poor. Murder and theft are still punished a
little, for they must do this. Otherwise no sin is too great for them." . . .

[As a young professor in Wittenberg] "the words 'righteous' and 'righteousness of God' struck my conscience like lightning. When I heard them
I was exceedingly terrified. If God is righteous [I thought], he must punish.

244 Makers of the Western Tradition

But when by God's grace I pondered, in the tower [1] and heated room of this building, over the words, 'He who through faith is righteous shall live' [Rom. 1:17] and 'the righteousness of God' [Rom. 3:21], I soon came to the conclusion that if we, as righteous men, ought to live from faith and if the righteousness of God should contribute to the salvation of all who believe, then salvation won't be our merit but God's mercy. My spirit was thereby cheered. For it's by the righteousness of God that we're justified and saved through Christ. These words [which had before terrified me] now became more pleasing to me. The Holy Spirit unveiled the Scriptures for me in this tower." . . .

"That works don't merit life, grace, and salvation is clear from this, that works are not spiritual birth but are fruits of this birth. We are not made sons, heirs, righteous, saints, Christians by means of works, but we do good works once we have been made, born, created such. So it's necessary to have life, salvation, and grace before works, just as a tree doesn't deserve to become a tree on account of its fruit but a tree is by nature fitted to bear fruit. Because we're born, created, generated righteous by the Word of grace, we're not fashioned, prepared, or put together as such by means of the law or works. Works merit something else than life, grace, or salvation—namely, praise, glory, favor, and certain extraordinary things—just as a tree deserves to be loved, cultivated, praised, and honored by others on account of its fruit. Urge the birth and substance of the Christian and you will at the same time extinguish the merits of works insofar as grace and salvation from sin, death, and the devil are concerned."

"Infants who have no works are saved by faith alone, and therefore faith alone justifies. If the power of God can do this in one person it can do it in all, because it's not the power of the infant but the power of faith. Nor is it the weakness of the infant that does it, otherwise that weakness would in itself be a merit or be equivalent to one. We'd like to defy our Lord God with our works. We'd like to become righteous through them. But he won't allow it. My conscience tells me that I'm not justified by works, but nobody believes it. 'Thou art justified in thy sentence; against thee only have I sinned and done that which is evil in thy sight' [Ps. 51:4]. What is meant by 'forgive us our debts' [Matt. 6:12]? I don't want to be good. What would be easier than for a man to say, 'I am a sinful man' [Luke 5:8]? But thou art a righteous God. That would be bad enough, but we are our own tormentors. The Spirit says, 'Righteous art thou' [Ps. 119:137]. The flesh can't say this: 'Thou art justified in thy sentence' [Ps. 51:4]." . . .

"God led us away from all this in a wonderful way; without my quite being aware of it he took me away from that game more than twenty

---

[1] The tower was the "privy" of the cloister, and it was there that Luther suddenly saw the significance of justification by faith. Hence Lutheran scholarship refers to his *turmerlebnis*, or "tower experience."—ED.

years ago. How difficult it was at first when we journeyed toward Kemberg [2] after All Saints' Day in the year 1517, when I first made up my mind to write against the crass errors of indulgences! Dr. Jerome Schurff [3] advised against this: 'You wish to write against the pope? What are you trying to do? It won't be tolerated!' I replied, 'And if they have to tolerate it?' Presently Sylvester,[4] master of the sacred palace, entered the arena, fulminating against me with this syllogism: 'Whoever questions what the Roman church says and does is heretical. Luther questions what the Roman church says and does, and therefore [he is a heretic].' So it all began." . . .

"At the beginning of the gospel [5] I took steps only very gradually against the impudent Tetzel. Jerome, the bishop of Brandenburg, held me in esteem, and I exhorted him, as the ordinary of the place, to look into the matter and sent him a copy of my *Explanations* [6] before I published them. But nobody was willing to restrain the ranting Tetzel; rather, everybody ventured to defend him. So I proceeded imprudently while others listened and were worn out under the tyranny. Now that I got into the matter I prayed God to help me further. One can never pay the pope as he deserves."

The Catholic Luther
HARTMAN GRISAR

The traditional Catholic view of Luther is a hostile one. For Luther's Reformation set the new Protestantism against the old Catholicism with a bitterness and animosity that are apparent even to this day.

The following selection is from Martin Luther, His Life and Work, *by the German Jesuit scholar Hartmann Grisar (1845–1932), a shorter and somewhat more pointed work based upon his more famous,*

[2] A nearby monastery where, presumably, they were traveling on some routine parish business.—ED.
[3] A colleague of Luther's in the faculty of law.—ED.
[4] Sylvester Prierias, a papal official and a Dominican, the first dignitary in Rome to attack Luther.—ED.
[5] Luther often used this phrase for the beginning of the Reformation.—ED.
[6] The book Luther wrote explaining and defending his ninety-five theses.—ED.

six-volume Luther. Although Grisar does abandon some of the more outrageous charges of the Catholic polemical tradition and displays an awesome knowledge of the detail of his subject, he is still openly partisan in his account and openly hostile in his interpretation. The passage below focuses on the last years of Luther the Catholic, the years at Wittenberg when Luther, as a young professor of theology, was struggling toward his understanding of justification by faith. Grisar insists that even then Luther was a "bad" Catholic. Instead of the frightened and solitary figure striving against "the terror of the holy," we find a truculent rebel, willfully distorting the rules of his own order and arrogantly preferring his own interpretation of scripture and ecclesiastical tradition to that of the church. Grisar makes Luther seem a selfish and overbearing man, neglectful of his proper religious duties. He finds him misled by his attraction to mysticism and excessive in his ascetic exercises. In short, what Grisar builds is a case for Luther's suffering from "a serious aberration."

THE YOUNG PROFESSOR of Sacred Scripture displayed a pronounced inclination towards mysticism. Mysticism had always been cultivated to a certain extent in the religious orders of the Catholic Church. The reading of Bonaventure had pointed Luther, even as a young monk, to the pious union with God at which Mysticism aims. Toward the close of his lectures on the Psalms, he became acquainted with certain works on Mysticism which he imbibed with great avidity. They were the sermons of Tauler and the tract *"Theologia deutsch."* They dominate his thoughts in 1515. Although these works were not designed to do so, they helped to develop his unecclesiastical ideas. His lively experience of the weakness of the human will induced him to hearken readily to the mystical voices which spoke of the complete relinquishment of man to God, even though he did not understand them perfectly. His opposition to good works opened his mind to a fallacious conception of the doctrines of those books of the mystical life. It appeared to him that, by following such leaders, his internal fears could be dispelled by a calm immersion in the Godhead. . . . In brief, he tried to transform all theology into what he called a theology of the Cross. Misconstruing Tauler's doctrine of perfection he would recognize only the highest motives, namely, reasons of the greatest perfection for himself as well as for others. Fear of divine punishment and hope of divine reward were to be excluded.

These were extravagances which could not aid him, but, on the contrary, involved great danger to his orthodoxy; in fact, constituted a serious aberration. But he trusted his new lights with the utmost self-confidence. . . .

In the spring of 1515, Luther was elected rural vicar by his fellow Augustinians.

At stated times he visited the monasteries thus entrusted to him. There were eleven of them, including Erfurt and Wittenberg. After the middle of April, 1516, he made a visitation of the congregations of the Order at Dresden, Neustadt on the Orla, Erfurt, Gotha, Langensalza, and Nordhausen. The letters written by him during his term of office as rural vicar, which normally lasted three years, contain practical directions and admonitions concerning monastic discipline and are, in part, quite edifying. Some of his visitations, however, were conducted with such astonishing rapidity that no fruitful results could be expected of them. Thus the visitation of the monastery at Gotha occupied but one hour, that at Langensalza two hours. "In these places," he wrote to Lang, "the Lord will work without us and direct the spiritual and temporal affairs in spite of the devil." At Neustadt he deposed the prior, Michael Dressel, without a hearing, because the brethren could not get along with him. "I did this," he informed Lang in confidence, "because I hoped to rule there myself for the half-year."

In a letter to the same friend he writes as follows about the engagements with which he was overwhelmed at that time: "I really ought to have two secretaries or chancellors. I do hardly anything all day but write letters. . . . I am at the same time preacher to the monastery, have to preach in the refectory, and am even expected to preach daily in the parish church. I am regent of the *studium* [*i.e.,* of the younger monks] and vicar, that is to say prior eleven times over; I have to provide for the delivery of the fish from the Leitzkau pond and to manage the litigation of the Herzberg fellows [monks] at Torgau; I am lecturing on Paul, compiling an exposition of the Psalter, and, as I said before, writing letters most of the time. . . . It is seldom that I have time for the recitation of the Divine Office or to celebrate Mass, and then, too, I have my peculiar temptations from the flesh, the world, and the devil."

The last sentence quoted above contains a remarkable declaration about his spiritual condition and his compliance with his monastic duties at that time. He seldom found time to recite the Divine Office and to say Mass. It was his duty so to arrange his affairs as to be able to comply with these obligations. The canonical hours were strictly prescribed. Saying Mass is the central obligation of every priest, especially if he is a member of a religious order. If Luther did not know how to observe due moderation in his labors; if he was derelict in the principal duties of the spiritual life; it was to be feared that he would gradually drift away from the religious state, particularly in view of the fact that he had adopted a false Mysticism

which favored the relaxation of the rule. As rural vicar, it is probable that
he did not sustain among the brethren the good old spirit which the
zealous Proles had introduced into the society. Of the "temptations of the
flesh" which he mentions we learn nothing definite. He was not yet in
conflict with his vows. His wrestlings with the devil may signify the fears
and terrors to which he was subject. . . . At times, in consequence either
of a disordered affection of the heart or of overwork, he was so distressed
that he could not eat or drink for a long time. One day he was found
seemingly dead in his cell, so completely was he exhausted as a result of
agitation and lack of food. . . .

Did Luther subject himself to extraordinary deeds of penance at any
period of his monastic life, as he frequently affirmed in his subsequent
conflict with the papacy and monasticism, when he was impelled by
polemical reasons to describe himself as the type of a holy and mortified
monk, one who could not find peace of mind during his whole monastic
career? Holding then that peace of mind was simply impossible in the
Catholic Church, he arbitrarily misrepresents monasticism, in order to exhibit in a most glaring manner the alleged inherent impossibility of
"papistic" ethics to produce the assurance of God's mercy. "I tormented my
body by fasting, vigils, and cold. . . . In the observance of these matters
I was so precise and superstitious, that I imposed more burdens upon my
body than it could bear without danger to health." "If ever a monk got
to heaven by monkery, then I should have got there." "I almost died
a-fasting, for often I took neither a drop of water nor a morsel of food
for three days." . . .

The above picture of singular holiness is produced not by early witnesses,
but by assertions which Luther made little by little at a later period of life.
The established facts contradict the legend. Perhaps his description is
based partly on reminiscences of his distracted days in the monastery, or
on eccentric efforts to overcome his sombre moods by means of a false
piety. His greatest error, and the one which most betrays him, is that he
ascribes his fictitious asceticism to all serious-minded members of his
monastery, yea, of all monasteries. He would have it that all monks con-
sumed themselves in wailing and grief, wrestling for the peace of God, until
he supplied the remedy. It is a rule of the most elementary criticism finally
to cut loose from the distorted presentation of the matter which has
maintained itself so tenaciously in Protestant biographies of Luther.

It may be admitted that, on the whole, Luther was a dutiful monk for
the greatest part of his monastic life. "When I was in the monastery," he
stated on one occasion, in 1535, "I was not like the rest of men, the
robbers, the unjust, the adulterous; but I observed chastity, obedience, and
poverty."

Yet, after his transfer to Wittenberg, and in consequence of the applause
which was accorded to him there, the unpleasant traits of his character,
especially his positive insistence on always being in the right, began to

manifest themselves more and more disagreeably. . . . His opposition to
the so-called doctrine of self-righteousness caused him to form a false conception of righteousness; instead of attacking an heretical error, he com-
bated the true worth of good works and the perfections of the monastic life.
Voluntary poverty, as practiced by the mendicants, was one of the
foundations of his Order. The inmates of monastic houses were to live on
alms according to the practice introduced by the great Saint Francis of
Assisi and for the benefactions received were to devote themselves gratis
to the spiritual needs of their fellowmen. Many abuses, it is true, had
attached themselves to the mendicant system; self-interest, avarice, and
worldly-mindedness infected the itinerant mendicants. But in his explanation
of the Psalms Luther attacks the life of poverty *per se:* "O mendicants! O
mendicants! O mendicants!" he pathetically exclaims, "who can excuse
you? . . . Look to it yourselves," etc. He places the practice of poverty
in an unfavorable light. In his criticism of the "self-righteousness of his
irksome enemies, he confronts them with the righteousness of the spirit
that cometh from Christ. These people, whom he believed it his duty to
expose, were guilty, in his opinion, of a Pharisaical denial of the true righteousness of Christ. His righteousness, and not our good works, effect our
salvation; works generate a fleshly sense and boastfulness. These thought-
processes evince how false mysticism, unclear theological notions, a darken-
ing of the monastic spirit, and passionate obstinacy conspired in Luther's
mind. . . .

The germ of Luther's reformatory doctrine is plainly contained in this
species of Mysticism. Step by step he had arrived at his new dogma in the
above described manner. The system which attacked the basic truths of
the Catholic Church, was complete in outline. Before giving a fuller exposition of it, we must consider the individual factors which cooperated
in its development in Luther's mind.

Confession and penance were a source of torturing offense to the young
monk. Can one obtain peace with God by the performance of penitential
works? He discussed this question with Staupitz [7] on an occasion when he
sought consolation. Staupitz pointed out to him that all penance must begin
and end with love; that all treasures are hidden in Christ, in whom we
must trust and whom we must love. . . . Nor was Staupitz the man who
could thoroughly free Luther from his doubts about predestination, although Luther says he helped him. His general reference to the wounds
of Christ could not permanently set the troubled monk aright. . . . Re-
calling Staupitz's exhortations, he says, in 1532: We must stop at the
wounds of Christ, and may not ponder over the awful mystery. The only
remedy consists in dismissing from our minds the possibility of a verdict
of damnation. "When I attend to these ideas, I forget what Christ and

---

[7] Johann Staupitz was a superior of Luther and one of his most trusted friends
and confidants. Though Staupitz remained Catholic and in orders, they remained
friends for many years.—ED.

God are, and sometimes arrive at the conclusion that God is a scoundrel.
. . . The idea of predestination causes us to forget God, and the *Laudate*
ceases and the *Blasphemate* begins." The part which these struggles had
in the origin of his new doctrine, is to be sought in Luther's violent efforts
to attain to a certain repose in the fact of his presumptive predestination.
. . . In his interpretation of the Epistle of St. Paul to the Romans, given
during the years 1515 and 1516, Luther completely unfolded his new
doctrine.

Luther Between Reform and Reformation
ERWIN ISERLOH

*A phenomenon of the last generation or so of Luther scholarship has been
the emergence of a new, more balanced, and more charitable Catholic
view of him. The polemical tone has almost disappeared, the shortcomings
of the old church have been recognized, and Luther himself is interpreted
in ways other than simply as a bad Catholic and a worse monk, led by
his own overweening hubris to an inevitable apostasy.*

*One of the best of the new Catholic critics is Erwin Iserloh, professor
of church history at the University of Münster in Germany. The following
selection is taken from his liveliest and most widely read book,* The Theses
Were Not Posted, Luther Between Reform and Reformation. *It is,
quite apart from its point of view, a stunning demonstration of how a
thoughtful scholar may use a precise event to reach a general conclusion.
The event in this case is the "primal image" of Luther nailing the ninety-five
theses to the door of the Castle Church in Wittenberg, thereby defiantly
proclaiming the beginning of his rebellion from the church. Iserloh
presents evidence that this treasured picture appeared only after Luther's
death, that it came not from Luther himself but from his younger associate
Philipp Melanchthon, and that Melanchthon had not even witnessed
the event. Iserloh goes on to point out that, far from an act of rebellion,
Luther's handling of the matter of the theses shows him to have been,
at this crucial point, both a good Catholic and a responsible theologian,*

in Iserloh's phrase, "an obedient rebel." Iserloh argues further that it
was not necessary for Luther to have been driven to rebellion; he might
well have been kept within the church to its great advantage, as well
as his own.

OUR INVESTIGATION of the sources and the reports concerning October 31, 1517, compels us to conclude that the drama of that day was notably less than what we would suppose from the jubilee celebrations which have been held since 1617 and from the Reformation Day festivals since their inception in 1668. In fact the sources rule out a public posting of the ninety-five theses.

Although October 31, 1517, lacked outward drama it was nevertheless a day of decisive importance. It is the day on which the Reformation began, not because Martin Luther posted his ninety-five theses on the door of the castle church in Wittenberg, but because on this day Luther approached the competent church authorities with his pressing call for reform. On this day he presented them with his theses and the request that they call a halt to the unworthy activities of the indulgence preachers. When the bishops did not respond, or when they sought merely to divert him, Luther circulated his theses privately. The theses spread quickly and were printed in Nürnberg, Leipzig, and Basel. Suddenly they were echoing throughout Germany and beyond its borders in a way that Luther neither foresaw nor intended. The protest that Luther registered before Archbishop Albrecht [8] and the inclusion of the theses with the letter eventually led to the Roman investigation of Luther's works.

Some will surely want to object: Is it not actually of minor importance whether Luther posted his theses in Wittenberg or not? I would answer that it is of more than minor importance. For October 31 was a day on which the castle church was crowded with pilgrims taking advantage of the titular feast of All Saints. Luther's theses on the door would have constituted a public protest. If Luther made such a scene on the same day that he composed his letter to Archbishop Albrecht, then his letter loses its credibility, even when we take into account its excessive protestations of submissiveness and humility as conventions of the time.

Above all, if Luther did post his theses, then for the rest of his life he knowingly gave a false account of these events by asserting that he only circulated his theses after the bishops failed to act.

If the theses were not posted on October 31, 1517, then it becomes all the more clear that Luther did not rush headlong toward a break with the church. Rather, as Joseph Lortz has never tired of repeating, and as Luther

---

[8] The Archbishop of Mainz, who had authorized the particular sale of indulgences.—ED.

himself stressed, he started the Reformation quite unintentionally. In the preface to an edition of his theses in 1538 Luther gave a detailed picture of the situation in 1517. It is as if he wanted to warn the Protestant world against dramatizing the start of the Reformation with false heroics. First he stresses how weak, reticent, and unsure he was; then he tells of his efforts to contact church authorities. This is something he knows his readers cannot appreciate, since they have grown used to impudent attacks on the broken authority of the pope. . . .

If Luther did turn first to the competent bishops with his protest, or better, with his earnest plea for reform, and if he did give them time to react as their pastoral responsibilities called for, then it is the bishops who clearly were more responsible for the consequences. If Luther did allow the bishops time to answer his request then he was sincere in begging the archbishop to remove the scandal before disgrace came upon him and upon the church.

Further, there was clearly a real opportunity that Luther's challenge could be directed to the reform of the church, instead of leading to a break with the church. But such reform would have demanded of the bishops far greater religious substance and a far more lively priestly spirit than they showed. The deficiencies that come to light here, precisely when the bishops were called on to act as theologians and pastors, cannot be rated too highly when we seek to determine the causes of the Reformation. These deficiencies had far more serious consequences than did the failures in personal morality that we usually connect with the "bad popes" and concubinous priests on the eve of the Reformation. Archbishop Albrecht showed on other occasions as well how indifferent he was to theological questions, and how fully incapable he was of comprehending their often wideranging religious significance. For example, he expressed his displeasure over the momentous Leipzig debate of 1519 where famous professors were, as he saw it, crossing swords over minor points of no interest for true Christian men. This same Albrecht sent sizable gifts of money to Luther on the occasion of his marriage in 1525 and to Melanchthon after the latter had sent him a copy of his commentary on Romans in 1532.

A whole series of objections might arise here: Do not the indulgence theses themselves mark the break with the church? Do they not attack the very foundations of the church of that day? Or, as Heinrich Bornkamm wrote, do they not decisively pull the ground from under the Catholic conception of penance? Was a reform of the church of that day at all possible by renewal from within? Is not the Luther of the ninety-five theses already a revolutionary on his way inevitably to the Reformation as a division of the church?

Our first question must be whether Luther's indulgence theses deny any binding doctrines of the church in his day. And even if this be true, we cannot immediately brand the Luther of late 1517 a heretic. This would be justified only if he became aware of holding something opposed to the teaching of the church and then remained adamant in the face of correction. It is especially important to recall this in view of Luther's repeated assertions that the theses do not express his own position, but that much in them is doubtful, that some points he would reject, and no single one out of all of them would he stubbornly maintain. . . .

Still, a truly historical judgment on the theses will not consider their precise wording only. We must further ask in what direction they are tending and what development is already immanent in them. Luther's theses can only be understood in the context of late medieval nominalism. This theology had already made a broad separation of divine and human activity in the church. For God, actions in the church were only occasions for his saving action, with no true involvement of the latter in the former. Regarding penance and the remission of punishment, Luther simply carries the nominalist separation of the ecclesiastical and the divine to the extreme in that he denies that ecclesiastical penances and their remission even have an interpretative relation to the penance required by or remitted by God. I see here one root of Luther's impending denial of the hierarchical priesthood established by God in the church.

The theological consequences of the ninety-five theses were not immediately effective. The secret of their wide circulation and their electrifying effect was that they voiced a popular polemic. Here Luther touched on questions, complaints, and resentments that had long been smouldering and had often been expressed already. Luther made himself the spokesman for those whose hopes for reform had often been disappointed in a period of widespread dissatisfaction.

Theses 81–90 list the pointed questions the laity ask about indulgences. If the pope can, as he claims, free souls from purgatory, why then does he not do this out of Christian charity, instead of demanding money as a condition? Why does he not forget his building project and simply empty purgatory? (82) If indulgences are so salutary for the living, why does the pope grant them to the faithful but once a day and not a hundred times? (88) If the pope is more intent on helping souls toward salvation than in obtaining money, why is it that he makes new grants and suspends earlier confessional letters and indulgences which are just as effective? (89) If indulgences are so certain, and if it is wrong to pray for people already saved, why are anniversary masses for the dead still celebrated? Why is the money set aside for these masses not returned? (83) Why does the pope not build St. Peter's out of his own huge wealth, instead of with the money of the poor? (86) These are serious and conscientious questions posed by laymen. If they are merely beaten down by authority, instead of being met with good reasons, then the church and the pope will be open to the ridicule of their enemies. This will only increase the misery of the Christian people. (90)

Here Luther's theses brought thoughts out into the open that all had more or less consciously found troublesome. . . .

The rapid dissemination of his theses was for Luther proof that he had written what many were thinking but, as in John 7:13, they would not speak out openly "out of fear of the Jews." (WBr 1, 152, 17)

Luther regretted the spread of the theses, since they were not meant for the public, but only for a few learned men. Furthermore, the theses contained a number of doubtful points. Therefore he rushed the "Sermon on Indulgences and Grace" into print in March 1518 (W 1, 239–46) as a popular presentation of his basic point on indulgences, and he wrote the *Resolutiones* (W 1, 526–628 and LW 31, 83–252) as an extensive theological explanation of the theses. . . .

[The] prefatory statements accompanying the explanations of the theses have been singled out for a remarkable combination of loyal submissiveness, prophetic sense of mission, and an almost arrogant conviction of their cause. Meissinger saw here the maneuverings of a chess expert. This does not strike me as an adequate analysis. I see rather the genuine possibility of keeping Luther within the church. But for this to have happened the bishops who were involved, and the pope himself, would have to have matched Luther in religious substance and in pastoral earnestness. It was not just a cheap evasion when Luther repeated again and again in 1517 and 1518 that he felt bound only by teachings of the church and not by theological opinions, even if these came from St. Thomas or St. Bonaventure. The binding declaration Luther sought from the church came in Leo X's doctrinal constitution on indulgences, *"Cum postquam"* (DS 1447ff.), on November 9, 1518. . . .

The papal constitution declares that the pope by reason of the power of the keys can through indulgences remit punishments for sin by applying the merits of Christ and the saints. The living receive this remission as an absolution and the departed by way of intercession. The constitution was quite reticent and sparing in laying down binding doctrine. This contrasts notably with the manner of the indulgence preachers and Luther's attackers. . . .

Silvester Prierias, the papal court theologian, exceeded his fellow Dominican Tetzel in frivolity. For him, a preacher maintaining the doctrines attacked by Luther is much like a cook adding seasoning to make a dish more appealing. Here we see the same lack of religious earnestness and pastoral awareness that marked the bishops' reaction to the theses.

This lack of theological competence and of apostolic concern was all the more freighted with consequences, in the face of Martin Luther's zeal for the glory of God and the salvation of souls in 1517–18. There was a real chance to channel his zeal toward renewal of the church from within.

In this context it does seem important whether Luther actually posted his theses for the benefit of the crowds streaming into the Church of All Saints in Wittenberg. It is important whether he made such a scene or whether he simply presented his ninety-five theses to the bishops and to some learned friends. From the former he sought the suppression of practical abuses, and from the latter the clarification of open theological questions.

I, for one, feel compelled to judge Luther's posting of the ninety-five theses a legend. With this legend removed it is much clearer to what a great extent the theological and pastoral failures of the bishops set the scene for Luther to begin the divisive Reformation we know, instead of bringing reform from within the church.

Suggestions for Further Reading

LUTHER WAS HIMSELF a voluminous and powerful writer, and students should sample his writings beyond the brief excerpt from the *Tabletalk* presented in this chapter. The standard English edition of his works is in many volumes and sets of volumes, each edited by several scholars, elaborately cross-indexed and with analytical contents so that individual works are easy to find. Of particular interest should be the set *Martin Luther, Career of the Reformer*, vols. 31–34 (Philadelphia: Muhlenberg Press, 1957–1960). Some of the same works will be found in another edition, Martin Luther, *Reformation Writings*, tr. Bertram L. Woolf, 2 vols. (New York: Philosophical Library, 1953–1956).

The career of the young Luther, which is emphasized in this chapter, has been of particular interest to Luther scholars. Heinrich Boehmer, *Road to Reformation, Martin Luther to the Year 1521*, tr. John W. Doberstein and Theodore S. Tappert (Philadelphia: Muhlenberg Press, 1946), is the standard work by a great German authority. The same ground is covered by Robert H. Fife, *The Revolt of Martin Luther* (New York: Columbia University Press, 1957). DeLamar Jensen, *Confrontation at Worms: Martin Luther and the Diet of Worms. With a Complete English Translation of the Edict of Worms* (Provo, Utah: Brigham Young University Press, 1973), gives a detailed look at the terminal event in young Luther's career. Erik H. Erikson, *Young Man Luther: A Study in Psychoanalysis and History* (New York: Norton, 1958), is a famous and controversial book that students find provocative.

Of the many works on Luther's theology and thought, two especially are recommended. Heinrich Bornkamm, *Luther's World of Thought,* tr. Martin H. Bertram (St. Louis: Concordia, 1958), is one of the most influential works of modern Luther literature. It is fundamentally a theological rather than an historical work and is difficult but also important. Of particular interest to the background of the young Luther is Bengt R. Hoffman, *Luther and the Mystics: A Re-examination of Luther's Spiritual Experiences and His Relationship to the Mystics* (Minneapolis: Augsburg Press, 1976).

Of the many general biographical works, James Atkinson, *Luther and the Birth of Protestantism* (Baltimore: Penguin, 1968), places emphasis on his theological development. Probably the best and most readable of all the Luther biographies is Roland H. Bainton, *Here I Stand: A Life of Martin Luther* (Nashville: Abingdon Press, 1950). Three books are recommended for the broader topic of Luther and his age. Two are very large and comprehensive: Ernest G. Schwiebert, *Luther and His Times, the Reformation from a New Perspective* (St. Louis: Concordia, 1950), and Richard Friedenthal, *Luther: His Life and Times,* tr. John Nowell (New York: Harcourt, Brace, 1970). The third, A. G. Dickens, *The German Nation and Martin Luther* (New York: Harper & Row, 1974), is really an attractive, authoritative extended essay.

For the still larger topic of Luther in relation to the Reformation, see A. G. Dickens, *Reformation and Society in Sixteenth-Century Europe* (New York: Harcourt, Brace, 1966); Lewis W. Spitz, *The Renaissance and Reformation Movements,* vol. 2 (Chicago: Rand McNally, 1971); and Harold J. Grimm, *The Reformation Era,* 2nd ed. (New York: Macmillan, 1973).